Sweet Talk

Emerging Frontiers in the Global Economy

Sweet Talk

Paternalism and Collective Action in
North–South Trade Relations

J. P. Singh

Stanford University Press
Stanford, California

Stanford University Press
Stanford, California

Printed in the United States of America on acid-free, archival-quality paper

Library of Congress Cataloging-in-Publication Data

Names: Singh, J. P., 1961– author.
Title: Sweet talk : paternalism and collective action in North-South trade relations / J.P. Singh.
Other titles: Emerging frontiers in the global economy.
Description: Stanford, California : Stanford University Press, 2016. | Series: Emerging frontiers in the global economy | Includes bibliographical references and index.
Identifiers: LCCN 2016036586 (print) | LCCN 2016037327 (ebook) | ISBN 9780804794121 (cloth : alk. paper) | ISBN 9781503601048 (pbk. : alk. paper) | ISBN 9781503601055
Subjects: LCSH: Developing countries—Foreign economic relations—Developed countries. | Developed countries—Foreign economic relations—Developing countries. | International economic relations. | Paternalism.
Classification: LCC HF1413 .S54 2016 (print) | LCC HF1413 (ebook) | DDC 382/.3—dc23
LC record available at https://lccn.loc.gov/2016036586

Typeset by Thompson Type in 10.25/15 Brill

To my mother
for her immense courage, curiosity, and optimism

Contents

List of Illustrations ix

Preface xi

List of Acronyms xvii

1 Introduction: The Subtext of North–South Relations 1

PART I: Understanding History

2 Who Is Served by Paternalism? 21

3 GATT and the Developing World before the Uruguay Round 55

PART II: The Uruguay Round and After

4 Unequal Partners in Merchandise Trade 83

5 An Uneven Playing Field in Agricultural Negotiations 111

6 Big Disparities in Services and Intellectual Property 139

7 Conclusion: The End of Sweet Talk 171

Appendix A: Node Classification Descriptions for the
U.S. Tone/Sentiment toward Trading Partners 187

Appendix B: Codebook and Data Sources 189

Notes 193

References 209

Index 231

List of Illustrations

Figures

1.1 Percentage Agriculture Concessions Received and Official
   Development Assistance as a Percentage of GNP 12

4.1 Uruguay Round Merchandise Concessions Received Minus Those
   Given Explained with Paternalism 102

5.1 Uruguay Round Agricultural Concessions Received Minus
   Those Given Explained with Paternalism 114

6.1 Relationship between GTRIC-e and 2010 GDP per Capita 148

Tables

1.1 Total Merchandise and Commercial Services Exports 7

1.2 Applied Tariff Rates and Frequency of NTBs in OECD Countries
   (1994–1998) in Select Products 8

1.3 Concessions Given and Received during the Uruguay Round 9

1.4 Uruguay Round Tariff Concessions, All Merchandise 10

1.5 Paternalism versus Trade Liberalization Concessions 12

3.1 British Imports and Exports to the Empire 59

3.2 Value, Volume, and Price of Imports and Exports (FOB)
   of the Nonindustrial Countries 64

3.3 Tariff Rates in North America and Western Europe: Commodities
   and Stages of Processing, 1960 66

4.1 Characterization of Sentiment toward Trading Partners in
   USTR Press Releases, 1982–1993 88

4.2 Country Groups and Trade Sector References in USTR
   Press Releases 92

4.3 Country Groups and Trade Policy and Issue References in
   USTR Press Releases 92

4.4 U.S. Trade Sentiments in Press Releases through the Uruguay Round   93

4.5 Variables and Expected Signs of Coefficients   97

4.6 Paternalism Strength Index Values   98

4.7 Descriptive Statistics   101

4.8 Merchandise Concessions Received Explained with Paternalism
     and Negotiation Indicators   104

4.9 Textile and Clothing Export Growth Rates for Select Countries   107

4.10 Characterization of Sentiment toward Trading Partners in USTR
     Press Releases, 1982–1993, on Textiles and MFA and VERs and OMAs   109

5.1 The U.S. Trade Sentiments toward Trading Partners in Agriculture   112

5.2 Uruguay Round Agricultural Concessions Received Minus Those
     Given Explained with Paternalism   113

5.3 Agricultural Concessions Received Explained with Paternalism
     and Negotiation Indicators   113

6.1 U.S. Trade Sentiments toward Trading Partners in Intellectual
     Property   143

6.2 GATS Commitments Explained with Paternalism and
     Negotiation Indicators   154

6.3 Differences in GATS and PTA Commitments Explained with
     Paternalism and Negotiation Indicators   157

6.4 Existing WTO and GATS Commitments in Services Sectors   158

6.5 Comparisons between the WTO Telecommunication Liberalization
     Offers and Domestic Telecommunication Liberalization Programs
     of Developing Countries   164

6.6 GATS Commitments in Telecommunications Explained with
     Paternalism and Negotiation Indicators   165

7.1 An Empirical Summary of Sweet Talk   172

7.2 Effects of UNGA Voting Alignment with the United States on
     Manufacturing and Agricultural Concessions Received for
     Poor Countries   180

7.3 Effects of Export Market Diversification on Agricultural
     Concessions Received for Poor Countries   182

Preface

Without a sense of identity, there can be no real struggle.

Paulo Freire, *The Politics of Education* (1985: 186)

THIS book puzzles about trade reciprocity. It explores the conditions under which the trade concessions countries of the Global North–South make to each other deviate from reciprocity. The puzzle developed from two "real-world" prompts that made me reflect on identity issues underlying reciprocity. One was about a trade diplomat and the other about the marketplace, both about the Global South.

During 2006, I was a visiting scholar at the World Trade Organization in Geneva. An anecdote circulated about a trade diplomat from Sub-Saharan Africa who complained about not being invited to a particular meeting until the chair noted that he was sitting in the meeting from which he thought he had been excluded. Poor diplomat! He didn't even know he was there. His nationality changed as I heard the story repeated but the identity affixed on him remained the same. That of not knowing, of incompetence.

Around the same time, back in the United States, struggles raged on how the developing world was pirating secrets, inventions, and creative digital works. It was even stealing outsourced high-tech jobs, grounds on which the United States had stood confident with its competitive advantage. Several xenophobic and racist comments circulated through the media. Poor developing world! It suffers even when it knows.

I resolved to write *Sweet Talk*—it would deal with an old conflict, sugar, and a new one, telecommunications or information technologies. As I researched, my ambitions both tamed and multiplied. Merely providing a structured, focused comparison of two issues was not going to be persuasive. I had to be thorough. This book, therefore, presents a history of North–South trade negotiations in the postcolonial era. In doing so, it addresses issues in agriculture, manufacturing, and high technologies. However, I retained the title *Sweet Talk*, which came from thinking about sugar and telecommunications.

I argue that the North paternalizes and gives little to the developing world at trade negotiations. The developing world is better off when it helps itself, either through collective action at negotiations, or best off when it diversifies its exports in products and markets. Although rooted in the political economy of trade, this is ultimately a narrative about cultural identities, which starts with a clash of civilizations, or at least one "civilization." In the colonial days, the colonial powers set out to civilize the unenlightened other. In the postcolonial era, they benevolently dole out sweet talk, trade-capacity building assistance, and a few nonreciprocal trade preferences, while withholding on the meaningful trade concessions the developing world needs.

Empirically, the book employs mixed methods for providing evidence from several perspectives. The book develops an index for measuring paternalistic strength, and multiple regressions test the effects of paternalism and negotiation indicators on degrees of reciprocity. The official rhetoric of the United States in trade, specifically twelve years of press releases from the US. Trade Representative, is also analyzed using manual coding through NVivo content analysis software. Qualitative and historical descriptions trace the processes through which reciprocity works. The book narrates the North–South trade story in cultural terms and the rootedness of trade preferences in historically derived cultures; therefore, the book returns to colonial era history in a few places. Specific issue area cases—textiles, sugar, cotton, telecommunications, and outsourcing—provide a granular view.

Ultimately, the book is about the present, not the past. The WTO's Doha Round of trade negotiations launched in 2001 is practically dead, and the future of multilateral trade negotiations and North–South interactions is unclear. Developed countries fear exports from emerging powers such as Brazil, China, and India and seek to exclude them from their preferential trade agreements. Outside of trade negotiations, in the post-9/11 era, many have asked in the West: Why do they hate us? This book explores the underlying cultural conditions in the rarified halls of trade diplomacy. If cultural clashes can happen there, they can happen anywhere.

In the last decade as I worked through the ideas for this book, I incurred many debts to students, friends, family, colleagues, and policy practitioners (not mutually exclusive categories by any means). I began conceptualizing the subject with a graduate seminar on "The International Politics of Race" when I taught at Georgetown University. It was one of the most intense courses I have ever taught.

Four years ago, I retrained myself in quantitative methods and went for two summers to the Inter-University Consortium for Political and Social Research (ICPSR) at the University of Michigan. Several instructors and TAs—especially Bill Jacoby, Shawna Smith, Rebecca Grady, and Kelly Gleason—were remarkably helpful. They are people who believe in empirical data but think of quantitative analysis both as an art form and a science. I related to their worldview and empathized with the technique.

Margo Beth Fleming, my editor at Stanford University Press, persuaded me to place this book in my own series, "Emerging Frontiers in the Global Economy." Her argument was that I would be making a credible commitment to the voice of the series with my own work. Instead of sounding like an easy bargain, her words put the pressures of academic branding in me! I hope the book helps to vindicate a few of these fears. Nevertheless, it was a privilege to have Margo's guidance throughout the writing process, and I "dumped" my fears on her more than I would ever dare with another editor. I would also like to thank James Holt at Stanford University Press for his timely and perceptive assistance throughout the process, Margaret Pinette for careful copyediting, and Mariana Raykov for production assistance.

It takes several villages to write a book. I am thankful to many academic communities. Several colleagues provided feedback, and I am immensely grateful to them for engaging with my ideas. These colleagues include Susan Aaronson, David Armor, Jennifer Ashley, Renée Bowen, Dan Druckman, Manfred Elsig, Ben Graham, Surupa Gupta, Tamar Gutner, Virginia Haufler, Eric Helleiner, Tobias Hofmann, Niklas Hultin, Holger Janusch, Chris Kilby, Soo Yeon Kim, Mark Langevin, Laura Mahrenbach, Renée Marlin-Bennett, Aaditya Mattoo, Maximilian Mayer, Axel Michaelova, John Odell, Anh Pham, Peter Rosendorff, James Scott, Susan Sell, Gabriel Siles-Brügge, Paul Smith, Silke Trommer, Mayra Velez, and Bill Zartman. I extend a special thanks to my colleague Byunghwan Son for his incisive insights, for our lengthy conversations on international economics, and for being my Stata guru in the department. Two referees from Stanford University Press provided detailed and constructive feedback on each of the chapters and challenged a few precepts. This feedback was extremely important toward addressing loopholes in the book and for fleshing out unclear arguments. I am grateful to the referees for empathizing with my argument, while at the same time challenging me.

I also presented papers or chapters from this book at various conferences and academic seminars, and gained from these interactions. These include the American Political Science Association, the Du Pont Summit of the Policy Studies Organization, International Studies Association, Midwestern Political Science Association, Political Economy of International Organizations, and the Washington Interest in Negotiations. At George Mason University I benefited from two presentations to the brown bag seminar of the School of Policy, Government and International Affairs; the doctoral studies colloquium in the Cultural Studies Program; and a presentation to the faculty at the Global Affairs Program to help me address counterarguments.

The Emerging Frontiers in the Global Economy series promotes interdisciplinarity, methodological rigor, and accessibility. On the latter point, I presented my ideas at several undergraduate and graduate classrooms in the Washington, DC, area to discern students reactions. These institutions are George Washington University, the Global Politics Fellows at George Mason University, University of Mary Washington, and the University of Maryland, College Park. The students engaged passionately with the issues, and I would like to thank many for pursuing me with their questions inside and outside the classroom. My undergraduate honors seminars and graduate classes have heard several informal or formal presentations on this book. They have been some of my worst critics and best supporters. Daphne St. Jean's research assistance in the early stages of the project was invaluable especially on the Freedom of Information Requests to the U.S. Trade Representative's Office. I am grateful to USTR for timely compliance with my requests and for supplying large amounts of materials.

Thanks to two institutions for resources. Georgetown University, where I taught until 2012, allowed me to set up a graduate program in Trade, Technology and Development at the Graduate Institute for International and Development Studies in Geneva. The experience of taking my students every summer to Geneva and engaging with the community associated with the WTO and other international organizations was crucial for understanding the cultural gestalt conveyed in this book. George Mason, where I taught 2012–2016, and where I am currently on a leave of absence, provided research funds for me to undertake many tasks, including the ICPSR coursework and to learn NVivo. George Mason was also a perfect home for me to undertake the writing. This book's ontology is situated in international liberalism, but I hope it comes with a critical con-sciousness, which borrows from many colleagues' reactions to anything smack-ing of "neoliberalism." My appointments at the interdisciplinary Global Affairs Program, the doctoral Cultural Studies Program, and the Schar School of Policy and Government allowed me to engage in differing perspectives as an everyday practice. As the book goes through the publication pipeline I look forward to my appointment as Chaired Professor of Culture and Political Economy and as the Director of the Centre for Cultural Relations at the University of Edinburgh. My new appointment provides further opportunities for analyzing cultural prefer-ences and relations.

My partner Chuck Johnson is my rock. He has stood by me for every project, and provided me assistance with just about every page and piece of data. His support means the world to me. Chuck is my muse. There is another person who fills me with love for the world, and makes me smile. I learned my first lessons on fairness and justice from her. Chuck and I agreed that my mother would endorse the provocations in this book. Chuck and I, therefore, dedicate this book to my mother.

We all have our personal stories that make us think of the research ques-tions and puzzles that we do and that motivate us to pursue our dreams. My experiences include both hope and distress. A steadfast belief in the world of scholarship is always the next step forward.

7-5-17

List of Acronyms

ACP	African, Caribbean and Pacific countries
ACTA	Anti-Counterfeiting Trade Agreement
ACTPN	Advisory Committee on Trade Policy and Negotiations
AGOA	African Growth Opportunity Act
ASEAN	Association of South East Asian Nations
ATC	Agreement on Textiles and Clothing
ATPA	Andean Trade Preference Act
BATNA	Best Alternative to a Negotiated Agreement
BIT	Bilateral Investment Treaty
BPO	Business Processes Outsourcing
BRICS	Brazil, Russia, India, China, and South Africa
CAP	Common Agricultural Policy
CEES	Central and East European States
CMO	Common Market Organization for sugar
CSA	Commonwealth Sugar Agreement
DR-CAFTA	Dominican Republic-Central American Free Trade Agreement
EBA	Everything-But-Arms
EC	European Community
ECLA	Economic Commission for Latin America
EEC	European Economic Community
FAO	Food and Agriculture Organization
FBI	Federal Bureau of Investigation
FCC	Federal Communications Commission
FDI	Foreign Direct Investment
FDR	Franklin Delano Roosevelt
FIP	Five Interested Parties
GATS	General Agreement on Trade in Services

GATT	General Agreement on Tariffs and Trade
GNP	Gross National Product
GSP	Generalized System of Preferences
IBRD	International Bank for Reconstruction and Development
IMF	International Monetary Fund
IP	Intellectual Property
IPC	Intellectual Property Committee
ISI	Import Substitution Industrialization
IT	Information Technology
ITO	International Trade Organization
LDC	Least Developed Country
LICs	Low Income Countries
LMG	Like-Minded Group
LTA	Long Term Arrangement
MFA	Multi Fiber Arrangement
MFN	Most Favored Nation
MNC	Multinational Corporation
NAFTA	North American Free Trade Agreement
NAM	Non-Aligned Movement
NAMA	Non-Agricultural Market Access
NIEO	New International Economic Order
OECD	Organization for Economic Cooperation and Development
OMA	Orderly Marketing Arrangement
PSI	Paternalism Strength Index
PTA	Preferential Trade Agreement
RTA	Regional Trade Agreement
RTAA	Reciprocal Trade Agreements Act
SDT	Special and Differential Treatment
SPS	Sanitary and Phytosanitary measures
STA	Short Term Arrangement
SSM	Special Safeguard Mechanisms
TiSA	Trade in Services Agreement
TPA	Trade Promotion Authority
TPP	Trans-Pacific Partnership
TRIPS	Trade-related Aspects of Intellectual Property Rights
TRQ	Tariff Rate Quotas

TTIP	Transatlantic Trade and Investment Agreement
UNCTAD	United Nations Conference for Trade and Development
UNESCO	United Nations Educational, Scientific, and Cultural Organization
UNGA	United Nations General Assembly
URAA	Uruguay Round Agreement on Agriculture
USSR	Union of Soviet Socialist Republics
USTR	United States Trade Representative
VER	Voluntary Export Restraints
WIPO	World Intellectual Property Organization
WTO	World Trade Organization

Sweet Talk

Chapter 1

Introduction

The Subtext of North–South Relations

When asked for his views on Western Civilization, Mahatma Gandhi is famously supposed to have said it would be a good idea. Poor countries are equally cynical about western governments' commitment to free trade. With good reason: America and Europe are forever lecturing developing countries about the need to open their markets, yet they do their best to keep out many poor-country exports.

The Economist, "White Man's Shame," September 23, 1999

THIS book explains the degree of reciprocity in North–South trade relations. Specifically, it explains the lack of reciprocal tariff and nontariff concessions toward the Global South and the presence of a small amount of nonreciprocal trade concessions.[1] These meager concessions are analyzed in the context of the postwar rhetoric of benevolence toward the Global South and the West's exhortations to them to join the global liberal order.

The argument situates the lack of reciprocal concessions in the Global North's paternalism, defined here as a patronizing discourse resulting from a position of economic and political strength and cultural distance from the Global South. This paternalism can be historically traced back to colonial-era racism. Nevertheless, we would expect paternalistic countries, with a discourse laden with benevolence, to make trade concessions. Unfortunately, the paternalistic countries do not do so. The study employs mixed methods, two original data sets, and findings at various levels to validate its central supposition on the negative correlation between paternalism and trade concessions. The following pages examine every major issue in North–South trade: agriculture, manufacturing, services trade, and intellectual property. The book analyzes these issues at various levels: macroquantitative studies to provide a broad picture; case study methods for historical analysis; microcases such as sugar, cotton, textiles, and high-tech outsourcing that allow for granular process tracing. One of the original data sets is a paternalistic strength index (PSI), which measures the economic, political, and cultural distance of the Global South from the Global North. This index confirms that paternalistic strength is negatively related to trade concessions. At multiple levels and in multiple issue areas, the book con-firms that paternalism is not benevolent; it does not result in trade concessions to the paternalized.

We would expect that sweet-talking benevolent or paternalistic countries would make trade concessions to the Global South. We would expect that there would be some truth in the benevolent rhetoric about the concessions the Global North promises to make. This turns out to be a benevolent lie. The second original data set codes 1,925 pages of press releases from the U.S. Trade Representative's Office in the 1982–1993 period, roughly equivalent to the begin-nings and end of the Uruguay Round of multilateral trade negotiations. It finds that 93 percent of the paternalistic references, mostly about U.S. benevolence in trade policy, were toward the developing world. Yet there is very little to show in terms of meaningful concessions to correlate with this moral rhetoric.

The Global South's negotiation strengths explain the presence of even the minimal trade concessions, including nonreciprocal trade concessions that the developing world receives. Negotiation factors explored in this book include co-alition building, multilateralism, and the ability of the Global South to leverage its trade portfolios for obtaining concessions. Through multiple issue areas at multiple levels, the book validates that the few trade concessions the develop-ing world receives result from its negotiation advantages and not paternalistic benevolence.

This chapter and the next make a broad case for the lack of reciprocity and the presence of cultural preferences traced to historical racism in international trade relations. The subsequent chapters provide the empirical evidence. This introduction explains the argument in brief but first provides the reasoning against the main counterfactuals.

The Departures

Sweet Talk's findings are surprising and counterintuitive. Strategic trade theory and related concepts provide the counterarguments closest to the theoretical leanings in this book. These are examined here, although others follow later.

Strategic trade analysts would accept the case for lack of concessions but explain it differently as the pursuit of strategic interests in trade (and security policy).[2] Strategic trade theory predicts that trade concessions (or an open trade policy) are contingent on utility maximization strategies that employ specific import restrictions and export incentives, sometimes linked to a conception of

PTA "preference trade agreements"

the national interest.[3] We can expect prosperous states in the Global North to negotiate reciprocal concessions with Global South countries with large markets in seeking increasing returns and benevolently offer reciprocal or nonreciprocal trade access, as needed, only to those with small markets. Empirically, neither proposition is found to be valid in this book. The United States and the European Union (EU) now resist reciprocal trade concessions to Brazil, China, and India at the multilateral level and exclude them altogether in preferential trade agreements (PTAs). This book also provides some evidence that the Global North may have sought to "punish" trade coalitions such as the G10 to which Brazil and India belonged in the Uruguay Round by making even smaller concessions to them than to the rest of the developing world. In the PTAs with small states, there is no evidence of great power benevolence. The consensus is that PTAs do not offer small states a better deal than those negotiated multilaterally. Both the United States and the EU have squeezed every little concession they could from a small power, whether it is Costa Rica, Morocco, or Brunei.[4]

The security variant of the strategic trade explanation would predict trade rewards for allies and benevolence for small states that are important for Global North's strategic interests (Gowa and Mansfield 1993, 2004; Mansfield and Bronson 1997). Again, these are empirically dubious propositions. At the macroquantitative level, we find some evidence that the Global North might reward countries that are strategic allies, as measured through the UN General Assembly Strategic Index (Voeten 2015). However, when these data are parsed further into countries that are developing versus developed, the affinity index predicts concessions only to prosperous allies, mostly in the Global North (Chapter 7). David Lake's (2009) supposition regarding benefits to the subordinate states as the price to pay for the global order provided from superpowers also does not hold for North–South trade reciprocity.

There are also many examples in this book where the United States cast aside its strategic interests to not make any concessions or, worse, withdraw concessions to strategically important small countries. The inability of the affinity index to predict trade concessions to allies in the Global South is an instance at the macrolevel. At a microlevel, one example may be sufficient for now. In the 1980s, the U.S. President Ronald Reagan was trying to check against communist insurgency with the Caribbean Basin Initiative (CBI) launched in 1984. However, in 1987 the Reagan administration reduced the duty-free sugar quotas from the Caribbean from 2.7 million tons to 1.0 million tons, in responding to its sugar lobby, which led to a loss of 350,000 jobs and foreign exchange shortages in the Caribbean, which is counter to the logic of thwarting communism. Using the logic of the theory-infirming case study method, if the strategic interest argument does not hold in this most likely case of checking for communist insurgency under President Reagan, then it is unlikely to hold elsewhere (Eckstein 1975; Odell 2001).[5] There are many "elsewheres" described in the book.

A few findings in this book also deepen insights of strategic trade theory in showing how trade preferences may be culturally constituted (Mansfield and Mutz 2009). There are many products from the developing world—agriculture or textiles, for example—that would constitute a large share of the global trade volumes from the Global South if reciprocal concessions were allowed. We find that the developed world maintains protections on these products, thereby depriving the developing world the benefits of trade and economic advantages to consumers in the developed world. Here the book's findings may be consistent with a version of strategic trade policy that inefficiently rewards domestic producers (Grossman and Helpman 2002; Reinert 2008). The historical evidence presented in this book, in the protected agriculture and textile producers in these countries, shows the power of open deceit and manipulation, at times with the support of political leaders, and racist arguments against the developing world to keep out their exports. This book, therefore, veers toward culturally defined trade preferences while also showing that many models of strategic trade theory that take entrenched opposition of domestic trade interests are insufficient in explaining the puzzle posed in this book.

Finally, one might argue that the Global North's concessions toward the South are in the form of nonreciprocal preferences, such as that of sugar just mentioned. However, these concessions are very small, less than 2 percent of the trade volumes for the United States and the EU, and they result from the Global South's collective advocacy and not the Global North's benevolence. The story is complicated: The developing world did not initially seek preferences and accepted its provisions begrudgingly. Once the Generalized System of Preferences (GSP) was in place, it produced a system of dependency allowing the Global North to make claims about its benevolence, while restricting meaningful concessions. The book also shows that GSP system is conditional, and the North uses it strategically in another sense: to divide and rule. The 2015 services trade agreement directed at the least developed countries, offering them nonreciprocal market access, is an example. LDCs have miniscule services exports

GSP "Generalized Systems of preferences"

to the developed world, and the initiative for services preferences came from the North, not from the South.

Neither the "sweet talk" of paternalistic benevolence nor a majority of the "straight talk" of strategic trade theory explains the lack of trade concessions to the Global South. Instead the book advances an understanding of culturally constituted paternalistic trade preferences in the Global North, which only marginally include the developing world in the global liberal trading order. Trade concessions the developing world obtains result from its own negotiation advantages.

Other historical explanations—power politics and core–periphery relations—will be debunked in the conclusion and briefly later in this chapter. They fare even worse. There is one exception: The Global North has succeeded in creating dependencies in the South for certain products with preferential access. This is consistent with recent arguments on coercive diplomacy, where resource-rich states can manipulate the weak through trade dependence (Carnegie 2015). In doing so, the North thwarts attempts from developing countries for reciprocal concessions by either rousing dependent states to the cause of preferential access or shepherding the nondependent states toward such policies. Strategic trade theory might predicate that the paternalism that results in such manipulative preferences is in fact a strategic interest to keep out these countries' exports. If so, strategic trade theory's cultural underpinnings are underexplored.

Another significant counterfactual is David Lake's (2009) critical realist analysis of the international political order as one characterized by hierarchical relations, rather than anarchy. Lake argues that superpowers such as the United States exercise legitimate authority over the subordinates as an act of social exchange: While benefiting themselves, they provide a legitimate social order. He throws down a gauntlet in his preface: "If others believe that a social contract is an insufficient approach to understanding hierarchy between states, they should develop alternative theories, deduce their implications, and compare the evidence for and against their theory relative to mine" (p. xii). Lake deduces his perspective on authority and domination from above, from the perspective of superpowers.[6] This book posits paternalism and resistance from below, from the perspective of the Global South's "subordinate." For example, Lake's relational model does not allow for any bargaining and negotiation from the South—they are mostly "provided for." The theoretical suppositions and the evidence in this book demonstrate that the social exchange is unjust, possibly racist, and illegitimate in many ways. This does not mean that a social contract does not exist but that it is seriously broken.

Sweet Talk points out the broader issues of economic injustice inherent to North–South trade relations and the social meanings of these interactions. These meanings are important for understanding the longevity and legitimacy of the liberal world order. However, social meanings or cultural origins of trade preferences are important for another immediate reason: They predict North–South trade negotiation outcomes better than extant theory.

Explaining the Puzzle: Reciprocity

Cultural concerns are often missing from scholarly and media perspectives in the West on international trade. *The Economist* story quoted at the beginning of this chapter, about poor countries' cynical and collective beliefs regarding trade, is a departure. Gandhi references the cultural practices in the West that trumpet its civilization. Understood in the Global South, these historical references to civilization can carry the imprint of paternalism. In the past, they resulted in the North lecturing the South about economic development and making promises in return for adopting its prescribed market-oriented economic policies.

This book narrates a narrow story about trade reciprocity, but the broad meaning of the book's puzzle lies in the cultural context that intersects and departs from the empirical evidence about the developing world and international trade. The intersections provide a happy ending in which middle-income countries of the Global South begin to garner a bigger share of international trade to capture ever-growing shares of traditional and new high-tech services products (Table 1.1). However, this book also elaborates on a tragic story in which the West continually bars the Global South from flourishing in international trade despite exhorting it to participate in the global economy. The South's assigned position: Either accept the deal the North offers or be cast as obstreperous and unwilling. Table 1.1 captures this story for developing countries, whose share of world trade remains slow despite the benevolent "preferential treatment" they have received in trade from the developed world. For the low-income countries (LICs), the share of merchandise exports has declined from an already low figure of 0.7 percent to 0.5 percent. In fact, although high-income countries might claim that their "average tariffs" are low, the low-income countries of the Global South continue to face protectionist barriers for products for which they might

Table 1.1. Total merchandise and commercial services exports.

us$ billion rounded (current prices) and percentage of total world exports (in parentheses/rounded)

		2010	2000	1990	1980	1970	1960
Merchandise exports	World	15,228	6,456	3,473	1,973	304	124
	High-income countries	10,284 (67.6)	5,082 (78.7)	2,903 (83.6)	1,559 (79.0)	246 (80.9)	93 (75.0)
	Middle-income countries	4,858 (31.9)	1,350 (20.9)	548 (15.8)	409 (20.7)	54 (17.8)	29 (23.4)
	Low-income countries	82 (0.5)	24 (0.6)	16 (0.5)	14 (0.7)		
Commercial services	World	3,862	1,531	826	386		
	High-income countries	3,081 (79.8)	1,305 (85.2)	731 (88.5)	337 (87.3)		
	Middle-income countries	766 (19.8)	223 (14.6)	94 (11.4)	47 (12.2)		
	Low-income countries	21 (0.5)	6 (0.4)	4 (0.5)	2 (0.5)		

SOURCE: The World Bank, World Databank. Retrieved on February 26, 2013, from http://databank.worldbank.org.

claim comparative advantage. This applies to most agricultural commodities and, until 2005, to textiles. Table 1.2 shows that for primary foods (from meat products to oil seeds in column one), although the applied tariffs are low in Organisation for Economic Co-Operation and Development (OECD) countries, the frequency of nontariff barriers is high compared to that in low-income countries. On the other hand, the OECD maintains low tariffs and nontariff barriers (NTBs) for mineral ores and fuels that are crucial for its economies. Although both OECD countries and LICs employ tariffs, the frequency of NTBs on primary foods shows that the North has liberalized much less than the South in these important export products for the developing world.[7]

Two contrasting views frame this book's puzzle regarding reciprocity in the context of the happy and tragic circumstances of trade described in the preceding paragraphs. They obliquely reference the cultural conditions within which international trade takes place. Both deal with the World Trade Organization (WTO) or its prior incarnation, the General Agreement for Tariffs and Trade (GATT), which since 1948 has provided the negotiation forums for crafting the multilateral rules governing international trade. The first view enhances the image of the rule-based system that the WTO offers to note that these rules are inherently fair and result from the moral and ethical concerns of the developed world, in this case mostly the West. Ethan Kapstein (2008) represents this story

Table 1.2.   Applied tariff rates and frequency of NTBs in OECD countries (1994–1998) in select products.

Products category	OECD countries		Low-income countries	
	Applied tariff rates	Frequency of nontariff barriers	Applied tariff rates	Frequency of nontariff barriers
Live animals	47.4	28.4	16.5	2.3
Meat products	7.9	32.1	30.3	6.7
Dairy products	45.5	62.1	25.8	2.8
Cereal grains	2.7	39.3	14.0	7.1
Vegetables	3.5	30.8	25.5	8.0
Fruits and nuts	2.5	27.9	30.7	6.6
Sugar and honey	8.0	34.3	25.9	3.5
Animal feedstuffs	0.7	21.6	14.3	2.1
Oil eeds	1.2	23.0	18.8	4.8
Mineral ores	0.2	0.6	11.9	5.1
Mineral fuels	0.9	7.6	12.8	5.2
Leather and travel goods	5.4		26.0	
Textiles and clothing	10.0		30.2	
Footwear	11.9		29.8	

SOURCE: Merlinda D. Ingco and John D. Nash, eds., *Agriculture and the WTO: Creating a Trading System for Development* (Washington, DC: The World Bank, 2004), pp. 12–15.

in writing: The global economy is a hard case for "fairness economics," Kapstein admits, but he seeks to demonstrate that principles rooted in fairness and justice have guided even the strategic considerations of powerful states in framing WTO rules. Great powers make fair propositions because they believe unfair ones would be rejected. Therefore, Kapstein exhorts scholars to move beyond the prisoner's dilemma beggar-thy-neighbor policies in the game theoretic models used for understanding international strategic conduct. As evidence, he cites data that show that the European Union and the United States made far bigger concessions in millions of dollars in tariff cuts than the developing world at the Uruguay Round (Table 1.3). Kapstein's case is partially or wholly corroborated in, and follows from, other findings from negotiation theory and normative concerns in trade policy. Negotiations studies now frequently show that multilateral forums such as the WTO allow the weak to make gains against the strong (Singh 2000; Odell 2006). Studies of normative concerns also show that ethical considerations can guide negotiators (Albin 2001).

The counterpoint about reciprocity is that developing countries, as in the *Economist* story cited earlier, make few gains in international trade negotiations; consequently, they are stuck in unequal exchanges whereby they open

Table 1.3. Concessions given and received during the Uruguay Round (in millions of dollars).

Country/region	Concessions received	Concessions given
European Union	578,816	627,939
United States	214,791	283,580
Argentina	6,331	0
Brazil	38.037	98
Indonesia	6,323	81
Malaysia	36,108	28,966
Sri Lanka	1,595	33

SOURCE: Ethan Kapstein (2008), "Fairness Considerations in World Politics." Kapstein statistics cited from J. Michael Finger et al. *Market Access Bargaining in the Uruguay Round: Rigid or Relaxed Reciprocity?* (Washington, DC: World Bank Publications, 1999).

their import markets more than their gains through exports. Scott and Wilkinson (2011) note that both the past and current multilateral trade rounds offer the developing world precious little by way of meaningful concessions. They start their evaluation with econometric computational general equilibrium models that predict the effects of tariff liberalization or gains from trade on the economy. Given the variation in estimates, the total global gains from trade between 1996 and 2006 vary between $376 billion and $2,080 billion in the decade following the close of GATT's Uruguay Round of trade talks from 1986 to 1994 (614). The gains to the developing world from these econometric models are meager, note Scott and Wilkinson, and they continue to fall because developed countries neither fully honored the agreements they made in GATT's Uruguay Round of trade talks nor have they agreed to make deep concessions in products of value to the developing world in agriculture and nonagricultural market access (NAMA). In the now defunct Doha Round, launched in November 2001, the developed countries offered duty-free and quota-free access to 97 percent of the products coming from the least developed countries. However, the excluded 3 percent includes most of the products that make up a bulk of exports from least developed countries. In Bangladesh's case, the United States offer to liberalize its trade is worthless: It lists products that Bangladesh does not export (623). This story is widely corroborated in other accounts where developed countries are able to obtain concessions in products such as intellectual property (Sell 2003) and services (Kelsey 2008; Narlikar 2003) but are loath to make concessions in products that matter to the developing world (Jawara and Kwa 2003; Srinivasan 1998). Table 1.4 provides additional data showing that the

NAMA   Non-agricultural Market Access

Table 1.4.   Uruguay Round tariff concessions, all merchandise.

Industrial economies		Developing economies	
Percentage of imports	*Depth of cut**	*Percentage of imports*	*Depth of cut**
30	1.0	29	2.3
30	1.6	29	2.3

* Depth of cut: $dT/(1 + T)$ comes from the weighted average across all products, including where no tariff reductions were made.
SOURCE: Michael J. Finger and Ludger Schuknecht. "Market Access Advances and Retreats: The Uruguay Round and Beyond." In Bernard Hoekman and Will Martin, eds., *Developing Countries and the WTO: A Pro-Active Agenda* (Oxford, UK: Basil Blackwell, 2001).

concessions the developing world made at the Uruguay Round were more than twice those of the developed world.

Both of these narratives about the presence and lack of reciprocity are par-tially correct, but taken together they are contradictory. In the first instance, the WTO is a rule-based system and offers many advantages to developing coun-tries, both through their inclusion in its negotiation forums to effect trade con-cessions in the future and also through the WTO's legalistic dispute settlement mechanism to correct present and past unfair trade practices and injustices. Fairness and justice considerations, even those motivated with self-interest, as Kapstein argues, may be widely prevalent. In general, scholars have also dem-onstrated that ethical and humanitarian considerations have historically been on the rise (Barnett 2011; Crawford 2002). However, the limits and connections between the narrative of reciprocity and the one about its absence are crucial. There is only scattered empirical evidence that justice and fairness consider-ations have led to meaningful and effective concessions in trade negotiations (Singh 2010). The data that Kapstein provides are not persuasive: As the sec-ond narrative and the empirical evidence provided later validates, developing countries have often not received concessions in products in which they can claim an advantage. A careful look at the original sources from where Kapstein cites his figures (Finger, Reincke, and Castro 1999: 22) also paints another story. In percentage terms (concessions received minus given), many developing countries in the world (India, Korea, Malaysia, Thailand, Turkey) fared much worse than the EU or the United States. Second, the data do not include trade preferences, making the option of lower tariffs in the United States and EU un-available to them, thereby overstating the value of the concessions that the de-veloping world received (Finger, Ingco, and Reincke, 1996: 13, 20).

Sweet Talk shows that most of the concessions developing countries have received—especially the ones that the developed world casts as benevolent—have resulted from hard-fought negotiations. Chapter 4 details how even the GSP, taken to be an exemplar of the Global North's benevolence, resulted from (or deflected) demands for market access from the developing world. The developing countries have taken advantage of multilateral processes to advance their interests and, if they have the resources, to redress their grievances through dispute settlement in challenging sugar, banana, cotton, underwear, and gambling rules in the developed world that are arrayed against them. Sweet talk continues. The latest example is the now-moribund trade round that started with the sweet talk of development aspirations when it began in November 2001 and was termed the Doha Development Agenda.

A Brief Cultural Context of the Argument

This book advances supplementary hypotheses, rooted in cultural factors, which resolve the tension between the binaries of justice and bullying mentioned in the preceding section. The following question provides the context: Under what conditions can the developing world effect concessions in its favor in international negotiations governing trade? This leaves open the possibility that there are gains to be made and losses to be faced.

Two broad hypotheses result from the theoretical literature discussed in the next chapter: (1) Developed country paternalism results in few trade concessions to the developing world; (2) The developing world's advocacy and negotiations facilitate the trade concessions that it receives. The second hypothesis is rooted in the collective advocacy and negotiation strategies from the developing world that are seen to positively affect the concessions developing countries receive. The first speaks to the spectrum of developed world discourse, from fairness to paternalistic, the former leading to concessions whereas the latter is problematic (even racist) in terms of concessions. Paternalism often results in trade measures that over the long run do not make developing country exports competitive. Foreign aid might be an example.

Smart negotiations from the developing world coupled with developed country paternalism collectively explain both the concessions gained and lost and the rhetoric of benevolence that often accompanies Western behavior at international negotiation forums such as the WTO. Nevertheless, paternalistic sweet talk and handouts or side payments eclipse the negotiated trade

Table 1.5.   Paternalism versus trade liberalization concessions.

Paternalistic concessions	Combination: Paternalism and trade concessions	Negotiated trade liberalization concessions
· Side payments · Moral statements · Trade capacity-building assistance · Affixing developing world in dependency narratives · Foreign aid	· Preferential schemes (often negotiated) · Special and differential treatment · Some forms of quotas (e.g., sugar)	· Reduction of subsidies · Decreasing tariffs · Eliminating quotas · Elimination of other tariff and nontariff barriers

SOURCE: Adapted from J. P. Singh, "Development Objectives and Trade Negotiations: Moralistic Foreign Policy or Negotiated Trade Concessions?" *International Negotiation* 15 (2010): 367–389.

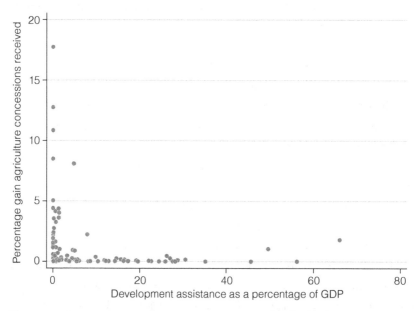

Figure 1.1.   Percentage agriculture concessions received and official development assistance as a percentage of gross national product (GNP).

concessions that the developing world receives (Table 1.5). Figure 1.1 makes this argument visually: Countries that receive foreign aid do not receive trade concessions in agriculture, suggesting that foreign aid may be a side payment. Studies acknowledge that foreign aid is inherently political.[8] I add to these understandings in showing that paternalistic countries would rather provide foreign aid than trade concessions.

The case for smart negotiations is well documented but will be spelled out in detail in the next chapter. For now it is important to note that global institutions do allow developing countries a fair playing ground. However, from the discussion so far it does not seem that the Global North plays fair. Evidence points to the contrary: Tariff peaks, nontariff barriers, and low levels of tariff cuts on products of interest to the developing world speak contrary to the rhetoric of benevolence and paternalism. The unsuccessful Doha development round of trade talks (2001–2015) at the WTO featured coalition building and often empirically well-informed claims from the developing world about unfulfilled promises and effects of unilateral trade liberalization. The United States and the EU responded through seeking regional and preferential trade agreements (RTAs and PTAs) with select and, until recently, weak trading partners against whom they can make substantial gains. This phenomenon is known as forum shopping in negotiation literature. A new trend is to hold negotiations in secret, such as the Anti-Counterfeiting Trade Agreement (ACTA) on intellectual property, which began in 2008 and concluded in 2011, and the Trans-Pacific Partnership trade negotiations signed in 2015 between the United States and trading partners mostly in East Asia. ACTA has endorsed highly restrictive intellectual property practices, after the modest gains the developing world made at the beginning of the Doha Round on intellectual property. Moreover, in the case of many RTAs and PTAs, the developed world has sought to exclude countries such as Brazil, China, India, and South Africa who provide leadership to other developing countries in the WTO. Kapstein (2008) argues that neoliberal global institutions have an in-built fairness, but it seems that the developed world navigates around the fairness of multilateral institutions.

The case *against* fairness considerations is not hard to make, but the case *for* paternalism does not follow automatically. The scope and consequences of postwar paternalism are gauged in this book by modeling it as a latent variable whose influence can be sifted through a variety of behavioral factors.[9] For these purposes, the book develops the paternalism strength index (PSI). The index will be fully explained in Chapter 4. In short, it measures the strength of the paternal countries in terms of their export market diversification (WITS 2015), ability to make other countries vote with them in the UN General Assembly (UNGA) (Voeten 2015), and their cultural distances from former European colonies (Hofstede 2015). Export market diversification is opposite of colonial patterns where colonies were locked into exporting few primary products to former colonizers. The UNGA affinity index addresses the political condition of the weak in international politics, whereas the cultural distance variables are self-explanatory.

ACTA — Anti counterfeiting Trade Agreement

The negative correlation between the PSI and the inability of the Global South to receive trade concessions in this book is indicative of the broad supposition. However, to show *how* paternalism informs trade negotiations, historical process tracing is important for causality, which this book provides in each of its issue areas and case studies. In doing so, this book seeks to demonstrate that paternalism and unfair practices are intrinsically linked and rooted in historical racism. Paternalism comes couched in the language of fairness and justice. Such *sweet talk* sounds good, but, as the following pages will show, the blocking of developing country interests at the WTO smacks of injustice and, arguably, racism.

A focus on paternalism connects postcolonial history with colonial racism. The connection is intuitive if we ask ourselves the following rhetorical question: Did the colonial masters switch from policies of domination and racism to those of liberal internationalist benevolence when they left the lands they occupied? Ethical arguments that ended colonialism may not be sufficient to demonstrate that racism ended with decolonization (Crawford 2002). Although not coterminous, colonial racism and postcolonial paternalism are related.

A nuanced conceptual explanation on paternalism follows in the next chapter because elements of racism and benevolence have always coexisted. As summary, the famous debate in the early sixteenth century regarding the status of the colonized as human beings affixed the ways in which Europe "imagined" and acted on its interactions with the colonized world until the twentieth century. Shortly after the Spanish conquest of the Indies, Juan Gines de Sepulveda argued that the "Indians" were savages and fit to be enslaved, although Bartolome de Las Casas noted that they were humans who needed to be converted to Christianity and introduced to "civilization" as the Europeans imagined it. The colonized world was assigned an inferior and dehumanizing status in both narratives. The dispute centered on human faculties for the reason that Europe had recently discovered among its own inhabitants. The early sixteenth-century debate was never quite settled, but the idea that Europe was bringing civilized conduct to the savages or natives informed the moral justifications for colonialism for three centuries, although within Europe there were strong protests. Nevertheless, even at the time of decolonization, the European elite continued to argue that the colonies were unfit to govern themselves. The postcolonial projects of economic benevolence—foreign aid, preferences in trade, persuasions to "modernize," technical schemes for catching up, exclusions from

U.S.–EU decision making—are all ontologically connected to colonial and paternalistic reasoning. If postcolonialism settled the sixteenth-century debate in elite quarters, it favored Bartolome de Las Casas: Colonies needed civilization, and the developed world would be the benefactor for these efforts.

A stark rejoinder to the civilizational narrative is Europe's sense of its moral superiority, in which the need to construct a civilizational "other" rationalized its actions in the colonies. However, Europe did not wake up to its racist policies until Hitler. The word *racism* stood for Hitler's policies of racial purity; colonial policies were never understood as racist. Again, a full exposition must await, but the following quotation from Aimé Césaire's (2001: 36) classic *Discourse on Colonialism*, lays bare the European project of racism, which was introduced to Europe in the form of Hitler: "He [Hitler] applied to Europe colonialist procedures which until then had been reserved exclusively for the Arabs of Algeria, the 'coolies' of India, and the 'niggers' of Africa."

Paternalistic rhetoric is, therefore, understood in this book in the context of colonial and interwar histories of racism. Liberal international institutions such as the United Nations were partly prompted out of the need to counter Hitler-like racism, and many agencies such as the United Nations Organization for Education, Science and Culture (UNESCO) explicitly undertook studies to counter racism. Nevertheless, racists themselves informed these lofty purposes. Cordell Hull, the Secretary of State under President Roosevelt, widely credited with providing the impetus to create GATT, strongly believed that only superior nations such as the United States had a right to colonize. Winston Churchill and his negotiators defended trade preferences they gave to the colonies, not because they brought benefits to the colonized but because the Tories among them viewed imperial preferences as the continuation of the British Empire. Churchill's racist references to the colonies and dominions abound in history books.

Differences and Frames

Paternalism and racism in international trade negotiations have never received the book-length treatment they deserve. Various disciplines present partial and ideological treatments that either misconstrue or ignore such claims. Cultural studies construes "neoliberalism," vaguely understood as degrees of free trade in this case, as a grand ideology that explains all contemporary forms of injustice, evil, and inequality. Neoliberalism is seldom defined, and its central claims are mischaracterized. In the Marxian variant of cultural studies arguments, race or paternalism, if mentioned, are always secondary to claims about class. As Chapter 7 will show, such claims are theoretically grand and empirically tenuous. An equally grand claim is that of power politics assuming that the developing world gets a bum deal because they do not have a better alterative. This book shows that the weak can get better deals from their negotiation alternatives and that the shape and scope of the bum deal is better explained through paternalism. International trade negotiations literature, of course, understands preferences in a political economy context, although the next chapter records the hints of social and cultural meanings of trade preferences among officials and interest groups that scholars now record. Nevertheless, racism, or prejudice toward a group of people based on the color of their skin, is excluded a priori in most models, and its inclusion here would probably, and frustratingly, make a trade theorist gasp.

The book mostly attends to the effects of paternalism, a follow-up to colonial racism. This book takes intellectual risks but also situates them in the growing awareness and literature on the cultural origins of preferences and institutions (Akerlof and Kranton 2010; McCloskey 2010; Mazower 2009). The intellectual risks are necessary. Sweet-talking developed nations continue to create the impression that their hearts and pockets bleed for the developing world. Meager foreign aid budgets and the dwindling resources of multilateral development organizations are often sugarcoated with this rhetoric. This ignores the hard-fought concessions that the developing world effects for itself in international trade negotiations. Negotiation strategies underscore the ways in which the developing world can ensure that international rules approach reciprocity and fairness.

The next chapter details the case for paternalism and the details on the conceptual and causal links important for this book. The puzzle or the dependent variable in the book is the degree of reciprocity that results from North–South trade negotiations. Paternalistic rhetoric provides a false sense that trade relations are governed through the North's benevolence and empathy to the South's development concerns. If paternalistic countries were really benevolent, we would expect developing countries to do better than reciprocity in trade concessions. In actuality, they fare worse. The chapter, therefore, provides an analysis of the negotiation strategies used by the Global South to steer trade concessions in their favor.

Empirical evidence for the effects of paternalism and negotiation strategies is provided through mixed methods: Multiple regressions techniques test the argument at the macrolevel, historical, and case study methods provide both process tracing and a granular look, and content analysis of official trade documents searches for presence of paternalistic rhetoric in trade policy. The book's logic is situated in causal inference but enriched both through quantitative variables and cultural contextualization.[10] Chapters 3 through 6 provide the empirical substantiation for the propositions advanced in this book. Chapters 3 and 4 examine North–South trade negotiation at the broadest level. Chapter 3 attends to the GATT era up to the beginning of the Uruguay Round. Chapter 4 deals with merchandise negotiations during the Uruguay Round and the Doha Development Agenda that was launched in 2001. In both chapters, the negotiation concessions resulted mostly from developing country negotiation strategies. It is important to note that Chapter 4 also provides quantitative evidence for paternalism and links it with the lack of reciprocity in merchandise trade negotiations. The presence of benevolence and paternalism should lead us to expect the opposite. Chapters 5 through 6 detail evidence for three broad issue areas in trade drawn from opposite ends of extant theories regarding developing country comparative advantage. Chapter 5 discusses trade in agriculture and then specifically trade in commodities such as sugar and cotton. In both, as the developing world gained a comparative advantage, the developed world became increasingly protectionist. Chapter 6 details the case of high-tech issue areas: intellectual property and trade in services, with a special reference to telecommunications and business process outsourcing (BPO). Trade in services, with less historical baggage, offers the best instance in this book for the ability of developing countries to join international markets. Intellectual property rights offer the best illustration of the coercive and manipulative ways in which the developed world foisted an international agreement on the developing world.

Part I

Understanding History

Chapter 2
Who Is Served by Paternalism?

Take up the White Man's burden, Send forth the best ye breed
Go bind your sons to exile To serve your captives' need;
To wait in heavy harness, On fluttered folk and wild—
Your new-caught, sullen peoples, Half-devil and half-child.

Rudyard Kipling, *The White Man's Burden*

COLONIAL histories often stress the paternalistic relationships between the rulers and the ruled: The white man talks sweetly; he speaks caringly for his subjects, half devil and half child; the folklore and poetry sing of his hardships and his helping hand.

Postwar Europe and the United States continued the paternalism, at least rhetorically, promising economic assistance and partnerships in a new world of international organizations to the newly formed nation-states out of former European colonies. The pertinent question for this book becomes: *Did the paternalistic rhetoric translate into meaningful trade concessions?* The white man's burden translated bluntly into economics meant the following: Would he make trade concessions to the less fortunate as reciprocity or as benevolence? The colonial world had produced vast amounts of grains and minerals, and its "infant industries" produced processed goods such as sugar, cotton, and textiles. Trade concessions for the developing world were imagined in postwar organizations only in abstraction. Neither was there much support historically for trade justice or benevolence. The foundational texts of international relations (IR) instead quote Thucydides: The strong do what they can and the weak suffer what they must. Interstate justice or benevolence is hard stuff.

This chapter first analyzes arguments in favor of, and against, interstate justice and paternalism—the strong helping the weak—before turning to the conditions in international negotiations that allow developing countries to obtain concessions in their favor. Empirically, the book will show that the Global North by and large has adhered neither to norms of justice nor to meaningful paternalistic assistance. Paternalistic concessions are examined as departures from reciprocity to the extent that they are unilateral concessions made to the developing world, often in lieu of trade concessions that the developing world needs. Examples of sweet talk without providing any trade concessions are also easy to document (look again at Table 1.5).

Paternalistic cultural preferences among the strong predict the lack of trade reciprocity in North–South trade negotiations and hence the shape of injustice in global trade relations. The argument for justice and cultural preferences in this book is made at several levels, chief among which is the empirical institutional context of the WTO and its salient norm of reciprocity in trade concessions. Justice results from a fair exchange of concessions that benefits both the strong and the weak (Albin 2001; Armstrong 2012), whereas paternalistic assistance follows from placing the weak in a disadvantaged or inferior position, lacking agency to change their circumstances on their own (Baker 2015; Barnett 2011; VanDeVeer 2014/1986).[1] The arguments in favor of justice arise from procedural or institutional norms that facilitate fair exchange, but they also rest on societal preferences for fair exchange that the elite reflect.[2] Similarly, paternalism reflects societal or elite preferences to assist or enable those perceived to be in a disadvantaged position. The argument for benevolence is unsustainable from the perspective of a theory of preferences, from the ground up among individuals, or among great power societies or interest groups, though there is some descriptive and experimental evidence to support such claims in economic history. In fact, it is easier to make a case for paternalism and cultural prejudices in trade discrimination, although paternalism and acts of benevolence are also not mutually exclusive. Idealism among the elite also does not translate easily into favoring the weak. The history of racism and paternalism, therefore, limits the case of elite or societal preferences for benevolence.

The case for negotiation concessions through multilateral processes is possible, even if difficult, when involving the strong and the weak. This chapter explores several types of conditions leading to such concessions. Paternalistic concessions include continuation of historical preferential schemes (though these also benefit the "patrons"), whereas "just" reciprocal concessions include features of international institutions that allow weak powers to gain concessions in their favor. Except for a brief period in the late 1960s and early 1970s, the developing world mostly opposed paternalistic concessions before the Uruguay Round.[3] Moreover, the evidence shows that neither paternalism nor justice have resulted in many concessions to the developing world. Negotiated trade concessions have mostly reflected economic advantages in the developing world (comparative advantage and trade diversity, for example) but also coalitional strength among weak powers. These negotiation conditions explain the concessions the developing world obtained at the Uruguay Round (1986–1994) and the beginning of the Doha Round (2001–). In turn, these concessions explain forum shifting among the great powers. Although the Doha Round has sputtered on, negotiations on substantive issues effectively ended in July 2008 when India refused to accept the deal on agriculture that the United States offered. To continue the Doha Round would have meant reciprocal concessions; instead, the developed world shifted to preferential and bilateral trade agreements, where the weak have a harder time getting concessions, and to exclude countries such as China and India.[4] Taken together, the theories of liberal preferences and negotiation discussed in the following pages, in the context of great-power paternalism, underscore the minimal conditions under which the developing world obtains trade concessions.

Understanding Trade Concessions

The argument in this book is that developing countries received trade concessions not from the benevolence of the powerful but due to the collective strength of the weak at international negotiations. The term *benevolence* ideally encompasses the willingness of the powerful to play by trade rules that are just and fair.[5]

Trade concessions are hard to measure, especially when trying to compare them across several countries and multiple issues (and subissues) through long periods of time. In multilateral negotiations, involving many issues and parties, understanding the vocabulary of concessions takes various forms. This includes tariff and nontariff measures and, in the case of services and intellectual property, various forms of market access measures and regulatory enforcement. Furthermore, concessions can also be measured through their incidence on the shares of trade for particular products for different countries. An average tariff of 3 percent for all products in an importing country would mean little for an exporting country facing a peak tariff of 30 percent for its primary export product.

The degree of reciprocity, or the give-and-take of trade concessions, serves as the dependent variable for my analysis. Reciprocity is not only a widely understood principle within trade negotiations but also informs notions of international ethics and law. There are roughly two literatures on reciprocity, the normative (ethics) and the strategic (efficiency) traditions, both of which regard reciprocity to be desirable for international justice or utility maximization reasons respectively. The normative tradition examines the rise of fairness and exchange in international relations to discover mostly the social meanings of reciprocity with embedded notions of justice; the strategic tradition examines the empirical substance of reciprocity in light of the utility-maximizing conduct of economic actors.[6] This section starts with empirical observations on trade that intersect with notions of strategic efficiency and ends with societal reciprocity to make a case for the missing (normative) understanding of the pathological social biases such as racism that lead to divergences from reciprocity.

Reciprocity is an ambiguous concept to measure in strategic terms. Despite the difficulty of measurement, specific trade concessions and their implementation provide a first-order glimpse of negotiation outcomes. At a broader level, these measures can be further understood in the context of social exchange norms and enforcement of international law. Berridge and James (2003: 224), in *A Dictionary of Diplomacy*, note reciprocity as a "very influential" principle governing state conduct and "observance of legal obligation." In the context of trade concessions at negotiations, reciprocity provides a sense of the winners and losers. Those who argue in favor of GATT/WTO multilateral processes providing mutual benefits for everyone point to "reciprocity" as the most important principal governing trade concessions (Albin 2001, 2015). The GATT preamble exhorts states toward "reciprocal and mutually advantageous arrangements directed to the substantial reduction of tariffs and other barriers to trade and to the elimination of discriminatory treatment in international commerce." Article XXVIII bis of GATT, subsequently incorporated into the WTO, provides the legal basis through "negotiations on a reciprocal and mutually advantageous basis" and notes that tariff reductions "are of great importance to the expansion of international trade."[7] However, GATT texts are ambiguous as to what reciprocity means, leaving it to negotiating parties to work out the framework at each negotiation within which concessions would be made.

Reciprocity has been variously understood in negotiations, but the consensus is that it implies some balance either in the approach or in the actual trade concessions states make to each other (Rhodes 1989). In practice, this can mean equal concessions or sacrifices among negotiators, a tit for tat, or responding to an overall pattern of concessions among negotiators (Albin 2015: 44–45). Reciprocity is often explained in the context of GATT/WTO's Article I on most favored nations (MFN), the most famous principle governing international trade, which emphasizes that any advantage, favour, privilege or immunity granted by any contracting party to any product originating in or destined for any other country shall be accorded immediately and unconditionally to the like product originating in or destined for the territories of all other contracting parties.

This abjures parties from not only according specific privileges to a subset of parties or products but also from seeking these privileges only for themselves. Bagwell and Staiger (2001) argue that reciprocity understood in the context of MFN provides the most efficient economic outcome. They also interpret the GATT history and literature to note that reciprocity is meant to be a "broad manner in which governments seem to approach trade negotiations" (299).[8] Negotiation practice may be different.

International negotiations are strategic and sequential. In practice, states trade concessions and hold favors until the other party responds or, in Keohane's (1986: 4) terms, involve "specific reciprocity" where negotiating parties "exchange items of equivalent value." Axelrod's (1985) model of cooperation, which arises out of iterative strategic interactions, is an example. Keohane writes that "diffuse reciprocity," where states contribute to provision of public goods without expecting immediate returns, is rare and follows only where international regimes are strong.[9] International trade principles have a long history, and the WTO is an important international institution, but trade negotiations, reflecting underlying national interests and employment numbers and incomes, mostly feature highly strategic conduct, and thus diffuse reciprocity is indeed rare.[10] This also means that, in evaluating trade concessions, the researcher can stay close to the ground, as negotiators do, and try to measure reciprocity within trade rather than in exchange for concessions elsewhere. Foreign aid programs directed to the developing world to mitigate effects of trade liberalization or carrots and sticks in foreign policy to induce developing countries to make concessions can, therefore, be understood within the context of specific reciprocity. Finger and Winters (2002: 50) note: "Participants and commentators use reciprocity, or its functional equivalent, 'balance,' as a standard against which to evaluate an outcome. The rules, however, do not define that standard; determining the standard is part of the evaluation itself." Writing at a broader level, Jackson (1997: 27) reiterates the rationale for the adherence to this ambiguous rule: "Notions of reciprocity and a desire to depend on other nations' observance of rules lead many nations to observe rules even when they do not work."

Trade reciprocity is strategic precisely because it is mutually advantageous, especially in the way that it thwarts inefficient outcomes in multilateral negotiations. Bagwell and Staiger's (1998 and 2002) rigorous proof of this insight rests on state motivations to increase national welfare while facing political temptations to increase tariffs. Their model illustrates that states are motivated to enter into trade agreements to avoid the terms of trade externality from their market power, which moves part of the cost of the tariff to foreign producers but can also result in a high unilateral tariff that is inefficient. They note that if this externality did not exist, there would be no need for GATT. Governments escape the terms of trade externality temptation (or pressure) through trade agreements, while increasing national welfare.

The language of interests and the legitimacy of agreements from the WTO are not mutually exclusive. Of paramount importance here is the forum through which negotiations take place. Bagwell and Staiger (2002) borrow from Jackson (1997) in describing the rules-based approach toward bargaining at the WTO that diminishes the power-based asymmetries at the WTO. One of their central conclusions has been to emphasize that reciprocity and nondiscrimination (MFN) when taken together increase global welfare the most. The absence of MFN also explains their opposition to PTAs and GSP that will be examined later.

Therefore, trade reciprocity, even when strategic, carries an internal legitimacy and offers a baseline for examining if trade negotiations cater to a notion of justice (Albin 2001: 44). Other terms like *fairness*, *quid pro quo*, and *overall package* are also used to describe reciprocity. All negotiated agreements are considered legitimate because of at least minimal convergence of interests among all parties (Albin 2001).[11] The WTO's consensus rule for all agreements lends a further sense of legitimacy. However, agreement does not mean reciprocity, of course, which is an additional condition implying some give-and-take among negotiators. For example, Sylvia Ostry (2001) notes that the Uruguay Round was a grand bargain in which the developed countries phased out quotas in textiles and clothing in exchange for the developing world agreeing to concessions in a variety of manufactured and services products and agreement on intellectual property. Reciprocity was also important within issue areas: The United States and the European Community sparred over agriculture, and some fairness within these negotiations was important (Albin 2001: chapter 4).

Trade literature is also replete with direct or indirect references to nonfulfillment of reciprocity in developed–developing country trade relations. Scott

(2007: 103–104) opposes the Ostry thesis mentioned earlier to note that the Uruguay Round "was not a balanced agreement." Richardson (2009: 204) calls the Uruguay Round a "bum deal" rather than a "grand bargain."[12] The developing world has also questioned the record of Uruguay Round implementation, for example in agriculture, as not reflective of reciprocity.

Looking for specific reciprocity can also lead states to look for concessions in specific products from particular countries. Preeg (1995: 187–188) writes that, during the Uruguay Round, the United States looked for specific reciprocity in new issues such as telecommunications and financial services. But the country does not shy away from denouncing such specificity from other demanders. When a group of four cotton-exporting countries demanded an end to cotton subsidies at the Doha Round ministerial in Cancun in 2003, U.S. Trade Representative Robert Zoellick reacted against such narrow reciprocity by referring to the overall package in which cotton would be a part of the overall agreements.

Reciprocity or the balance among concessions becomes even more difficult to gauge considering nontariff barriers and new issues in trade negotiations. The list of nontariff barriers includes quantitative (quotas, preferential schemes) and nonquantitative measures such as regulatory, distribution, and health standards. Again, the negotiators' sense of balance in concessions traded with each other—whether tariffs or NTBs—remains important. Larson (1998: 129) notes that during GATT's Kennedy and Tokyo Rounds of trade talks, negotiators often used rules of thumb to calculate the total trade that would be covered by the percentage reductions in tariffs. Toward the end of the Uruguay Round, negotiators also widely expected developing countries to make tariff cuts averaging 25 percent, and 33 percent for developed countries (Finger, Reincke, and Castro 1999: 8).[13]

There are several studies that try to measure reciprocity or the concessions that countries make to each other during trade negotiations.[14] Finger and Winters (2002: 57) calculate concessions both in terms of the weighted averages of tariffs before and after the Uruguay Round negotiations and the value of trade to the importing country applying the tariffs. These data are used for the dependent variable in this book (Chapters 4 and 5). Their summary statistics confirm the win-win of multilateral negotiations: The sum of absolute differences in tariff concessions is 86 percent, and the sum of absolute differences in concessions received for overall imports versus exports is 58 percent. These win-win statistics confirm Bagwell and Staiger's (1998) insight regarding the welfare maximizing motivation for state to sign a reciprocal trade agreement. However, as Table 1.4 in the introductory Chapter 1 showed, the depth of cuts developing countries made was greater than the cuts made by the industrial economies (Finger and Winters 2002: 58). The latter finding does not negate Bagwell and Staiger's insights, which predict that, lacking market power, for terms of trade externality, small states would move toward zero tariffs. This book, however, confirms an alternative explanation, consistent with the cultural history of North–South trade relations.

There are not many studies that calculate services concessions or liberaliza-tion commitments, as they are known. Roy, Marchetti, and Lim (2007) compare the liberalization commitments thirty-six WTO members made in services dur-ing the Uruguay Round and initial concessions in the Doha Round and compare them against the concessions that these countries made in recent preferential trade agreements. They demonstrate that the concessions the developing coun-tries made to the United States in the PTAs are much greater than those made at the WTO. These data are used in Chapter 6.

Given the difficulty of calculating reciprocity quantitatively, it is hardly sur-prising that the evidence for the balance of concessions between the developed and developing world tends to be partial as in the quantitative studies previ-ously cited, and qualitative studies to follow, often times rooted in norms of fairness or justice. Sell (1998) notes that in intellectual property negotiations the developed world got 95 percent of what it wanted. Although not speaking of reciprocity, Jawara and Kwa (2003) note that developing countries are generally bullied in trade negotiations and give more than what they receive at the WTO.

A mixed-method approach is, therefore, necessary to measure and describe trade concessions and reciprocity. This book analyzes quantitative data, where available, to describe trade concessions, but most of these data address Uru-guay Round concessions. The book also borrows from historical and compara-tive methods. The empirical chapters provide a history of reciprocity since the formation of the GATT. This historical context, in turn, informs the theoretical hypotheses generated for this book. The quantitative and qualitative evidence presented later shows that the North–South concessions have not been recipro-cal with the gains tilted in favor of the North.

The evidence later also provides a structured focused comparison of two issues since the Uruguay Round at two levels (Lijphart 1971; Odell 2001). The issues examined at the broadest levels are agriculture and high-tech issues (services and intellectual property). I analyze quantitatively the macro outcomes in agriculture and intellectual property and services, but each chapter also provides details with a particular case to deepen my argument: sugar and cotton in the case of agriculture and telecommunication and business processes outsourcing in the case of services. The two sets of independent variables in this study, degree of paternalism and the negotiation strength, vary in the two issue areas examined, and the method of structured focused comparison allows an evaluation of the conditions that produce variable outcomes in reciprocity. We would expect strong paternalism and seasoned negotiation strategies in agriculture and less in new issues. Across the two issues, the biggest finding is that concessions have been reciprocal in services but not in agriculture. The developing world has sought market access concessions in both, even undertaking unilateral liberalization in services, but its attempts have been thwarted in agriculture where the Global North needs to make concessions. Given the common and strong negative effect of paternalism in both cases, the difference lies in the negotiations tactics.

The difficulty of analyzing reciprocity needs some additional context in the normative tradition of reciprocity mentioned earlier, especially if we are to link broad theories of justice and cooperation with strategic and empirical studies of reciprocity. In analyzing the imbalance in trade relations, many analysts have focused on norms parallel to reciprocity such as ethics, fairness, and justice (Armstrong 2012; Wraight 2011; Narlikar 2006). Most of these studies acknowledge the difficulty of sustaining these norms and address the underlying global understandings and political theories and raise questions of global justice from the distributive impact of trade policies. Cecilia Albin (2001, 2015) is an exception because she takes reciprocity to be an aspect of justice norms *within* negotiations. These are the microdistributions on which rests the macro case of justice and fairness; therefore, calculating the degree of reciprocity is important. This book follows a similar strategy, taking into account existing quantitative studies dealing with trade concessions but also providing a description of the major trade concessions the developing countries made and received. This is necessary for connecting the micro empirical and strategic substance of reciprocity with higher-order questions of justice and ethics.

Advances in international political economy, especially developments in formal theories of reciprocity and strategic trade theory, can also help to bridge the gap between the normative and strategic observations of reciprocity. The

first step in this direction would be to point out the need to move beyond numbers, despite their importance. Not surprisingly, negotiators and policy makers
themselves care about the numbers attached to concessions and the volume
of trade that they affect. As already mentioned, many economists have calculated these concessions. A WTO official once told me, "Everything has a dollar
value here." Given these numbers, economic studies generally make a case for
or against trade based on welfare or global collective gains or losses (Bagwell
and Staiger 1998; Bhagwati 2002; Bayard and Eliott 1994). One of Bagwell and
Staiger's contributions is to show that market access concessions traded at the
WTO can be easily translated into the language of overcoming terms of trade
externality, which motivates states to undertake such bargaining.

Nevertheless, these studies have not answered all the questions about the
political and the social dimensions of reciprocity. For example, Bagwell and
Staiger (2013) argue that the Doha Round could be a development round if developed countries move away from special and differential treatment (SDT) and
the developing countries come to the bargaining table to negotiate reciprocally.
Their insight is that with SDT developing countries have no way to check against
demands for protection in their home markets or employ reciprocity commitments to liberalize their markets effectively. Therefore, preferential treatment
is trade distortionary and economically inefficient. My conclusions support this
thesis but only after investigating the North–South motivations for creating
SDT: a set of cultural preferences in the North that deflected demands in the
1950s and 1960s for infant industry and market access, while coercing the Global
South to a historically derived system of European "imperial preferences" for
colonial products. Anderson's (2013) review of Bagwell and Staiger's SDT thesis,
although mostly about efficiency, also notes that for the developing world SDT
is a moral concern. Jackson (2000: 232) points out that Bagwell and Staiger's
global efficiency criterion may not be culturally universal. Krugman (1997) goes
further to note that economics by itself cannot understand negotiation motives
and behavior.[15] A second example is also important for examining the underlying motivations. Bagwell and Staiger (2002: chapter 10) explain the presence
of export subsidies in agriculture with recourse to strategic trade theory (specifically Brander and Spencer 1985). Although export subsidies increase global
welfare, through reduction of prices for consumers, subsidizing governments
nevertheless want to reduce them to release the burden on their national budgets. However, if strategic trade theory can explain the incidence of subsidies

that are welfare maximizing, then why cannot its insights be equally applicable to those that are welfare reducing? McGillivray (2004), for example, shows that governments are maximizing a political function in protecting goods and that they respond to a variety of factors in doing so, including the type of industry and the political system. At this point, the question is no longer about the desirability of reciprocity but the causal factors that will make it diverge from efficiency. The next subsection will situate negotiation motivations in the historical legacy of colonial racism.

Concessions that states make to each other at international trade negotiations provide incentives or disincentives for producers and consumers. They are forms of property rights that require enforcement. Trust and legitimacy are well-known conditions in institutional political economy for the voluntary enforcement of property rights (North 1990; Greif 2006). Although legitimacy could be induced through coercion, voluntary due obedience is both efficient and ethical (Hurd 1999: 188). Lake (2009: 188) notes that "legitimacy originates in the opinions of the subordinate." However, as I will argue later, Lake himself reverses this causality: He takes subordination to be the opinion of the subaltern. Therefore, to understand the degree of trust or legitimacy in trade concessions, it is necessary to analyze the underlying political economy of their negotiation and the social context of benevolence or strategic conduct that informs these negotiations.

A political economy of reciprocity helps to connect the microfiber of concessions to the broader case for social exchange and enforcement. The broad vision of a pluralist international society of states or a solidarist society of global actors is embedded in cooperation around shared ideals and norms of reciprocity.[16] Historical norms of diplomatic conduct invoke reciprocity even though the word does not enter the lexicon of international treaty language until the late eighteenth century. The following oft-cited passage from one of the foundational texts in diplomacy from Francois de Callieres (1716/1963: 11) can be read as invoking reciprocity:

To understand the permanent use of diplomacy, and the necessity for continual negotiations we must think of states of which Europe is composed as being joined together by all kinds of necessary commerce, in such a way that they may be regarded as members of one Republic, and that no considerable change can take place in any one of them without affecting the condition, or disturbing the peace, of all others. The blunder of the smallest of sovereigns may indeed cast an apple of discord among all the greatest powers, because there is no state which does not find it useful to have relations with the lesser states and to seek friends among the different parties of which even the smallest state is composed.

Theories of society or of markets both speak to reciprocity as the condition that provides trust to interactions. Adam Smith's moral political economy of the invisible hand in markets relies on socially understood exchange (Smith 1991/1776) that can include or exclude people (Akerlof and Kranton 2010; Finn 2006). Sociologists have long noted that forms of social exchange provide the basis of legitimacy for any social order (Elster 1989). It is in this sense that reciprocity provides the legitimacy of enforcement to international law (Jackson 1997: 27; Larson 1998: 126).

Understanding Trade Preferences and Paternalism

A valid theory of trade concessions that the North grants to the South—resulting from the cultural context of negotiations, namely paternalism—needs to account for the underlying motivations and objectives in trade policy, which guide negotiators in making concessions. The economic basis for trade lies in comparative advantage, but its realization through trade policy is a political process that deals with the economic and cultural preferences of those affected positively or negatively by trade. Biased cultural preferences, for example, are evidenced most immediately in the many xenophobic attacks that can accompany media coverage of trade. However, xenophobic attacks in media or society may or may not result in a xenophobic trade policy. A historical examination implicates racism as the original sin or causal variable that shapes colonial occupation, postcolonial paternalism, and the associated "racial codes" that have accompanied international North–South international trade policies.[17]

The myth of trade policy is that the North demonstrated plentiful benevolence in according trade privileges to the South in the postcolonial era. This myth starts with the idealism that informed the creation of global institutions that would provide opportunities for the South to improve its social and economic circumstances. Before dealing with preferences specifically related to trade, a brief review of the literature on the North's benevolence destroys the case for idealism and links trade preferences with the same paternalism and racism that regulated relations among the colonial masters and the colonized. Some idealism is definitely evident in the creation of postwar trade institutions, but its actual translation into a benevolent trade policy that overcomes the colonial past is hard to discern.

Racism and Paternalism in Economic Relations

International economic relations scholarship has accorded paltry attention to racism and paternalism. This is shocking. More than two centuries of colonial occupation, including that of the Americas, resulted in the worst genocide and dehumanization ever recorded in world history. International trade was exploitative. Acemoglu and Robinson (2012: 251) note that the burgeoning sugar plantations in the Caribbean and in Latin America led to Africa trading 300,000 slaves in the sixteenth century. This increased to 1.35 million in the seventeenth century, and 6 million in the eighteenth century. Add to this indentured servitude in the nineteenth century, after the abolition of slavery, and the exploitation of resources in the colonies, often with the assistance of local rulers, and the story becomes the heinous in its proportions.

Marginalizing race issues is not a case of paradigmatic conceptual jails or normal science.[18] It is conscious and willful neglect, even within paradigmatic and normal science traditions. The beginnings of American political science, and the American Political Science Association, were intricately connected to research on the science of colonial governance (Vitalis 2010). These political scientists believed that "hierarchy was natural, it was biologically rooted, and it could be made sense of best by such concepts as higher and lower races, natural and historic races, savagery and civilization, and the like" (Vitalis 2010: 929). William E. B. Du Bois had called attention to the twentieth century as the "problem of the color line." Following Du Bois, Henderson (2013: 72) notes that international relations were "interracial relations." The influential journal *Foreign Affairs* was known as *Journal of Race Development* between 1910 and 1919 (and *Journal of International Relations* between 1919 and 1922). The lead-up to the foundation of postwar international institutions was replete with references to racism from the Nazi era when this word began to be used with reference to the fate of the Jews in Germany. Postwar international institutions such as UNESCO carried out significant studies of racism during the 1950s. The issue was well and alive during the time of the Uruguay Round of trade talks through successive global resolutions and conferences on racism.

Given the origins of international relations in race issues, its neglect in the postwar era is surprising. This omission is well recorded. Vitalis (2000, 2010) explains both the "norm against noticing" race and silencing of those who do. Hobson (2012) notes that racism has taken on a subliminal dimension in the study of international relations but manifests itself in "colonial-racist guilt syndrome" and through an almost exclusive focus on Western relations to the neglect of North–South relations. Persaud and Walker (2001: 374) underscore "the epistemological status of silence" given to race issues in international relations. Doty (1993: 445) surveyed five influential international relations journals between 1945 and 1993 and found that only one of them mentioned the word *race* in the title to an article. Mittelman (2009: 100) surveyed the titles of papers presented at the International Studies Association between 2000 and 2008 and found that only 0.37 percent of the papers contained the word *race* or its extensions such as *racialized* and *racism*. I found that the 2015 American Political Sciences Association Annual Convention with the theme "Diversities Reconsidered" had several papers with the word *race*, *racial*, or *racism* for American and comparative politics and political theory but not a single paper dealing with racial politics (or paternalism and xenophobia) in any section traditionally made up of international relations scholars, or presented by an IR scholar outside of IR sections. There was one panel on "Empire, Imperialism, and Race" in the political theory section.

Race remains a secondary or silent category in global political economy analyses in analyzing trade preferences of the elite, businesses, or individuals. Critical theorists accord some attention to race (Chowdhry and Nair 2013; Chin 2008). But they relegate it to serving the aims of capital-owning classes, whereas liberals often celebrate the foundation of international institutions in the mid-twentieth century that fostered global cooperation, therefore sidestepping a horrid evil in human history. A few studies have now moved beyond this exclusive link with class to try to provide a more nuanced and pluralistic perspective (Anievas et al 2015; Hobson 2012).

The neglect of racism in international relations is consequential. It ignores the presence of racism, or its operational counterpart paternalism, in trade relations. The term *paternalism* refers to granting of nonreciprocal trade favors or a moral discourse while harboring strongly negative or stereotypical feelings toward sets of people and, as the term implies, acting as a parental authority toward another understood as an infant. A brief account of racism and paternalism in the colonial era thus facilitates an understanding of these latent factors that shaped North–South trade relations in the postwar era.

Recent scholarship has begun to address paternalism, but most of it has addressed issues of colonialism and, in the postcolonial context, of humanitarian intervention. Crawford's (2002) majestic study on the processes of argumentation in global politics shows how arguments against colonization produced a cultural change in Europe. This study is important but does not document sufficiently the continuation of racist or paternalistic practices in the postcolonial era. Michael Barnett (2011) addresses the issue of postcolonial paternalism. He accords attention to feelings of superiority that undergird paternalism, but his broad conclusion is that current weak paternalism, tempered with the presence of global institutions and technocrats, is both benevolent and beneficial. "Love it or hate it, paternalism is an enduring feature of global life" (Barnett 2012, 520). Hobson's (2012) study is an exception, not only in documenting the racist and antiracist intellectual history of international relations but in explaining postwar paternalism much the same way that this book does. Hobson (2012) regards paternalism to be a subliminal influence, disguising colonial racist discourses about bringing civilization to the inferior races with a postwar language of benevolence and superiority, which remain Eurocentric.

This book is a departure from current studies of paternalism in three methodological ways. First, as noted, my method departs from scholars such as Hobson (2012), who rejects hypothesis testing, or Barnett (2011), who provides only thick description. As paternalism is latent (or subliminal), we need rigorous empirical techniques that uncover this bias.[19] Second, as the empirical results will show later, paternalism has not resulted in any meaningful material concessions to the developing world. This runs counter to the findings from the implications of paternalism in humanitarian and foreign aid literatures (Baker 2015; Barnett 2011). Third, ontologically, this book shows that the paternalistic Global North actively resists attempts from the Global South to not play the subservient "other." This is consistent with analyses that note that the Global South is playing by global market rules but that the dominant lens in the North tends to be to reserve the Global South for trade preferences rather than trade concessions (Ford 2003; Singh 2010; Hopewell 2016). Intellectually, most studies of paternalism cited earlier, with the exception of a few essays in Anievas et al (2015), have a rather incestuous Eurocentric bias in documenting paternalism only in the West and hardly ever studying the resistance to paternalism, or its consequences, in the colonies or the Global South. Crawford (2002) draws on feminist scholarship to note that an ethic of care that accords equal dignity to the caregivers and the cared could result in beneficial humanitarianism. This ideal future has not arrived yet in the world of humanitarian giving, let alone trade relations.

A Brief History

Racism in political economy of colonial–colonized relations was part of a grand ideology of superiority. The hallmark of nineteenth-century racist thought was to posit the colonized as racially inferior. This was validated through extant measurements of science, differentiating skull types and body features, and reinforced through other intellectual enterprises. Darwin's theory of evolution and natural selection created tremors among the religious views of human life, but it also created a bogus science of racial differences. This scientism ran in parallel to racist ideas: "Most non-Europeans were regarded, even by Darwin, as 'barbarians': he was astonished and taken aback by their wildness and animality" (Shipman 1994: 19). It was relatively easy for nineteenth-century science to make a case for the superior evolution of Europeans in racial terms, a case taken to extremes in the Nazi era.

Political theory in the nineteenth century spoke eloquently either to dismissing the barbarians or, conversely, to caring for them. Liberal political philosophers such as John Locke, James Stuart Mill, and John Stuart Mill sanctioned the idea of tutelage for the colonized to make them civilized (Mehta 1999). Said (1979: 40) summarizes the European case with due irony:

The Oriental is irrational, depraved (fallen), childlike, "different"; thus the European is rational, virtuous, mature, "normal." But the way of enlivening the relationship was everywhere to stress the fact that the Oriental lived in a different but thoroughly organized world of his own, a word with its own national, cultural, and epistemological boundaries and principles of internal coherence.

Henderson (2013) notes that the presence of the racial and savage "other" was essential to the political thought of Hobbes, Locke, Kant, Rousseau, and Mill: The anarchic condition, salient to realist political analysis, applied more to the uncivilized racial other than to the civilized West.[20] In other words, the problem of the global order and civilization was that of the racially inferior populations. A late example of this was Wilsonian internationalism, which advocated self-determination for the colonies in his "Fourteen Points" speech to the U.S. Congress in 1918. Hobson (2012: 168) notes that the celebration of self-determination in Wilsonian idealism "obscures the racist side of his politics that issued in no uncertain terms the need for the Western imperial civilizing mission in the primitive East."

Racism as a word was introduced in the 1930s to refer to anti-Semitism in Germany and its *Juedenrein* project to rid the country of Jews (Rattansi 2007: 4). Outside Germany, intellectual ideas that made the case for innate human differences, holding particular groups to be biologically or morally inferior, were being debunked but not widely accepted. Barkan (1992) provides an account of the efforts between social and natural scientists in the interwar era to debunk scientific racism that had gained steam since Darwinian ideas. However, although racist ideas were in decline in the United States, there was initially little opposition to Nazism. Barkan (1992: 288) notes that whereas science and anthropology had questioned racial abstractions in the past, the prejudices within science and scientists were not fully addressed. In 1938, Alfred Boas from Columbia University, who had led the intellectual fight against racism, returned disappointed from the International Congress of Anthropological and Ethnological Sciences. He had received support from members, but no formal antiracist platform was adopted at the Congress. American anthropologists also pointed out that Jim Crow blood banks in the United States were not that different from Nazi classifications on race (Barkan 1992: 334). The League of Nations' idealism did not rise above racism: Its scientific studies on the effects of climate differences further institutionalized racism (Tambe 2011). It was only after global institutions like UNESCO took up the cause against racism that *The New York Times* reported in 1950 that there was no scientific basis for racial classification or discriminations. It had become relatively easy by then to accept the claim that biologically all human beings were the same and that their intermixing did not lead to any sort of racial dilution. After 1950, "It was no longer possible to make crudely racist statements without challenge" (Crawford 2002: 309). However, as Barkan (1992: 241) notes, attempts to demonstrate that race was a social myth continued to meet with opposition.

Nazi propaganda was countered at the Council for Allied Minister on Education (CAME), which began to meet in 1942. The United Nations Educational Scientific and Cultural Organization, which formally came into being November 1945, developed as an idea out of these meetings. UNESCO has featured the most intense intellectual history of all global organizations and sought to address racial and cultural conflict at the deepest level (Singh 2011). Its

Preamble is based on a speech by Clement Attlee, adapted from words by the poet Archibald Macleish: "Since wars begin in the minds of men, it is in the minds of men that the defences of peace must be constructed." Julian Huxley, who was UNESCO's first director-general, was a biologist but also a scientific humanist. He helped to forge the link between culture and science at UNESCO (Huxley 1947).

Among global organizations, UNESCO is at the forefront in confronting racism. The fourth line of UNESCO's Preamble states that denials in dignity and respect for human beings lead to conflict and war; in particular, it mentions "the doctrine of the inequality of men and races." The issue of race came up often in UN resolutions. In 1948, a resolution from the UN Economic and Social Council asked UNESCO to study the issue scientifically, and UNESCO resolutions in 1949 adopted this agenda. UNESCO (1950) issued a powerful but controversial statement—*The Race Question*. Several social scientists, educators, and biologists signed the statement, which addressed *Homo sapiens* as one species with no differences or racial purities. The statement was, in fact, critiqued for ignoring intellectual and social differences. However, several other studies followed, including one from Lévi-Strauss (1958), who also signed the 1950 statement. UNESCO has addressed race on several occasions. The monumental eight-volume *General History of Africa* sought to counteract prejudices and stereotypes in history. The 1966 International Covenant on Economic, Social and Cultural Rights, supported by the Soviet Union and the Eastern bloc, focused on group rights as opposed to individual rights. Article 2 addressed forms of discrimination, including race. In 1978, UNESCO adopted a Declaration on Race, but its context was informed by the anti-Israel advocacy at UNESCO in the 1970s. The declaration did lead to four World Conferences on Racism in 1978, 1983, 2001, and 2009, most of which have been marked with anti-Israel and anti-Semitic remarks. UNESCO's program on cultural diversity has also broadly addressed issues of human diversity, but the limited implementation of the 2005 Convention on the Protection and Promotion of the Diversity of Cultural Expressions has mostly focused on "national" cultural products such as films and television programs.

Personalities and power politics have tempered and even vitiated noble aims to address racism at the global level through UNESCO or at the United Nations in general. Julian Huxley, UNESCO's first director-general, was well known for his views on eugenics even as he espoused a humanist vision for UNESCO.

The studies in the 1950s encountered not just intellectual resistance but popular opposition to respecting the dignity and equality of human beings as the often-violent civil rights movement in the United States reminds us. As already noted, the UNESCO program on race since the 1970s has been hijacked by Arab countries' opposition to Israel.

The quest to create postwar institutions is often related as a struggle between power politics and ideology and omits references to colonial racism. Even UNESCO's reference to race arises in the context of Nazism; therefore, Aimé Césaire's cynical comment that Europe's discovery of racism within its borders was not news in the colonies. Banton (2002: 42–46), in fact, notes that the attribution of racism to pathology among the Nazis only was a noble lie. Racism had been and was rampant all over Europe.

The presence of racism and racists in the strategic calculations of great powers, or a silent category in the historical categories idealists count, is a grievous omission in accounts of international institutions but one that continues to rankle the canonical explanations. E. H. Carr's (1964) *The Twenty Years' Crisis*, originally published in 1939 as World War II began and often viewed as a foundational text of the study of international relations, balances the utopian ideology of global intellectuals who believed in international institutions against the bureaucratic reality of power politics that informed their creations and practice. The latter more or less win. Similarly, Inis Claude's (1956) *Swords into Plowshares* charts the evolutionary trends toward the foundation of international organizations since the nineteenth century against the presence of power politics. The presence of power politics in the creation of postwar institutions is indisputable, and a tug-of-war exists between the historical recesses of realism and emerging utopias. But they miss the question of race.

Racist ideologies and prejudiced people informed the creation of the United Nations. Mazower's (2009) history of the origins of the United Nations connects its creation to racism and colonialism of the past rather than as a departure from these processes. British imperial interests were grafted into even Wilsonian principles, as the United States overlooked British racial practices in the colonies, and Britain continued to oppose resolutions that would lead to racial equality well into the 1940s. In the 1940s, Gandhi noted that the Nazis and the British were indistinguishable in many respects. He was responding to a letter from an Indian in South Africa who wrote: "Many of us think that the British are sweet-tongued but they pursue their own ruthless policy in spite of honeyed words, whereas Hitler would be more frank" (quoted in Mazower 2009: 163). Therefore, the United Nations, in Mazower's account, would civilize the emerging colonial nations: "A democratic imperial order had been preserved, thanks to the formation of the UN, even as fascist militarism had been defeated. The world of civilizing inferior races, and keeping them in order, could continue" (Mazower 2009: 21).[21]

Racism shaped the paternalistic underbelly of postwar international development, a case that is beginning to be documented. Barnett's (2011) analysis of paternalism in the context of humanitarian assistance—particularly the shift he describes from imperial humanitarian to postwar neohumanitarianism—is relevant for international development in general: "Humanitarianism was still something done for and to others, not with them" (105). Similarly, Crawford (2002: 409) notes that "the failure to treat the intervened upon as if they were active agents, links colonialism and present-day humanitarianism." Vitalis (2010) blasts scholars such as Martha Finnemore (1996) who overlook the racist origins of humanitarianism for conflating humanity and humanitarianism with equality of peoples. Humanitarian efforts have always been reserved for nonwhite peoples and non-Western states.

The end of colonialism did not mean the end of racism. Duncan Bell's (2013) recent introduction to a special issue on race and international relations for *The Cambridge Review of International Affairs* acknowledges the silence on race but notes that scholarship in the special issue and elsewhere "concerns the extent to which racism, and in particular white supremacism, continued to permeate and shape practices and conceptualizations of global politics after 1945 and into our present time" (2). Roxanne Doty (1993) treats racism as a "site" to note that "oppression, domination and power are at the very core of the concept of race" (452). In particular, Doty calls attention to "racial codes" that "have facilitated the rearticulation of racism disguised with ostensibly non-racist rhetoric" (453). In the U.S. context, these codes apply to social welfare, urban inequalities, and affirmative action. At this broad sociological level, Desmond and Emirbayer (2009) record several fallacies that relegate racism to the past, of which two are particularly important: the legalistic fallacy, which notes the end of racism because of the presence of laws and institutions that constrain racism; and the ahistorical fallacy, which relegates discrimination to the past. "But racial domination survives by covering its tracks, by erasing its own history" (Desmond and Emirbayer 2009: 338).

At the international level, racial codings can be discerned in studies of international development. In fact, international development emerged as the macropaternalistic worldview within which the North's efforts to help the South would be located. Development vocabularies were invented to guide these efforts and connected them to paternalism. The Global South was underdeveloped, backward, or traditional, and it became, as before, the white man's burden to bring modernity and modernization. Escobar (1995) documents "the messianic feelings and the quasi-religious fervor" in the report of the World Bank's first-ever mission to a developing country, Colombia, in 1949. Escobar's point: "Development was—and continues to be for the most part—a top-down, ethnocentric, and technocratic approach, which treated people and cultures as abstract concepts, statistical figures to be moved up and down in the charts of 'progress'" (Escobar 1995: 44). Ferguson (1990) shows that international development efforts sought to connect places like Lesotho to markets and capitalism, when the country's history demonstrates otherwise; it was always connected to markets and capitalism—as part of the international division of labor and as a supplier of commodities. Similarly Guyer (2004) notes that transactional and exchange mechanisms, the essence of markets, have always existed in her account of Atlantic Africa: Africans are, therefore, not bewildered by such transactions, and only the Europeans who fail to understand them are bewildered. Development practitioners' worldviews did not allow them to see markets and transactions in the very places where they sought to introduce them because underdeveloped peoples could not possibly possess these higher-order institutions.

Paternalism was widespread and widely shared among the elite and their societies in the North. This section has analyzed the macrocontext of paternalism in colonialism and the creation of postwar global governance institutions. The next section now turns specifically to a theory of societal preferences in trade in which cultural biases, xenophobia, and paternalism play a central role.

Trade Theory and Cultural Preferences

Trade theory has undergone four important changes in the last 200 years. Its genesis lay in the international division of labor and factor-based comparative advantage. Starting with Schattschneider (1935), trade theory began to accord attention to the way comparative advantage must reckon with the industry-based interest group politics that accompany trade. Since the 1980s the political economy of strategic trade policy has raised important questions about sources of trade advantage. Finally, in the last two decades, trade theory has slowly started to accord attention to the role of cultural identity and preferences in trade. This last development, dealing with cultural identity, discussed in the following paragraphs, provides the context to make the link with paternalism and racism.

Trade theory predicts that the abundant factor in any economy provides the comparative advantage to nations relative to their trading partners and allows that factor to enhance its returns (Stolper and Samuelson 1941). Scarce factors lose from trade and thus their returns are lower. Trade theory is wistful about returns to an economy. It assumes that factors disadvantaged from trade will selflessly move out of the way and find alternative employment. This is the Hecksher-Ohlin model of trade theory. The Ricardo-Viner model of trade theory acknowledges the limits of labor mobility. Especially if labor mobility is low, import-competing sectors will resist trade. Furthermore, the costs of collective action for scarce factors are lower than those for the more numerous numbers of the surplus factor (Olson 1982).

Trade theory has provided the material basis for trade. Politics provides the reality. Kindleberger (1978: 49) points out that, even with a two-sector model of free trade, the abundant factor must have political power to overcome the scarce factor's protectionist stance. The political organization for trading sectors depends on the distributional gains or losses from trade. Those employed in import-competing industries will, therefore, organize in favor of protection, and the demand for protectionism will increase with decreasing levels of factor mobility among sectors. Schattschneider (1935) broke down this level of political organization to the industry level rather than broad-factor deployments in agriculture or industry. Nevertheless, Gourevitch (1986) and Rogowski (1989) explained the ways in which broad factors align themselves politically when exposed to trade. He demonstrates the existence of Germany's iron–rye coalition where Bismarck succeeded in cementing a coalition within four years between the free-trade Juncker landlords and protectionist heavy industry (39–40). The role that a cultural ideology plays (Kulturkampf in this case) is often overlooked in these analyses, but, in the context of this book, it is important, and I will return to it later. The political economy of cleavages and alignments provides an opening to examine the role of cultural factors. Hiscox (2002) predicts that class-based coalitions would follow where interindustry mobility among factors, impacted by trade, is high, whereas industry-based coalitions follow in cases where it is low. This analysis also omits references to cultural ideologies in cementing class or industry coalitions.

Political economy since the early 1980s has also shown the relationship between political institutions and the market for trade or protection among affected groups. Chapter 1 outlined strategic trade theory's central insight. It questioned the origins of trade in comparative advantage to show that imperfect competition and increasing returns to scale, along with government incentives such as subsidies, can both create and expand trade (Krugman 1987; Busch 1999). As argued earlier, Bagwell and Staiger's (2002) and Brander and Spencer's (1985) findings on agricultural trade subsidies are consistent with this argument. However, the case of "endogenous protection" may not always be efficient; Grossman and Helpman (1994, 2002) show that protection results not only from interest groups' contributions to politicians but also from the government's reliance on industry for the information it needs. McGillivray (2004) and Milner and Kubota (2005) both speak to the relationship between democracy and trade: In the former case to show the variety of factors the UK politicians take into consideration in providing protection while maximizing votes; in the latter case the support is for trade in democracies as leaders consolidate their support with emerging groups of labor, farmers, and capitalists who are the new beneficiaries of trade.[22]

This book adopts a cultural lens to deepen the understandings in political economy but also to depart from them with each set of my independent and dependent variables: degree of paternalism, negotiation advantages, and reciprocity. First, despite the weight of history, the political economy tradition refuses to explain the elephant in the room of North–South trade politics: namely, the presence and effects of paternalism on the interest groups and officials in the West. Milner (1997, 1999) has made a strong case for understanding preference formation and institutional influence. Milner and Kubota (2005) is one such study. This book's evidence on the effects of cultural preferences provides an alternative explanation for the provision and legitimacy of measures such as GSP, MFA (Multi-Fibre Arrangement), GATS (General Agreement for Trade in Services), and TRIPS (Trade-Related Aspects of Intellectual Property Rights). In doing so, the book provides an empirical foundation for connecting the politics of trade with broader questions about justice and oppression. Second, although the political economy literature does not rule out negotiations, it concentrates on determinants of trade policy at the national level. Few scholars have examined the empirical conditions under which developing countries can improve their trade alternatives at the international level (this will be taken up in the next section). This book argues that the cultural context of these struggles is important.[23] Finally, the consensus in the political economy literature favors reciprocity; this book provides a cue for examining the deviations from reciprocity albeit from a cultural lens.

The relationship between cultural factors and trade theory is about how groups view their own identity versus those of others and the weight to be assigned to material factors in these perceptions. Economic models described earlier, whether Hecksher-Ohlin or Ricardo-Viner, hold material factors to be predominant in shaping utility maximization calculations. Kindleberger (1978, chapter 2) astutely points out the group dynamics that underlie these material factors in trade: "The flexibility of a society in devising institutions to accomplish its purposes under changing conditions is a function of its social cohesion, which in turn depends upon its internal social mobility, system of communications, and set of values" (37).[24] Identity economics (Akerlof and Kranton 2010) does not throw away materialism but shows the extent to which utility-maximizing preferences are conditioned by material and nonmaterial or cultural considerations.[25]

The quantitative evidence for cultural considerations in preferences for trade (foreign economic policy) has come mostly from survey data or experiments. Mansfield and Mutz (2009: 3) note that anxiety about out-groups shapes trade preferences more than straightforward material considerations. They note that the key to understanding trade preferences lies in "sociotropic perceptions" that shape how trade affects the well-being of the entire country rather than in perceptions about the effects of trade on individual utilities. Using two large-scale national surveys that gauge perceptions about individual and national benefits, they show that latter dominates in considerations on trade preferences. They also construct indices of nationalism, ethnocentrism, and isolationism (though only the first two are statistically significant) for the populations surveyed in the United States. These data demonstrate that "there is little support for free trade among people who believe the United States is superior to other countries, hold isolationist views, and exhibit evidence of prejudice toward groups unlike themselves" (450). In a similar vein, Sabet (2012: 4) shows that "symbolic dispositions enjoy a higher level of priority in the formation of trade preferences." Sabet's results rest on findings from the Harvard Globalization Survey of 4,000 workers in twelve industries in the United States. Specifically, the study finds that positive and negative cultural sentiments, which measure the role of foreign influences on American society, are statistically significant in explaining support or lack of support for trade respectively. Only when these cultural sentiments are neutral do the material factors dominate.

Survey data point to individual-level preferences about trade, which may or may not translate well into trade policy. Guisinger (2009) finds that voters did not hold trade policy, specifically incumbent senators' votes on the 2005 Central American Free Trade Agreement (CAFTA), as a salient consideration in their voting behavior. At a broader level, one might note that the United States supported free trade policies in the postwar era regardless of the varying levels of support for trade at the grassroots.[26] The debate on the extent to which grassroots cultural preferences influence trade policy in general is beyond the scope of this book. However, despite the lack of quantitative evidence, there's plenty of qualitative evidence on how cultural identity influences trade negotiations (Singh 2008; Goff 2007).[27]

For the purposes of this book, the role of cultural considerations in North–South trade relations is important. Two cultural factors are especially examined. The first is a corollary to the surveys mentioned earlier. It would follow from the evidence presented that Americans would loathe making trade concessions to out-groups that they deem to be inferior.[28] On the basis of this evidence, it would be hard to show that the United States made reciprocal or benevolent trade concessions to the developing world. A second cultural factor, however, deals with paternalism in trade policy wherein Americans do make trade concessions or assist those less fortunate than themselves. Herrmann et al. (2001) describes the various mental models Americans deploy in thinking of trade. They conclude: "Free traders may dominate among the elite, but intuitive neorealists clearly represent an important minority." This is based on a survey of 512 American leaders and an experiment that tests how Americans arbitrate neoclassical economics, national security, and distributive justice claims. The survey showed that although conservatives favor free trade, liberals (97.5 percent of those surveyed) favored trade only when its benefits accrued to the poor (211). Skonieczny (2001) shows that Americans' acceptance of Mexico as an equal trading partner in the North American Free Trade Agreement (NAFTA) relied on discursively constructing Mexico as inferior:

A dominant NAFTA discourse emerged during the three-month public debate that reemphasized the U.S. self-image as one of strength, leadership, and an embodiment of the American Dream of a prosperous future. As an extension of a positive U.S. self-image, the NAFTA discourse overpowered the reigning negative image of Mexico without challenging the ingrained perception. Moreover, this negative image was actually utilized by the pro- and anti-NAFTA sides to argue each position. The dominant NAFTA discourse did not attempt to transform the image of Mexico, but relied on representational elements to create the possibility of NAFTA for the U.S. public despite the negative image held by the U.S. The NAFTA discourse allowed the simultaneous existence of both the possibility of economic integration with Mexico as an equal partner and the established image of Mexico as a dependent other. (451)

These conclusions are broadly supported in the recent findings on foreign aid and humanitarian literatures. Baker's (2015) experimental data show that subjects are more likely to provide foreign assistance when shown pictures of the racial other (Cameroon, Guyana) rather than the racially similar (Moldova, Armenia) even though the economic characteristics of the recipients are broadly similar. This paternalism is attributed to the belief in the lack of agency in the racial other: "The source of greater generosity toward those of African descent will not be a perceived deficit in their material welfare but rather a perceived deficit in their capacity to take action to improve their own welfare" (97). Baker validates this hypothesis through a "perception of foreign poor's agency" index constructed from three questions asked of the subjects that deal with racial stereotypes. The greater giving to the racial other remains highly significant statistically when "mediated" through this index. Baker's results are consistent with those of Skonieczny (2001), discussed in the preceding paragraph, for trade policy, and with Barnett (2011) on humanitarian assistance.[29]

The case for racial codings in international trade can be made at another level, which documents the end of the colonialism but relegates postcolonials to the same status that they were assigned in the colonial era. Studies of neo-colonialism and dependency that posit core–periphery relations where the developed core shapes and controls the periphery have long documented the economically inferior status to which colonies were assigned.[30] However, these works maintain a silence on race in favor of speaking to class relations. The notion of continuing colonialism through other means is, of course, not limited to dependency and neo-Marxian scholarship. Early advocacy from the developing world toward favorable terms of trade and protecting their infant industries was based on the unfavorable terms to which they were assigned in the international trade relations in the postcolonial era.[31] Gartzke and Rohner (2011) have recently located the end of colonialism in similar dynamics: international commerce could continue the colonial economic relations through noncoercive means. Gartzke and Rohner identify "to trade or to take" as "central to the logic of the empire" (12).

Racial codings are shared collective understandings among dominant groups about another group, usually with a different skin color, which is often understood as inferior. Their presence is most obvious in the mechanisms that maintain the codes and the fury from the dominant when the oppressed do not obey or try to break the code. This book will provide several examples later of the maintenance and breaks from these racial codes. At a broad level, the entire history of North–South trade may be read as a history of racial codes. The North rebuffs attempts from the South to protect infant industry and enacts high tariffs for manufactured goods but low tariffs for minerals, raw materials, and primary products. When the South manufactures textiles, it faces quantitative restrictions in the North. In the current era, attempts from countries such as India to break the racial code completely and compete in high-tech products through outsourcing practices have led to openly racist controversies.

The review of the literature given in the preceding paragraphs offers conceptual and historical support to the proposition that a sense of superior cultural identity can shape great power trade negotiating behavior. This literature also suggests that such paternalism shapes the granting of trade concessions to the developing world. The next section discusses the negotiating tactics the developing world employs to obtain trade concessions.

For the purposes of this book, the null hypothesis is that paternalistic states will tend to make favorable trade concessions, not because of welfare gains from trade but because they judge this to be fair and just for the infant. This book later develops a "paternalism strength index" as an indicator of paternalism. The null hypothesis is that states ranking low on the index, mostly developing countries, will make fewer concessions relative to those received, especially in agriculture.

The null hypothesis is not validated with the quantitative and qualitative findings presented later. Although this pattern also holds across merchandise trade, it is especially noticeable in agriculture where the paternalistic states receive more concessions than they give.[32] The historical evidence further shows that the paternalized are asked to make trade concessions based on received ideas from their patrons rather than their sources of comparative advantage. Instead of meaningful trade concessions, the developing world is forced to ask for trade preferences, which are both limited and often resented in the Global North.[33] Until the Uruguay Round, as Michael Finger's Foreword notes for Robert Hudec's (1987) classic work on North–South trade diplomacy, "the identity of the developing countries in the system became almost entirely a matter of them demanding non-reciprocal and preferential treatment and developed countries responding grudgingly to those demands." Apparently the developing countries had learned their lesson well. In seeking handouts, which they received "grudgingly," they had internalized the paternalism. Franz Fanon's polemics against racism rested on unraveling the psychological internalization of repression, in feelings of inferiority that he called the "dependency complex of the colonized" (Fanon 2008/1952: chapter 4).

Negotiation Tactics

The negotiation literature, rooted in trading of concessions, does not support any form of benevolence from the developed world. Instead of paternalism, the concessions the developing world receives result from its negotiations tactics. However, the developing world is disadvantaged a priori: Gains in negotiations belong to those with the most alternatives (often understood as bargaining power).[34] By definition, the developing world has fewer alternatives for its products and for the markets it can reach. Neither do ideas of justice or fairness, seen embedded in the preferences toward the developing world in the studies cited earlier, translate easily into concessions. This is readily apparent in the preferential trade agreements. The consensus is that the United States and the EU have extracted more concessions than they have given in these agreements (Roy et al. 2007). The negotiation literature supports the thesis that the developing world has to negotiate hard to obtain any concessions.

Negotiations involve a set of techniques or tactics that follow from diplomatic relations. These include exploration of alternatives prior to and during the negotiations and formal tactics such as coalition building, issue linkage, and trade-offs during the negotiation process. The obvious implication is that the concessions made at the negotiation follow from exploring alternatives and exercising tactics—rather than the benevolence of one party toward another. In fact, cases of benevolence in trade negotiations are hard to find.

The negotiation process can be explored in two steps. The first makes up the structure of negotiations that helps to specify the alternatives available to each party in the negotiation, and the second step involves the negotiation process that further constrains or expands these alternatives. These steps are explored in the following subsection with reference to North–South trade negotiations.

Negotiation Structure

Traditionally, scholars analyzed North–South negotiation in a power structure that resembled a hierarchical distribution of power among nation-states. Developing countries were relegated to "a definitional inferiority" in such a power structure (Zartman 1971). Unless developing countries possess crucial raw materials, the advantage belongs to the great power monopsonist. Even when the developing world might have materials that confer a certain degree of advantage, its advantages do not improve easily: In the case of oil, it took the organization of a coalition to organize price increases. Furthermore, the dependence among developing countries on foreign aid, technology transfers, foreign direct investment, and preferential access further constrains the alternatives. Lacking alternatives, the developing world can extract concessions for itself from either playing off one great power against another (Yoffie 1983; Wriggins 1976) or try to use coalitional tactics, as did the Organization of Petroleum Exporting Countries (OPEC), in an attempt to overturn the power structure. However, as Krasner (1985, 1991) has shown, such tactics from the developing world are likely to fail because great powers have nothing to lose.[35]

Fortunately, the developing world possesses a few more alternatives because the assumption of a distribution of power is not always empirically valid. North–South trade relations often take place in a power structure that may be described as a diffusion of power (Singh 2008, 2015). There are many features of a diffusion of power. There are not only multiple great powers (United States, the EU, Japan) but also sizable midlevel emerging powers (Brazil, Russia, India, and China—known as BRIC—and other blocs) that can often make a difference in negotiations because they have better alternatives. In general, as developing world economies have become diversified in the postcolonial era, they may not be tied to a single market in the North or beholden to a few products for their exports. Trade with and from China is an obvious example. Second, in the GATT/WTO era, multilateral negotiations dominated trade relations at least until the end of the twentieth century, and during the Uruguay Round the developing world ably took advantage of the diffusion of power to obtain some concessions in many issues areas.

Multilateral negotiations are made up of many issues and many actors allowing trade-offs and linkages during the negotiation process and allow for coalition building among trade partners.

The presence of a diffusion of power extends a few negotiation benefits to
the developing world, but, in doing so, other structural factors cannot be overlooked. First, the developing world was de facto excluded from most multilateral
trade negotiations in the postwar era (Winham 1986). Its inclusion in the Uruguay Round followed two decades of strident advocacy from the Third World,
mostly through the United Nations and its agencies. This history is discussed
in the next chapter. Second, Steinberg (2002) notes that many of the rules at
the GATT favor the great powers. In particular, the consensus voting rule came
at the behest of the United States, which viewed the inclusion of postcolonial
countries as a threat to its dominance; consensus voting, therefore, ensured
that there would be no coalitions of defectors, which in many UN agencies were
becoming a majority. Third, historically the period after the Uruguay Round has
been marked with bilateral and preferential trade agreements among the great
powers and many developing countries. The United States and the EU have a
negotiating advantage in these talks and, therefore, prefer this form of "forum-
shopping" (Busch 2007; Drezner 2008). The latter is technically a negotiation
tactic. The preference for forum shopping arises from the underlying structural
conditions, in this case great power preference for avoiding negotiations that
are marked with a diffusion of power.

There really is no such thing as bargaining power, but a party's advantage in
negotiations depends on its alternatives. The concept of the best alternative to
a negotiated agreement (BATNA) is most suited for understanding the "power"
of a negotiating party. Given their large markets and consumption incomes, and
their diversified product portfolios, great powers have many alternatives when
negotiating with a country that produces only a couple of export products for
a majority of its export revenues. Therefore, in most negotiations, the developing world faces an inferior BATNA. It can seek to improve the terms in its favor
through diffusion of power but under limited conditions.

Negotiation Processes

Negotiation processes such as coalition-building, trade-offs, and linkages improve alternatives for negotiators, allowing the outcomes to move toward reciprocity. In a bilateral negotiation between a great and a weak power over one

issue, the weak party is left with no recourse but to accept the great power's terms. When there are multiple issues and multiple parties in a negotiation, the weak can build coalitions to provide collective resistance to unfair negotiations terms or try to effect concessions in one area of importance to them in exchange for another.

The structural constraints within which the negotiation takes place are important. In this book, the structural constraint of a diffusion of power with multiple actors and multiple issues provides a hard test case: If developing countries must negotiate hard-to-gain reciprocal concessions in a diffusion of power, then their chances of trade concessions, such as in a bilateral negotiation environment, are limited. Diffusion of power is an encompassing concept that also includes the institutional environment within which multilateral negotiations take place. Davis (2004) emphasizes the institutional environment—that of multilateral institutions such as the GATT and WTO—as offering opportunities to negotiators to make joint gains through linking issues. Thus, multilateral institutions such as GATT/WTO are the most likely case to examine North–South trade reciprocity.[36]

With multiple parties and multiple issues in a negotiation, parties can improve their alternatives in two ways. First, they can enter into coalitions with other like-minded partners to promote their own agenda or stall another that will leave them worse off. Second, as just mentioned, parties can link issues in such a way that their compromise on one issue may be directly tied to gains in another. However, linkage depends on underlying trade diversity: Only if a country has something to "give" can it effectively link it to something it wants to "receive." The two negotiation tactics—coalition building and issue linkage— are key to understanding the multilateral negotiations processes. *The hypothesis is that coalition building and issue linkage increase reciprocity of trade concessions.* Each tactic is now briefly discussed.

Coalition Building   The types of coalitions in a diffusion of power scenario are different from those in the concentration of power; the former mostly featured a homogenous North negotiating with a homogenous South. Diffusion of power scenarios in particular posit flat power distributions at the top, thus leading to a considerable amount of jostling among great powers. This allows smaller or weaker powers to not only play great powers against each other but also to choose their coalitional partners carefully and align themselves, or be asked to align themselves, with different great powers. Narlikar (2003) calls these "cross-over coalitions" and traces their origins to the Uruguay Round.

Issue-specific negotiations, especially those in a multilateral setting, provide countries with the ability to form coalitions and increase their bargaining power (Singh 2006[37]). For Raiffa (1982: 255), "the interplay among shifting coalitions" is "the fundamental difference between two-party and many-party" negotiations.[38] He notes that the many parties and many issues during the Law of the Sea negotiations led to complex coalitions but also eventually resulted in a search for joint gains through compromises among these coalitions. In the Uruguay Round, negotiations were structured in such a way that coalitions could not be ignored because they often featured developed and developing countries together. Inasmuch as the parties stayed focused on issues, these coalitions were able to shape the negotiation process. Weak countries favor multilateral forums precisely because forming coalitions increases bargaining power by presenting them with (and allowing them to explore) better alternatives.

Multiple Issues and Issue Linkage   Several actors and many issues make negotiations complex because of the risk of no agreement and the risk of complexity. However, several actors and many issues can also allow for many trade-offs and issue linkages. For example, agreement can come about through compromising either on one issue for gains in another or vice versa (Aggarwal 1998). Bringing in potentially related issues to increase one's bargaining power can also increase alternatives, although that also risks deadlocks. Agreement may also come about on some issues and not others. Many times, if the underlying interests behind issues differ for negotiators, negotiators can effect several trade-offs or issue linkages, although they were not apparent on the surface.

Economic strength and trade diversity are important preconditions for exercising linkage tactics but operate in an overall cultural context. Yoffie (1983: 29) argues that, in the nineteenth century, British hegemony "was a real and usable threat in bargaining over trade" and issue linkages were all but impossible for weak states. Britain held its colonies hostage to imperial preferences. Conybeare (1985) also notes the ability of stronger powers to foster linkages in the nineteenth century whereas the weak were unable to do so. But, in the current context (diffusion of power), linkages leading to trade-offs may be becoming common. Linkage thus becomes effective if countries increase their trade diversity, on average increasing the number of their export products and markets. Trade diversity is thus positively linked to BATNA, but the causal path includes trade linkages and trade-offs that trade diversity enables.

Trade linkage also enables alternatives during the negotiations process. Sebenius (1983) shows that linkages, although a risky strategy (because of no agreement), can increase alternatives during the negotiation. These alternatives then can lead to, among other things, an increase of bargaining power, the possibility of mutual gains, solidifying coalitions, and strengthening commitments. Again, the Uruguay Round is a good example. The strength of developing countries' coalitions was through recognition of their common interests or compromise across several issue areas. Davis (2003, 2004) notes that agriculture liberalization, a concession on the part of countries, could take place during the Uruguay Round because it was linked to gains in other issue areas. Zartman (2003: 35) puts forward the concept of "issue-coalitions" in the context of trade-offs and linkages.

Measuring coalition building and issue linkage is hard because of the ever-shifting nature of both coalitions and issues in a negotiation. Therefore, mixed-method approaches are necessary. The macrohistory and case study chapters explain in detail how the coalition and linkages have operated historically for the developing world in particular. Coalitional pressures resulted in cosmetic changes to GATT rules until the 1960s. The trade preferences accorded to developing country products in the 1970s and 1980s, however, followed as much from developing country advocacy as they did from paternalism. Coalition building and linkages were most visible in the Uruguay Round. Therefore, quantitative measures are employed for the Uruguay Round to test for these explanatory factors for this period. In the case of coalitions, the results are mixed. A few are rewarded with concessions, whereas others seem to have been punished by the developed world. A full discussion on this must wait for the empirical chapters to follow; the case of "failed coalitions" might be complicated in practice—arguably, they could have fared even worse without the coalitions. The case of trade diversity is simpler. Higher levels of diversity are positively linked to higher levels of concessions received.

Conclusion

The concept of trade reciprocity provides a good yardstick not only for measuring trade concessions given and received among trade partners but also for a first glimpse at the ethical and justice issues in analyzing negotiations. This chapter has examined two sets of causal conditions at a theoretical level for trade reciprocity. The first set of causal conditions is situated in the benevolence of the powerful, which may result from (1) paternalistic benevolence, where the strong help the weak because the weak are believed to not possess agency of their own; or (2) strong concerns from justice or ethical considerations underlying North–South negotiations. The current literature on paternalistic benevolence, situated mostly in humanitarianism and foreign aid, leads us to expect a positive relationship between benevolence and trade concessions received by the Global South. However, the evidence presented later in this book does not validate this relationship. Instead, most of the trade concessions received are linked to the South's negotiation advantages. Two negotiation conditions are explored in-depth: trade diversity that improves the alternatives for the developing world and coalition building that allows for collective action on common concerns. The next four chapters detail the empirical evidence provided for the theoretical suppositions deduced in this chapter.

Chapter 3

GATT and the Developing World
before the Uruguay Round

Thus, reciprocal negotiations, conducted on a bilateral or multilateral basis
among members, and the extension of all negotiated "concessions" to the
entire group under the most-favored-nation (mfn) clause, formed the two
foundations of the GATT. These principles are still fundamental to the
agreement, although a number of exceptions were allowed from the start and
many new exceptions (often applying to developing countries) have been
allowed as time has gone on.

Kathryn Morton and Peter Tullock,
Trade and the Developing Countries (1977: 55)

Our cause is never heard. . . . Our co-operation over and over again just makes
us look as if we are not being assertive enough.

Nirmala Sitharaman, commerce minister of India,
quoted in *The Financial Times*, July 13, 2014

COLONIALISM organized trade relations between the Global North and
Global South before agitations for independence and their realization
reached their apogee in the postwar period. The creation of the GATT coin-
cides with the cessation of hostilities among Western countries and was part of
the postwar peace that was envisioned. GATT's creation and early history also
parallel the end of direct imperialism. GATT's founders were in fact not oblivi-
ous to the links between trade and peace. Neither were the Western negotiators
unaware of questions regarding trade with the colonies.

This chapter shows that postcolonial questions were not paramount in the
creation of GATT. Most of the demands from the developing world—infant-
industry protections, for example—were ignored in the founding of the GATT.
European colonizers preserved the imperial preferences in trade that assured
them cheap primary materials and minerals. Starting in 1962, the European
Community's Common Agricultural Policy began to chip away at these preferences, replacing them in Europe with quantitative quotas, a trend paralleled in
the United States.

The greatest difficulty in North–South trade negotiations continues to be
the extent to which the developing world makes and receives concessions. The
extent to which developing countries, especially the poorest of the poor, should

be asked to make concessions at trade negotiations remains not a problem just of trade but also one of ethics and justice. One of the most astounding moments in GATT's creation is that colonial and postcolonial countries, which made up more than half of the twenty-three founding members of GATT who signed the agreement in Geneva on October 30, 1947, received almost marginal consideration in terms of measures that could be beneficial to them.[1] The system of imperial preferences that emerged from GATT, ensuring preferential trade flows from former colonies, was in fact something the Tories in Britain entertained as a continuation of the idea of the empire.

This chapter presents an analysis of trade measures that affected the developing world from the creation of the GATT to the end of the Tokyo Round (1979). The primary aim is to examine how the most favored nation principle, which defines reciprocity, shaped North–South trade relations. Three trade measures are examined: the system of imperial preferences, trade status for infant industry in the developing world, and the generalized system of preferences that resulted in special and differential treatment for the developing world. The causal variables for examining the degree of reciprocity in each of these trade measures remain the same as before: North–South trade negotiations and the degree of paternalism from the North.

Imperial Preferences

The issue of tariff preferences from Britain to goods from the Commonwealth dominated the negotiations that resulted in the postwar trade organization. The often-heated diplomacy played at two levels. First, imperial preferences derogated from the most favored nation clause that had gained ascendance in American trade policy ever since Congress had authorized the president to undertake tariff cuts through the Reciprocal Trade Agreements Authorization Act in 1934. More important, the Americans and the British regarded imperial preferences, albeit with different national interests in context, as a continuation of colonial policies: Churchill's Britain celebrated notions of the Commonwealth and empire, whereas Roosevelt's officials scoffed and found it antithetical to American interests.

The negotiations that led to the International Trade Organization were essentially a bilateral exercise between the United States and Britain, although fifty-five countries' delegates were in Havana in 1948 for the signing of the agreement to create an International Trade Organization.[2] Winston Churchill was loath to consult with the dominions, "these people" as he called them, during the negotiations (quoted in Irwin et al. 2008, location 3844). The dominions were Australia, Canada, South Africa, and New Zealand. Colonies such as India, Kenya, or Southern Rhodesia ranked lower.

The plans for a postwar trade organization emerged from the Atlantic Charter, initially signed between President Franklin Delano Roosevelt and Prime Minister Churchill on August 14, 1941, but later endorsed among the Allied Powers. The Atlantic Charter also provided the basis for the postwar United Nations. For commerce, the International Trade Organization was conceived as a specialized agency of the United Nations. Point 4 of the Atlantic Charter noted: "They will endeavour with due respect for their existing obligations, to further enjoyment by all States, great or small, victor or vanquished, of access, on equal terms, to the trade and to the raw materials of the world which are needed for their economic prosperity." The term *existing obligations* referred to imperial preferences, and when Roosevelt tried to convince Churchill on free and multilateral trade, Churchill evoked "existing commitments." Other points in the Charter spoke to self-determination and the "abandonment on the use of force."

The Atlantic Charter would be invoked in the colonies to demand an end to colonialism. There was duplicity in two great powers speaking against Nazi evil while overlooking imperialism, although FDR did pressure Churchill on the decolonization of India. For his part, Churchill did not see any contradictions: Postwar organizations were meant only for the civilized world. The young Churchill regarded the colonized as barbarians and savages and, later, at the height of Indian struggles for independence in 1943, he noted: "I hate Indians. They are a beastly people with a beastly religion" (quoted in Toye 2010). He ignored pleas from India that could have prevented the Bengal famine of 1943, which claimed 3 million lives. He did not take seriously food scarcity in Bengal and infamously quipped that, if food was so scarce, why hadn't Gandhi died yet?

The American leadership espoused noble aims, but its own involvement overseas, or the history of racial prejudice in America, was hardly laudable. Cordell Hull, FDR's Secretary of State, led the negotiations for the postwar trade organization. Hull is famous for furthering the eighteenth-century belief that trade, peace, and prosperity are related; The Atlantic Charter was an enunciation of this. At one point in his memoirs, written in an almost folksy style common to the U.S. South, Hull writes of two neighbors, Jenkins and Jones, who are enemies but nevertheless realize that they must exchange corn for hogs to their mutual benefit (Hull 1948, 364–365):

As a result, it wasn't long before the two old enemies were the best of friends. A common-sense trade and ordinary neighborliness had made them aware of their economic need of each other and brought them peace.

Yes, war did come, despite the trade agreements. But it is a fact that war did not break out between the United States and any country with which we had been able to negotiate a trade agreement. It is also a fact that, with very few exceptions, the countries with which we signed trade agreements joined together in resisting the Axis. The political lineup followed the economic line-up.

However, the Tennessee-born Cordell Hull, the architect of trade and peace, was also "a subscriber to the idea that only Europeans have the right to colonize and exploit weaker peoples" (Meyers 2012). He was, as Susan Aaronson describes him, "a good old boy" (Aaronson 1996: 13) who knew how to carry Congress in service of FDR's foreign policy. Although Hull was generally supportive of the right to self-determination, it is hard to find positive references to the movements for independence in the colonial world in his memoirs (Hull 1948), and the writing reveals paternalism:

At no time did we press Britain, France, or the Netherlands for an immediate grant of self-government to their colonies. Our thought was that it would come after an adequate period of years, short or long depending on the state of development of respective colonial peoples, during which these peoples would be trained to govern themselves. (1599)

Hull was not prone to apply overt pressure on the British for Indian independence even after it was clear to the Roosevelt administration that Indian support for the war effort was important. The chapter titled "Independence for India" has hardly any words of praise for Gandhi or the Indian nationalist movement (Hull 1948: chapter 108).[3]

It is now becoming increasingly clear that in economic matters—including the tripartite negotiations that eventually resulted in the IMF, the World Bank, and the GATT—FDR's foreign policy sought to replace Britain as the global leader with most resources (Steil 2013; Kennedy 1987: 357–361). This foreign policy entailed that the United States would be the global leader in the post-war world, in which trade would contribute to peace. Imperial preferences were both political and economic in character and continued imperial connections

Table 3.1.   British imports and exports to the Empire.

	Percentage of British exports to Empire countries	Percentage of British imports from Empire countries
1913	37.2	24.9
1921	42.5	30.5
1927	46.5	30.1
1929	44.5	29.4
1931	43.7	28.7
1935	48.0	37.6
1938	49.9	40.4

SOURCE: Herbert Feis, "The Future of British Imperial Preferences." *Foreign Affairs.* 24(4, 1946): 668, 670.

while also being trade diversionary. Herbert Feis, who served as an economic advisor to the Hoover and Roosevelt administrations, described them as "born out of the union of political exaltation and economic uneasiness" (Feis 1946: 661). He also quotes Joseph Chamberlain in 1906 describing them as "a true *zollverein* for the empire" (661). The preferences affected Britain's trade with Australia, Canada, India, New Zealand, South Africa, and Southern Rhodesia. By the 1930s, these preferences discriminated against manufactured goods from the United States but also textiles from Japan. The Ottawa agreements of 1932 expanded the system of preferences and served as one of the impetuses for the 1934 RTAA that arose in the United States for whom Britain was a major trading partner; Britain accounted for 43 percent of American exports (Feis 1946: 664).

Britain's trade with its colonies and dominions was also substantial, with the net terms of trade in its favor (see Table 3.1).[4] Imperial preferences ensured Britain cheap imports of raw materials and a market for its products. The position had political support both with Labor and the Tories, although Churchill himself favored free trade policies. However, his Secretary of State for India, Leopold Amery, reflected the Conservative position in support of the preferences, and they threatened to withdraw support from Churchill's government (Irwin et al. 2008: Section 1.2, location 309). Publicly and in newspapers, Amery argued for the economic advantages of preferences, lest his position was perceived otherwise. However, American Ambassador to Britain John Winant characterized his position as reflecting that of "Empire preference Tories who in my opinion, are nothing more than imperialists" (quoted in Irwin et al. 2008: Section 1.2, location 3792). Furthermore, the colonies and the dominions were seldom consulted in Britain's position. Clement Attlee's Labor government, which succeeded Churchill, was even more favorably inclined toward multilateral trade than its predecessor but "found it difficult to relinquish imperial preferences under American pressure" (Irwin et al 2008: Section 1.6, location 732).

For their part, the Americans worked with two national interest goals in mind: The first was to ensure future peace with American leadership, and the other related to American prosperity through trade. John Odell states (2000: 162): "From the start, the International Trade Organization was an American idea." Britain's imperial preferences were chiefly understood in the context of American leadership of postwar economic institutions and need to assist the allied countries. Therefore, FDR was cautious not to apply too much pressure on Britain to abolish imperial preferences as a precondition for American assistance. Despite pressures from Hull's State Department, which was hostile to preferences in trade, the Atlantic Charter seemed to accommodate British interests, and FDR used the Charter only to prod the British toward a conversation on multilateral trade policy. In 1942, he did not make abolition of imperial preferences a precondition for the lend-lease arrangement. It was only shortly after the war ended in August 1945 that Assistant Secretary of State William Clayton specifically tied continued American assistance to the UK on revocation of preferences. The British regarded this as blackmail and resisted American attempts, and eventually the Americans backed down. After the war, the British economists James Meade and Lionel Robbins led the trade talks. Unlike John Maynard Keynes, who undertook the Bretton Woods financial negotiations, these men were predisposed to multilateralism but thought ill of American efforts to link financial assistance to the abolition of preferences. Robbins called the maneuver "crude and unimaginative" (quoted in Irwin et al 2008: Section 1.7, location 862).

American trade interests, rather than ethics, underscore the American demands for abolition of imperial preferences. U.S. trade as a percentage of GNP had grown from 3.9 percent in 1890 to 9.3 percent in 1940 and was expected to increase. Britain was America's chief trading partner and accounted for more than 40 percent of this trade. Imperial preferences discriminated against American products. Cordell Hull's State Department understood this well, and the technical team that Truman assembled for the trade negotiations— William Clayton, a cotton broker; Clair Wilcox, an economist; Winthrop Brown, an attorney—reflected this position. However, unlike Cordell Hull, they were neither well connected with the president nor with the Congress to eventually make their case for an agreement that was signed in 1948 for the International Trade Organization (Aaronson 1996: chapter 4).

Imperial preferences remained the most important issue in the negotiations, but the overall negotiations themselves took on a different character. Truman sensed that Americans had lost further appetite for international institutions after the exhausting Bretton Woods and UN negotiations. Furthermore, business, labor, and farm groups were not all unilaterally in favor of the extensions of the reciprocal trade agreements act, which made Congress increasingly reluctant on trade issues. An agreement to create the International Trade Organization was signed in March 1948 in Havana, but, after testing the waters with the Congress and American business groups, Truman withdrew it from congressional ratification. The ITO died with that move. Instead, a General Agreement on Tariffs and Trade among contracting parties had been drawn up in Geneva in October 1947, and this became the de facto trade governance mechanism. Like the ITO, it mentioned MFN in Article 1, but derogations for imperial preferences were continued.

It is hard to assess whether imperial preferences catered to the interests of the developing world. Brazil accounted for 2.8 percent of world trade in 1948 and India (Pakistan) for another 3.3 percent (Irwin 2009: Section 2.3.4, location 4515), but this trade was tied to former colonial masters. In this sense, their hands were tied, and this probably accounts for their lack of opposition to imperial preferences in the short run. Over the long run, though, the fact that this issue dominated the discussions on the status of colonies in trade meant that other issues, including those that the colonies raised, ranked lower on the negotiation agenda. The chief demand from countries such as India, Brazil, and China made in the negotiations that led up to Havana was to allow trade measures to be relaxed for the growth of infant industries. Eventually, these were allowed but with strict conditions. There is little evidence to suggest that Americans took seriously the concerns of technical trade teams from countries such as India, even though many of them had been educated in Keynesian economics. Although acknowledging the effectiveness of the Indian and Australian proposals, Clair Wilcox (1949) did not like what the developing world wanted and wrote critically of the challenges and objections it raised in the name of economic development. He noted in a confidential document: "The Indians came with a chip on their shoulder. They regarded the Proposals as a document prepared by the U.S. and the U.K. to serve the interest of the highly industrialized countries by keeping the backward countries in a position of economic dependence" (quoted in Irwin et al 2008: Section 1.9, location 966).[5] The foundation of GATT did not reflect any development aspirations. The developing world had thrown its weight behind the ITO negotiations. GATT promised them less. For example, Brazil, Chile, and Cuba were the only three of the seventeen Latin American countries that had signed the Havana Charter to also sign on to GATT (Helleiner 2014: 261).

Trade Interests and Infant Industry

The evolution of developing country trade interests in GATT took place within GATT, through additions to GATT's instruments, and in parallel through collective action and advocacy in other global forums. These efforts resulted in the addition of the Chapter on Trade and Development in 1964 (Part IV, articles XXXVI–XXXVIII). International trade theorists often emphasize developments within GATT, whereas many social scientists examine advocacy outside of GATT to provide the context for Part IV. From a negotiation perspective, both are important for understanding the way the developing world gained this concession. Chronologically, it is useful to return to the negotiations that created GATT.

The ITO negotiations were mostly bilateral between the United States and Britain, but shortly after the United States convened a "nuclear group" of fourteen countries to negotiate in January 1946, developing countries brought up the issue of protections for infant industry for the purpose of economic development. They disrupted what Narlikar (2005: 13) calls the "cozy consensus" between the two great powers to discuss only issues of importance to them. Article XVIII (c) of GATT allowed a contracting party to get permission for its government to restrict imports with specific measures to allow its domestic industry to grow. The measure was not easy to implement, and it took almost two decades of strident advocacy before GATT's contracting parties agreed in November 1964 to Part IV of the agreement, which recognized the special economic needs of the developing world. In 1964, developed countries also promised to open their markets to imports from the developing world and to relax their reciprocity condition in doing so.

Getting infant industry protections was the major thrust of the developing countries in the fourteen-member nuclear group that the United States convened to negotiate in January 1946.[6] India led the movement but received important support from Australia, Brazil, and Cuba. India asked for infant industry protections in a seventy-six-page response to the proposed ITO charter that the United States presented in September 1946. Specifically, India was concerned that rich countries could subsidize their industries to support them but that the developing world, lacking resources, would need quantitative import restrictions. Brazil presented another charter but one that acknowledged and supported India's position. Australia provided much of the intellectual rationale as well as the text for Article XVIII.[7] Cuba's support specifically addressed the need for NTBs. The developing world's stance on infant industry reflected unease with volatility with commodity prices and the legacy of colonial sentiments and distrust, but the developing world accepted the main principles of tariff liberalization (Scott 2010). However, the United States was "dismissive of the importance placed by developing countries on industrialization" (12).

Article XVIII (c) was not of much help to the developing world, and the contracting parties did not grant permission easily. Britain applied for permission to discriminate against Belgian Congo soaps to encourage domestic industry in Northern Rhodesia in July 1949, but the contracting parties were not convinced that products from another "underdeveloped" country posed much of a threat. Cuba's request to increase tariffs from 50 to 180 percent on textile imports was also denied on the grounds that Cuba had a textile industry dating back to the 1920s (Curzon 1965: 212–214).[8] The developing countries were especially upset that developed countries could undertake protections without notification for balance of payments reasons under Article XII: "The difference of treatment between highly industrialized countries, which could impose such restrictions in full conformity with Gatt, and the close control which was exercised over restrictions imposed for development purposes was an anomaly which was soon to cause friction" (Curzon 1965: 214). The developing world started to employ Article XII to its benefit: Twenty-four of the thirty-nine waivers granted for balance of payments difficulties between 1949 and 1963 were for the developing world (Evans 1971: 119).[9]

Several studies in the 1950s showed that developing countries faced inimical terms of trade. The early advocate of this view, starting with studies in 1949, was the Economic Commission of Latin America (ECLA) and the Argentinian economist Raúl Prebisch.[10] He reflected the disappointment that the developing world experienced from the marginalization of development goals from both GATT and the Bretton Woods institutions IMF and IBRD (Helleiner 2014:

268–269).[11] The early thrust of the studies was on infant industry, which encouraged import substitution industrialization in the developing world, but quite soon the emphasis shifted to international trade. The 1954 GATT Annual Report *International Trade* pointed out that exports from the developing world were decreasing, and this became an important topic of discussion among the contracting parties. A 1954–1955 amendment to GATT Article XVIII allowed developing countries to raise their tariffs for infant industry as long as they compensated the country affected by the tariff. This meant the developing countries seldom used Article XVIII (*Harvard Law Review* 1967–1968: 1809).

A panel of experts, known as Committee III, comprised of distinguished international trade economists, was appointed in 1957 to examine this issue (General Agreement on Tariffs and Trade 1958). This panel included the Austrian school economist Gottfried Haberler and also Roberto de Oliveira Campos, James Meade, and Jan Tinbergen. Meade had been involved from the UK in the negotiations that led to GATT. Their report, submitted in October 1958, which soon came to be known as the *Haberler Report*, was unequivocal in noting that the problem of developing countries' exports was chiefly due to protectionism in industrialized countries both for commodity and manufactured exports from the developing world. The report also notes that the preferences of imports from Europe's "overseas territories" were "predominantly trade diverting and not trade creating" (General Agreement on Tariffs and Trade 1958: 120).

The *Haberler Report* pointed out that the long-term exports from the developing world had not grown as much as their imports, which moved from a $1.7 billion export surplus in 1928 to a $3.4 billion surplus in imports in 1957 (see Table 3.2). The report made several recommendations, including foreign aid

Table 3.2.   Value, volume, and price of imports and exports (FOB) of the nonindustrial countries* (in thousand million dollars; index 1928 = 100).

	Imports			Exports		
	Value	*Volume*	*Price*	*Value*	*Volume*	*Price*
1928	8.71	100	100	10.39	100	100
1937–1938	6.84	99	80	7.80	108.5	69
1957	34.31	203	(194)	30.88	151	197

*USSR, Eastern Europe, and China are not included.
SOURCE: Adapted from General Agreement on Tariffs and Trade, *Trends in International Trade: Report by a Panel of Experts* (Geneva: GATT, October 1958, p. 26).

and provision of international liquidity, but the bulk of the recommendations pertained to protectionism in the industrial countries: "It will be observed that the implementation of these recommendations requires action primarily (and in some cases solely) by the highly industrialized countries" (General Agreement on Tariffs and Trade 1958: 123). Nevertheless, the report ends on the only possibility that exists to correct trade policies—"a negotiated settlement" (127).

GATT appointed several committees to examine trade issues, and Committee III was explicitly charged with trade between developing and developed countries.[12] One of its first tasks was to select trade barriers in eleven products, and this reflected arguments about commodity trade from the ECLA. The products were cocoa, coffee, copper, cotton, cotton textiles, jute products, lead, tea, timber, tobacco, and vegetable oils. Committee III found that duties on products became higher as the product went from primary to processed stages. Table 3.3 reports the differences among these tariff rates. Committee III concluded that, given the barriers to imports for processed products, the de facto rates of protection were much higher than calculated and discouraged industry in developing countries, in effect forcing them to be producers and exporters of primary commodities. These calculations are complicated, but the GATT Secretariat reported that the tariff rates of 10, 10, and 3 for copper wire in the UK, the EEC, and Sweden respectively meant protection rates respectively of 77, 77, and 23 for the processing industry that utilized copper wires. "The most sensible method of economic development, i.e. the transformation of the traditional exports of under-developed countries in to the first stage of manufacture, and the surest way of increasing their export earning was thus thwarted" (Curzon 1965: 231).

After the *Haberler Report* and the GATT Secretariat's findings on effective rates of protection on commodities, the developing countries met as a group for the first time in GATT's history and collectively submitted a note in May 1959.[13] The note outlined their exclusion from trade negotiations, pointed out tariff and nontariff barriers to their products, and requested unilateral concessions from developed countries. Committee III issued four other reports between October 1959 and September 1961. Although acknowledging marginal progress, the reports continued to call attention to trade barriers.[14] The last report was issued before a meeting of GATT ministers and examined the international trade goals in India's third five-year plan (1961–1966). It concluded that two-thirds of Indian exports were subject to high trade barriers. For example, Indian exports were

Table 3.3. Tariff rates in North America and Western Europe: Commodities and Stages of Processing, 1960 (percentage).

Commodity		EEC	United Kingdom	United States
Cocoa	Beans	9	1.5	0
	Powder	27	13	4.2
Copper	Mattes, unwrought copper, waste and scrap	0	0–10	7–8
	Tube and pipe fittings	15	20	21–24
Cotton	Cotton not carded or combed	0	0–10	0–8
	Fabrics of standard type	17	23	25
Iron and steel	Iron ore	0	0	0
	Pipes and fittings	13.5	17.5	10
Jute	Raw	0	0–20	0–15
	Fabrics	23	23	8
Oilseeds and vegetable oils	Oilseeds	0	0–10	0–49
	Vegetable oils	0–20	0–15	0–45
Rubber	Natural rubber	0	0	0
	Rubber tires and tubes	20	27	19
Wool	Sheep or lamb's wool	0	0–10	0–47
	Woolen or worsted fabrics	18	22	46

SOURCE: Adapted from Gerard Curzon, *Multilateral Commercial Diplomacy: The General Agreement on Tariffs and Trade and Its Impact on National Commercial Policies and Techniques.* New York: Frederick A. Praeger. 1965, pp. 229–230.

concentrated in a few items, with tea accounting for 20 percent of total exports. The EEC proposed to cut tea tariffs from 35 percent to 18 percent. The Indian representative told the contracting parties that the 18 percent tariff was still higher than what the UK had imposed earlier. Germany's cut in tariffs was accompanied with domestic taxes, which made the price of tea higher than before (Curzon 1965: 235–236).

Industrialized countries undertook a few tariff cuts—Sweden removed tariffs on coffee, for example—but by and large they were not moved. The ministers meeting in 1961 considered ten recommendations, of which there was nothing new in calling for removal of tariffs, quantitative restrictions, and nontariff restrictions and honoring reciprocity in trade negotiations. However, Curzon (1965: 238) notes that "the ministers tamely concluded their meeting by

giving moral support to the General Agreement as the basis for the trading relationships between their countries." The *Harvard Law Review* (1967–1968: 1810]
notes: "Little more than lip service was paid to these proposals by the developed
countries." Robert Hudec (1987: 44–45) notes that, by 1961,

GATT's work evolved into a slow and patient form of bureaucratic slogging—unending
meetings, detailed studies of trade flows and trade barriers and repeated declarations in
increasingly urgent but never-quite-binding language. The work was tedious, repetitive
and often absurd.

Several well-known economists continued the work Committee III had
begun on the differences in tariffs between raw materials and processed goods.
These came to be known as tariff differentials, which further showed that the
nominal rate of tariff was different from the effective rate: A product with only
10 percent value added paid effectively a higher rate of tariff than one with
70 percent value added. Further, studies from economists such as Bela Balassa
and Giorgio Basevi pointed out that these tariff differentials impacted the imports from the developing world more heavily than those from the developed
world (Evans 1971; Balassa 1965; Basevi 1966; Grubel and Johnson 1967).

The actual instruments that developed countries exercised were twofold.
The EEC continued its program of imperial preferences, in this case with France
and Belgium arguing for preferences for their existing and past African colonies
(Zartman 1971). Interestingly, Nigeria called for an elimination of these prefer-
ences on tropical products at the 1961 ministers' meeting with support from the
United States and even the UK, which had earlier argued for imperial preferences (see footnote 5 for a similar stance from Ghana earlier). However, France
attacked this proposal: "France therefore made herself the spokesman for the
French African territories and the E.E.C. countries and managed to have the
Nigerian resolution changed into a plan of good intentions" (Curzon 1965: 238).
The second instrument was what economists Pater Bauer calls the "soft option"
of foreign aid: Instead of overriding domestic interests opposed to lowering tariffs for the developing world, the developed countries began to provide foreign
aid to the developing world. President Kennedy asked Congress in March 1961
to increase this foreign aid in a special message. Bauer and Wood (1961) are clear
that foreign aid is given chiefly because developed countries cannot overcome
the opposition of domestic groups who benefit from import restrictions and
powerful groups who benefit from projects that are financed from foreign aid

funds. Therefore, consumers in these countries were now paying for the higher costs for products they consumed and paid taxes (that went into foreign aid) for the same products produced in the developing world that they did not consume. Bauer and Wood call foreign aid a form of "conscience money" and "an example of the familiar rule that benefits to sectional interests are obvious, while the cost to the community are obscured" (Bauer and Wood 1961: 407). Curzon (1965: 225) notes that this made "rich countries' exhortations to free trade sound hypocritical."

Developing countries worked within GATT to bring pressures on developed countries but the "postcolonial" moment of coalition building was especially evident outside of GATT. Twenty-nine Asian and African states came to Bandung from April 18–24, 1955, in a show of postcolonial unity, which examined Cold War questions from the perspective of colonized countries and reaffirmed their commitment to the United Nations. It included stalwarts such China's Prime Minister Zhou Enlai, Indonesia's President Sukarno, Indian Prime Minister Jawaharlal Nehru, Ghana's President Kwame Nkrumah, and Tanzania's President Julius Nyerere. Taylor and Smith (2007: 8) note that the *Haberler Report* was in part a reflection of GATT's acknowledgment of Bandung. One of the questions at Bandung was great-power interference in the developing world. This led to the convening of another conference in 1961 in Belgrade where the Non-Aligned Movement (NAM) was born, which resulted directly from processes begun in Bandung. The history of NAM is varied, but it served as a bulwark and a counterstrategy to address pressures from the United States and the Soviet Union. Among its prominent creators were Egypt's Nasser, India's Nehru, and Yugoslavia's Tito—each of whom employed the Non-Aligned Movement to either assert independence from the Cold War or to extract concessions from the great powers.

By the early 1960s, coalitional pressures from the developing world on international trade continued and had come to fruition both within and outside of GATT. In 1962, thirty developing countries in the UN General Assembly called for a United Nations Conference on Trade and Development (UNCTAD) by 1963 (UNGA Resolution 1785[XVII]). Earlier, thirty-six countries had met in Cairo for the Conference in Problems of Developing Countries. The Soviet Union lent support at both conferences and proposed a different trade and development organization. Negotiation literature acknowledges the way small powers can gain concessions by playing them off each other—in other words, increasing their alternatives (Wriggins 1976). Superpower competition also ties the "Suzerain's hands" in David Lake's (2009: 122–124) model of great-power authority and subordinate states. Western countries, facing weakened alternatives, lent support to the convening and creation of UNCTAD.[15]

UNCTAD established several principles to govern North–South trade relations in which Raúl Prebisch's intellectual weight was obvious. He became the first president of UNCTAD from 1964 to 1969. UNCTAD's principles argued for equality among sovereigns, free trade, and assistance for the development needs of postcolonial countries. There is increasing evidence that the West mischaracterized and misunderstood the developing world's aspirations and UNCTAD. Bockman (2015) notes that developing countries aspired to join the global economy, while the West marginalized the postcolonial world and resisted globalization. At the plenary session of UNCTAD on March 25, 1964, even Ernesto "Che" Guevara declared: "This conference must also establish in plain terms the right of all peoples to unrestricted freedom of trade, and the obligation of all states signatories of the agreement emanating from the conference to refrain from restraining trade in any manner, direct or indirect" (cited in Bockman 2015: 109).

The creation of UNCTAD allowed developing countries an alternative forum to coalesce and apply technocratic pressures on the developed world. GATT's submission to UNCTAD in 1964 is itself a technical document and a good summary of the measures undertaken since the creation of GATT to accommodate the needs of the developing world (General Agreement on Tariffs and Trade 1964). Instead of platitudes, the report offers details on amendments to GATT articles following the *Haberler Report* and Committee III work. Annex II (30–43) lists the measures adopted to expand the trade of developing countries on May 21, 1963, for particular commodities but also lists the objections of the EEC to these measures, which were mostly rooted in the case for imperial preferences.

There is little evidence to show that the movement to UNCTAD resulted in direct concessions. However, over the long run, it accomplished three things. First, UNCTAD increased the leverage the developing world could exercise on GATT. It was created out of postcolonial coalitions and led to further coalitions, the most important of which would be G77 and the New International Ecoomic Order (NIEO, discussed later). It was the precursor to bloc diplomacy that characterized North–South bargaining for two decades until the Uruguay

Round in 1986 (Narlikar 2003; Hudec 1987). Second, it created a technocratic forum for discussion of North–South trade and facilitated the presentation of positions that were rooted in an economic logic, data collection, and statistics.[16] For example, the International Trade Centre created at the GATT became a joint organization of the GATT and UNCTAD in 1968, to research trade issues. Hudec notes that GATT remained useful to the developing world and did not ever mean to replace it with UNCTAD: "Although it did not seem so at the time, developing countries actually used the UNCTAD threat with a great deal of caution and patience" (Hudec 1987: 40).

GATT's major shift in positions as a result of developing country pressures was the adoption of Part IV (Articles XXXVI–XXXVIII) as a "Chapter on Trade and Development." The articles address the objectives of trade and economic development through favorable tariff and nontariff concessions. However, developing countries were not effective participants in the Kennedy Round. Even before the Round, the Western countries had "negotiated" (rather imposed) a set of quantitative restrictions on cotton and manufactured cotton exports, starting in 1961, in a system that would later evolve into the Multi-Fibre Arrangement in 1974 (see Chapter 4). UNCTAD data showed that the average Kennedy Round tariff reduction for the developed countries was 36 percent; whereas for the developing countries it was 20 percent (quoted in *Harvard Law Review* 1967–1968: 1808). On the other hand, the incipient processes through the UNCTAD resulted in another set of preferences, ostensibly favoring the developed world—the Generalized System of Preferences (GSP).

Generalized System of Preferences

Throughout the 1960s, developing countries continued to emphasize protections for domestic industry, but their attention also moved slowly toward preferential access to developed country markets. Domestic protections and market access had become the twin pillars of developing country trade advocacy inside and outside of GATT. The shift from opposing preferences to accepting them as the best deal on the table was driven both by their historical dependency on such exports and by the moral and political efficacy of such a deal in the North, where it was a side payment to placate the developing world. Raúl Prebisch at UNCATD also helped line up the developing world for preferential access. The Generalized System of Preferences was designed to provide limited market access for developing country exports. From the end of the Tokyo Round, the GSP became part of special and differential treatment accorded to many parts of the developing world. The measures were hard fought but, as explained in the following paragraphs, they yielded few and questionable benefits.

After the creation of UNCTAD in 1964, the developing countries started to argue for preferential treatment, but the United States remained opposed until a 1967 GATT meeting in Punta del Este where in principle it agreed to consider favorable tariffs for the developing world (Dos Santos et al. 2005: 647). Subsequently, states at UNCTAD II in 1968 in New Delhi agreed to set up a Special Committee on Preferences to prepare the details. By 1970, developed countries pledged to introduce the GSP, which had "become a rallying point for developing country action" (Erb 1974: 88). However, the developed countries conferred at the OECD, an organization more responsive to their interests, to work through their differences and to decide on the coverage and exclusions for countries and products. Dos Santos et al. (2005: 648) note, "Their agreement sabotaged the creation of significant GSP schemes, giving developed countries 'loose commitments with strong escape provisions' rather than 'strong commitments with loose escape provisions.'" UNCTAD's advocacy for preferential access had been much broader in scope than the GSP provided.

A ten-year GATT waiver for preferences was worked out in 1971. The GSP granted zero or low nonreciprocal tariff preferences to specific products from designated developing countries. The Tokyo Round Declaration in 1973 made special mention of the GSP (General Agreement on Tariffs and Trade 1973: 2–3):

The developed countries do not expect reciprocity for commitments made by them in the negotiations to reduce or remove tariff and other barriers to the trade of developing countries, i.e., the developed countries do not expect the developing countries, in the course of the trade negotiations, to make contributions which are inconsistent with their individual development, financial and trade needs. The Ministers recognize the need for special measures to be taken in the negotiations to assist the developing countries in their efforts to increase their export earnings and promote their economic development and, where appropriate, for priority attention to be given to products or areas of interest to developing countries. They also recognize the importance of maintaining and improving the Generalized System of Preferences. They further recognize the importance of the application of differential measures to developing countries in ways which will provide special and more favourable treatment for them in areas of the negotiation where this is feasible and appropriate.

The GSP was voluntary, and the developing countries sought a permanent waiver through GATT to institutionalize this arrangement. At the 1968 New Delhi meetings, the developing world feared unilateral conditions imposed on GSP exporters of their products; therefore, they wanted to multilateralize the arrangement and subject it to GATT's MFN provisions (Tobin and Busch 2014). In the U.S. case, the GSP was authorized through the Trade Act of 1974, and it was the twenty-third country to adopt the scheme in 1976 (Dos Santos et al. 2005: 649) after overcoming misgivings about the derogations from MFN and reciprocity (Elumenthal 1970).[17] The Tokyo Round negotiations ended with the specification and adoption of a legal rationale for the GSP through the "Enabling Clause" in 1979 to provide for "Differential and More Favorable Treatment Reciprocity and More Fuller Participation of Developing Countries." Michalopoulos (2000: 12) writes:

In bringing together the key elements of preferential market access, nonreciprocity and flexibility in the implementation of rules and commitments, the Enabling Clause was a summation, rather than an extension, of the efforts made since 1954 to address the concerns of developing countries within the multilateral trading system.

The GSP was marginal and partial, but it resulted from developing countries' bloc diplomacy that matured in the late 1960s. At the formation of UNCTAD, seventy-seven developing countries coalesced into a group that would later act as the voice of the developing world in the United Nations and many of its specialized agencies. Following G77, which continues to exist to the present with 134 members in 2016, several other developing country groups pressed for economic advantage. In 1960 a group of oil-exporting countries, the Organization of Petroleum Exporting Countries (OPEC), came together and began to coordinate their strategies for oil production and prices, effectively challenging the power of an oligopoly of Western oil producers, the Seven Sisters. Following the Yom Kippur War of 1973, they raised the price of oil from $3 to $12 a barrel. Within UNCTAD, the fiercest advocacy came from the calls for a New International Economic Order (NIEO) starting in the early 1970s. The NIEO sought to redress colonial economic injustices and inequalities. It drew support from both G77 and the Non-Aligned Movement (NAM), leading to the Sixth Special Session of the United Nations in 1974 (see Rothstein 1979).[18]

Institutions such as the UNCTAD and the NIEO, and provision of measures such as the GSP, marked the apogee of developing countries' bloc diplomacy

(Whalley 1999; Narlikar 2003; Narlikar and Tussie 2004; Singh 2006). Their case in trade rested on a normative foundation of distributive and egalitarian justice; a redress of past exploitation and current international inequalities through a system of economic preferences (Beitz 1979; Armstrong 2012). The leverage for bloc diplomacy was manifold. First, G77 had sheer numbers. Small countries could cut transaction costs across several issue areas by joining a bloc like G77. Large countries could bear some of the costs of collective action while being able to count on large numbers for support. Second, the bloc diplomacy operated in the shadow of the Cold War and, as mentioned earlier, increased the developing world's negotiation leverage. The creation of UNCTAD undercut an alternative proposal from the Soviet Union, and the NIEO benefited from the support of the Eastern Bloc both materially in the United Nations and ideologically from radical worldviews. The developing world had already made some gains by playing off one great power against another (Wriggins 1976). Third, material interests informed the bloc and accounted both for its coherence and its clout. The developing world could simply not be excluded from the international trade system. It accounted for one-fourth of world trade and was intricately linked with supply chains to the global North. Fourth, developing countries made ideological demands on the international trade system for redistribution (see, for example Winham 1986; Krasner 1985), but these demands were rooted in sound economic analyses, a fact often ignored in international relations research. These demands had a technocratic and well-researched component; they carried intellectual gravitas and as acts of public reasoning; they invited deliberation.[19] From the *Haberler Report* to various UNCTAD studies, the developing world advocacy was not devoid of economic grounding and empirical data. The developed world feared, in fact, that the developing world would seek legal solutions to their grievances through bodies like GATT and threatened "to treat any resort to law as a hostile act" (Hudec 1987: 66). The developing world's legal and technical threat had a payoff: The developed world's pragmatism. By the 1970s, the developed countries accepted the fact that developing country participation in GATT would be on preferential terms.

The Enabling Clause of 1979, or formally the Decision on Differential and More Favourable Treatment Reciprocity and Fuller Participation of Developing Countries, as part of the Tokyo Round's Framework Agreement institutionalized this understanding. The Enabling Clause allowed market access for the developing world on nonreciprocal and nondiscriminatory bases, favorable treatment with respect to nontariff barriers, special provisions for least developed countries, and acceptance of preferential trade among developing countries. For the United States, the Enabling Clause would supersede the European Community's preference schemes, to which it had long been opposed. The United States also inserted the famous "graduation" clause for countries that would no longer be eligible for GSP if they became prosperous; eventually, the United States would use the World Bank classification for high-income countries to "graduate" developing economies to developed status. The first country to graduate was South Korea in 1989, while St. Kitts and Nevis graduated in 2014.

The economic rationale for GSP also reflected the dominant ideas of the day. The case for state interventions for industrialization and growth had found acceptance in both the Global North and the Global South.[20] The North also preferred the extent to which the developing world sought provisions for growth within the GATT rubric. Social policy in the West had also shifted in favor of creating exceptions and quotas for underprivileged groups. The advocacy for the GSP coincided with the civil rights movement and the great society programs in the United States. Regulatory agencies, for example, multiplied in the late 1960s and early 1970s in the United States (Horwitz 1991).

In hindsight, the developed world's pragmatism was another instance of sweet talk. GSP implementation reveals that it resulted in paltry benefits to the developing world. Hudec's (1987: 116) straightforward assessment is that the GSP was a "tool used to win friends and punish enemies." Meier (1980) notes that the developed countries granted these preferences "begrudgingly," noting them as instances of trade diversion and protection, and slipped in exceptions, escape clauses, and quantitative restrictions. However, Hudec (58–59) also admits that the GSP expressed "moral commitments" and the developed world danced to "the whip of these agreed principles."

The U.S. and European records summarize both the restrictive and the manipulative aspects of GSP implementation. An early study (Karsenty and Laird 1987) showed that GSP exports to the "donor" countries were only 2 percent higher than what they would have been without the preferences. In the United States, restrictions applied to the coverage of products, countries, and the scope of the agreement. In 1996, GSP applied to 4,500 products from 140 countries to a total of $16.9 billion, but this was less than 2 percent of the total U.S. trade and 16 percent of the total imports from developing countries (Holliday 1997: 8–11). It is frequently pointed out that a majority of the benefits accrued to a small number of countries, with the top ten countries accounting for 85 percent of the benefits (Holliday 1997: 13), and the top four (Hong Kong, Korea, Taiwan, and Brazil) accounting for 50 percent of the benefits (Karsenty and Laird 1987).

The GSP was a manipulative Faustian bargain. The preferences were provided unilaterally on a voluntary basis. The U.S. reasoning was that it did not want the developing world to ask anything in return, and it also weakened their legal case for any grievances to follow. In return for zero or no tariffs, the donor countries imposed quantitative restrictions, many times on products that would have been able to compete even without the preferences, in effect keeping out developing country exports (Holliday 1997). Furthermore, the granting of the U.S. GSP came with political conditions: (1) The GSP favored countries that were promarket; (2) it was revoked for those sought to appropriate or nationalize U.S. investment assets; (3) it was reserved for noncommunist countries; (4) it excluded OPEC because it employed nonmarket mechanisms for price controls. The United States also prohibited "reverse preferences" through its GSP that former colonies granted European countries; the inclusion of this feature was an impetus, in fact, for the United States to adopt GSP. Starting with the Trade Act of 1984, GSP provisions were tied to enforcement of intellectual property provisions and may have accounted for the acquiescence of many East Asian countries for the restrictive intellectual property agreement from the Uruguay Round (see the next chapter). Finally, the U.S. regional preference schemes such as the 1983 Caribbean Basin Initiative and the African Growth Opportunity Act of 2000 provide better preferences to countries than does the GSP.

The European Economic Community adopted the GSP in July 1971. Its adoption was limited to a few products for which the developing world was competitive. The Lomé Convention in 1975, which revisited the issue of imperial preferences, provided a better bargain for the former colonies, which came to be known as ACP (African, Caribbean, and Pacific) states. The Cotonou Agreement between the EU and ACP in 2000 replaced the four Lomé conventions from 1975 to 1995 and tied European preferences for ACP countries to their economic development. In 2001, the EU introduced the Everything-But-Arms (EBA) initiative, which provided duty-free access to products from LDCs. Other initiatives such as EU's "Special Incentives Arrangements" also privileged APC or LDC products. Summarizing EU's GSP record, Michalapoulos (2000: 24) notes:

Indeed, in the EU, which has put in place the largest number of regional preferential arrangements, to be extended GSP preferences is tantamount to being in the lowest rung in the EU preference pyramid which includes practically all countries, except those to which MFN tariffs are extended such as the US, Japan, Australia and a few other developed countries.

It is hard to evaluate the strengths and weaknesses of GSP from the perspective of developing countries. The GSP resulted from their collective advocacy, but its actual provision was not only underwhelming but also counterproductive. From the beginning, the developing world protested its restrictions and escape clauses and saw its benefits whither away with additional protections or political pressures. In actuality, the GSP became more of a distraction for addressing developing country interests. Agriculture remained excluded from GATT negotiations, and other products such as textiles and garments faced quantitative restrictions.

Recent studies on GSP have produced a lively debate. Andrew Rose's (2004) "infamous" article, which included an examination of preferential trade, noted that trade increases faster in countries that do not join the WTO. Tobin and Busch (2014) have countered that developing country advocacy to make the GSP conditionalities nondiscriminatory had the perverse effect of limiting trade for every GSP beneficiary in the WTO as opposed to those who were not WTO members. On labor conditionalities, Hafner-Burton (2005) notes that human rights groups have forum shopped to preferential trade agreements to enforce human rights practices, which have been effective. Mosley and Tello (2015) find that interest groups in the North trying to institute human rights or labor conditionalities are motivated more with material rather than moral concerns.

The GSP preferences are often defended on the grounds that developing countries are either not ready for reciprocity or would move away from free trade. Özden and Reinhardt (2005) test for 154 developing countries in the years 1976 through 2000 and find that trading countries that were removed from GSP adopted liberal trade policies. This provides an earlier confirmation of Bagwell and Staiger's (2013) hypothesis that developing countries need to be integrated into the WTO on a reciprocal basis: These authors find the GSP to be especially perverse for the developing world because it removes the moral hazard, or the credible binding, for the cost of protecting inefficient industry. Chapter 6 of this book also shows that the developing world can undertake reciprocal preferences even in high-tech issues such as services. However, the Trade in Services Agreement (TiSA) signed in 2015, mostly at the behest of the United States, instituted preferences for the LDCS in services.

The GSP has continued to become less useful to large parts of the developing world, but it has also divided countries along the lines of those who want multilateral tariff reductions and those who view "special and differential treatment" as their major goal. This division and also the preference for SDT has contributed to the Doha Round deadlocks as those accustomed to these unilateral preferences resist multilateral concessions (Low et al. 2005). In the United States, the GSP imports were one percent of the total imports, or $19.9 billion of its total $2.3 trillion of imports in 2012. For the GSP countries, the $19.9 billion represent 5.9 percent of their total exports to the United States of $338 billion (Jones 2014: 20–21). Thus, the share of GSP declined by half from the 2 percent calculated in 1986 (Karsenty and Laird 1987). Furthermore, GSP continues to benefit a few countries disproportionately: In 2012, five countries—India, Thailand, Brazil, Indonesia, and South Africa—accounted for 70 percent of the total GSP imports into the United States from a total of 122 countries (Jones 2014: 27–28). The economic value of the GSP to the United States itself is now increasingly recognized. This may be to assuage the antitrade groups in the United States, but it has forced the United States to elaborate on the benefits it receives.[21]

The Generalized System of Preferences strengthened the rhetoric of paternalism. It was more than the pious platitudes of the 1950s and 1960s. It was a unilateral and voluntary gift to the developed world. It is, nevertheless, apparent that the developing world gained little and may have done better in its exports without it. The GSP is another instance of sweet talk. The early evaluation from 1974 reflects this sentiment: Developed countries regarded the GSP "as a favor to the poor—a form of international charity that places developing countries in the position of supplicants" (Erb 1974: 93). Official texts are polite but now do acknowledge explicitly the value of the GSP to the United States. After the U.S. Congress renewed the GSP in June 2015, the U.S. Trade Representative (USTR) noted:

Renewal of the Generalized System of Preferences (GSP) program, which lapsed in July 2013, will promote economic growth in the developing world by eliminating duties on a wide range of products from developing countries, including some of the poorest countries in the world. GSP will also support U.S. jobs, help keep American manufacturers competitive, and benefit American families by lowering prices on many consumer goods.

The next chapter will also provide details of the content analysis of USTR press releases for the 1982–1993 period. Among other things, the GSP will be discussed again, specifically its use as a strategic trade policy instrument during the Uruguay Round. Srininvan writes that in opting for import substitution industrialization (ISI) and the GSP, the developing countries misguidedly stepped out of the GATT system:

Instead of demanding and receiving crumbs from the rich man's table, such as GSP and a permanent status of inferiority under the "special and differential" treatment clause, had they participated fully, vigorously, and on equal terms with the developed countries in the GATT and had they adopted an outward-oriented development strategy, they could have achieved far faster and better growth. (Srinivasan 1998: 27)

Conclusion

The developing world was a marginal player during the Kennedy and Tokyo Rounds. During the Kennedy Round, the average tariff reduction for developing countries was 20 percent and 36 percent for developed countries. After the Tokyo Round, the average reduction in tariffs in goods of interest to the developing world was 26 percent as compared to 33 percent for the developed world (GATT estimate quoted in Michalopoulos 2000: 7). The developing world was excluded from the benefit of the plurilateral agreements or codes that applied only to signatory countries at the Tokyo Round. Before the Uruguay Round, out of the sixty-five developing countries, only a handful had signed the Tokyo Round codes. These included fourteen for standards, thirteen for subsidies, ten for import licensing, nine for customs valuation, nine for antidumping, and three for procurement (Hudec 1987: 88). Therefore, the developing world's participation until the Tokyo Round can be summarized through an examination of the preferential tariffs system.

With the Tokyo Round, the developing world's bloc diplomacy also came to an end as the ideological and economic case for preferences weakened. Many developing countries realized that their exclusion from GATT mechanisms was because of their demands for exceptions. From the 1980s onward many of them would seek to play the same game as that of the developed world, namely reductions in tariff and nontariff barriers. This weakened the hand of the least developed and a few other developing countries, such as in the ACP, who by then were quite dependent on preferential treatment for their products. Second, starting in the mid-1980s, the macroeconomic policies in the developing world shifted from the import substitution to either a market-oriented or an export-led strategy. Mexico's entry into GATT in 1986, under a prolabor regime, was an instance of the market opening in the developing world. The "graduation" of East Asian Newly Industrializing Countries such as South Korea, Taiwan, Hong Kong, and Singapore (from the GSP and developing country status) were other reminders. There is a wealth of literature on the domestic political alignments and economic incentives and strategies that allowed these countries to reduce various forms of economic dependency (Hamilton and Kao, forthcoming; Amsden 1992; Haggard 1990). The rise of the East Asian NICs was a blow to arguments about economic dependency from Latin America (Cardoso and Faletto 1979). Their economic strength is also consistent with this book's argument that developing countries strive hard to change patterns of paternalism.

As developing countries moved from seeking preferences or exclusions from GATT mechanisms toward working for MFN benefits within GATT, it was not readily apparent whether the developed world would become any less paternalistic or if the developing world had the collective negotiation advantage to effect concessions in their favor.

Regardless of the limited positive impact of GSP, all trade concessions in the postcolonial era, including the GSP, were shaped with collective action from the developing world. This chapter also shows that each of the developing world's concerns was met with a great deal of sweet talk. The GSP emerged as the developing world's best hope at distributive justice. In hindsight, it remained a limited act of charity and a strategic trade policy instrument. A U.S. government evaluation in 2014 noted that the GSP is an "effective low cost means of providing economic assistance to developing countries" (Jones 2014: 25). This chapter has shown that this "effectiveness" must be understood both within the context of its limited applicability and its use as a strategic trade policy instrument.

Winham's (1986: 376) history of the Tokyo Round concludes that "the developing countries were not essential to the process and the accords did not directly address their perceived needs." However, keeping in mind the rising advocacy from the developing world in UNCTAD and GATT, Winham also notes that these countries "tend to make revolutionary demands" and that "negotiations are not an appropriate method" for such action (377). This chapter shows that such uncharitable and empirically partial assessments overlook the context of developing country advocacy for market access since the creation of GATT in 1947.

Part II

The Uruguay Round and After

Chapter 4
Unequal Partners in Merchandise Trade

> In the Uruguay Round North–South bargain the North's mercantilist sacrifice
> on tariffs and quotas is, in real economics, a gain for them—even larger
> because of recovering the MFA quota rents. The South's concessions, however,
> involve real costs to the South—significant costs to implement the policy
> changes, negative impacts in many cases of the changes themselves.
>
> Michael Finger "The Uruguay Round North–South Bargain:
> Will the WTO Get over It?" (2008: 304)

THE Uruguay Round brought in developing countries as active participants to the negotiating forums of the GATT. Agriculture, textiles, and garments were included in the negotiations, and, in return for the developed world's "reciprocity" for including these goods, the developing world agreed, after some protest, to negotiate new trade issues, namely intangible services and intellectual property. The "grand bargain" of the Uruguay Round's beginning was implicit in the terms of this reciprocity.[1]

The acceptance of reciprocity was a departure from the way things ended in the 1970s. The Tokyo Round closed with the Escape Clause in 1979, providing special and differential treatment, which marked both the apogee and the waning of developing country advocacy for differential treatment. However, the developing world boycotted the signing of the Tokyo Round agreement in April 1979 because of their dissatisfaction with the "safeguards" provisions (GATT Article XIX), which allowed countries to protect their producers from surges in imports. Developing countries argued that this provision was indiscriminately used against them, especially for textiles and clothing. As a result of their advocacy, developing countries became important players in the Uruguay Round, and the shift in their position toward market-oriented positions beginning in the early 1980s also made it hard to ignore their demands.

This chapter attends to the dynamics of paternalism at the Uruguay Round and the overall negotiations in merchandise trade at the three levels of evidence from mixed methods presented in this book. In doing so, this chapter also reports on the two data sets compiled for this book. First, the chapter attends to the presence of "sweet talk" as rhetoric. It provides the results of a content analysis of 1,925 pages of press releases for the period from 1982 through 1993 from the U.S. Trade Representative (USTR) for the years of the Uruguay Round

(1986–1994) and the efforts to start this round since 1982.[2] The data reveal that 69 percent of the references to the developing world were paternalistic, and another 14 percent were highly unfavorable references. Of the total 710 paternalistic references, 93 percent (or 662) of the total were toward the developing world. These findings confirm the presence of a sweet-talking United States, but they do not confirm the presence of any concessions given or received at the Uruguay Round, except for the systems of preferences covered in the press releases. Next, the chapter presents the overall findings on merchandise trade at the Uruguay Round with an index developed to measure paternalism from a factor analysis of three other indices. Countries ranking high on the paternalism strength index, not surprisingly many countries in the West, garnered higher concessions at the Uruguay Round than did the developing world. Qualitative analysis presented in this section also validates the broad macro findings. Finally, the textiles agreement from the Uruguay Round is examined as a case of North–South negotiations in manufacturing.

We would expect sweet-talking developed countries to make great cuts to their tariffs once the developing countries came on board with the idea of reciprocity (instead of seeking differential treatment). Data show otherwise. The grand bargain was lopsided in favor of the developed world and later affected the impasse of the Doha Round, which started in 2001. The gains made by the developing world at the Uruguay Round and thereafter resulted from their bargaining strategies. Paternalism continued.

Paternalism in U.S. Trade Policy

Documenting sweet talk or paternalism at the level of countries and all trade issues is a difficult proposition but empirically necessary for this book. The content analysis of twelve years of press releases from the U.S. Trade Representative's office addresses trade policy at the level of its rhetoric, which is important for this book's claim. This analysis documents sweet talk but also provides a first glimpse that this "talk" from the developed world has not resulted in meaningful concessions to the developing world.

The content analysis of 1,925 pages of press releases from USTR is a first attempt at operationalizing a measure for the rhetoric of the developed world toward the developing world.[3] Being the primary agenda setter for trade policy and outcomes, the official U.S. rhetoric on its international trade is important in its implications for the rest of the world. U.S. hegemony is often cast in benevolent terms (Mearsheimer 1991; Nye 1990), or as a social contract between authority and subordinates (Lake 2009). Among the developed states, the United States, without an extensive history of colonial domination, may be taken at least to not carry the historical baggage of paternalism as do the West European states. Michael Barnett's (2012) definition of weak paternalism is apt: It exists within a framework of "institutions, information and knowledge" (506) and is sanctioned through liberal democracies. Barnett seeks to develop an empirical category for this paternalism, but it is too broad to be implemented in any meaningful sense. Most of his empirical analysis accounts for the presence of paternalistic actions related back to sets of motivations for actors. There is a problem of endogeneity here: Good paternalistic things happen; therefore, paternalism is good. Furthermore, this good weak paternalism is unlike its coercive strong paternal predecessor. For this reason, it is necessary to first account for the presence of paternalism regardless of whether it is beneficial to the paternalized.

The section offers an independent measure for the presence of paternalism and then points out its implications in this section and next. Press releases from the USTR are an official record of the positions that the United States undertakes on trade issues. Although press releases may serve a strategic function of persuading trading partners, they are still a valid measure of the trade policy positions that the United States undertakes. Generally negotiation scholars rely on media accounts and interviews with negotiators to determine the actual position a country holds on a trade issue. It would be hard to uncover a latent measure such as "paternalism" through interviews and media accounts. Media and scholarly accounts do record paternalism but at a very broad level where it cannot be related to specific negotiation issues such as U.S. positions on intellectual property or the agricultural trade policy toward the developing world.[4] It is also hard to disaggregate such measures to the country, regional, or trade groups level. Similarly, although developing country diplomats speak to being paternalized, the evidence is anecdotal and piecemeal and often conveys opinion rather than an empirical measure (Jawara and Kwa 2003; Raghavan 2014). Certainly, it is hard to find an account of developed country negotiators talking about their paternalism in media or scholarly accounts. A content analysis of nearly 2,000 pages of press releases covering just about every issue area and trading partner gets around many of the empirical problems confronted in operationalizing and finding a valid measure of paternalism.[5]

The content analysis offered here mentions 129 countries and seven grouped trading partners (Andean countries, Caribbean or Caricom countries, Central and European countries, developing countries, the European Community, Latin American countries, and all trading partners taken collectively) in the USTR press releases. The content analysis or codings were conducted manually using NVivo software, where the classifications for data are called nodes, which can then be reclassified and aggregated for further analysis.

Coding Description

Four groups of classifications or nodes were used containing 208 individual nodes for countries, trade sectors, trade issues and policies, and sentiment toward trading partner. First, each press release was coded for each country mentioned. Each country or group was coded only once, even if the press release mentioned it more than once. The purpose was to determine which countries and trading groups prompt a press release, and multiple mentions of the same country within a press release were unnecessary. Multiple press releases involving the same country (on the same issue) demonstrate the importance of the issue or country, and each press release was recorded separately. Thus, for example, U.S.–EU steel negotiations in the mid-1980s produced several press releases as also did semiconductors and Japan. The second group of coding nodes covered the trade sector: agriculture, manufacturing, intellectual property, services, investment, financial or currency issues, and several issues. The several issues node covered many issues in the same press release: GSP mentions, for example, covered issues involving agriculture, manufacturing, and intellectual property. The third set of coding nodes covered trade policy and issues including U.S. trade policy instruments such as Section 301, bilateral trade talks and investment agreements, and U.S. versus trading partner restrictions.

Fourth, and central to this chapter's claim, the dominant tone or sentiment toward the trading partner was coded in each press release: favorable, unfavorable, mixed, neutral, or paternalistic. Appendix A provides an operational definition for each node, but that of paternalism is important enough to be listed here on its own:

Paternalistic

Moralistic, preachy, or patronizing statements toward the trade partner, often pointing out or providing benefit of nonreciprocal market access, or FDI from the United States.

Offers of assistance and measures that are also beneficial to the United States but announced as if it helps the other country only (including GSP, BITs). Most GSP press releases contain language of "help" to the developing world. Also includes patronizing and manipulative statements such as telling countries like China and India to be willing to bring their laws in tune with international rules.

After the manual coding, data for countries and groups were also categorized for some macrolevel results for trading partners into the following three groups: Organization for Economic Cooperation and Development (OECD), non-OECD, and Central and East European Countries (all in mutually exclusive categories). The OECD and non-OECD distinction is important. Most of the GATT agendas were set by the developed world in the OECD forums, including the Generalized System of Preferences in the 1960s and 1970s, or the services and intellectual property agenda in the 1970s and 1980s.[6] Often even the technical details were worked out at the OECD before being "multilateralized" over to the GATT and WTO. The OECD is, therefore, a relevant forum for determining if the United States was paternalistic toward other paternalistic states (OECD) and those that are developing (non-OECD).

Only countries that were members of the OECD prior to 1994 are included in this category for the tables in this book. This includes Australia, New Zealand, Japan, and Turkey, who were the only non-Western members of the OECD club prior to 1994. After 1994, Chile, Korea, Mexico, and several East European states were admitted to the OECD, but they are not counted as non-OECD in the tables presented here. The non-OECD group in this book, even though it includes two Western states (Cyprus and Grenada), also corresponds roughly to the conceptualizations of the Global South as comprising developing and middle-income economies in Latin America, Africa, and Asia.

Coding Results

The first set of results relates to the tone or sentiment toward the trading partner. Each mention of the 137 countries and groups was coded for the characterization of the trading country or group in one of the five following ways for tone: favorable, unfavorable, mixed, neutral, and paternalistic. The operational definition for each of these measures is provided in Appendix A. Only the dominant characterization was recorded, thus each press release warranted only one characterization for tone. This yielded 1,462 references for tone, which are summarized in Table 4.1. These data show that 69 percent of the total references

Table 4.1. Characterization of sentiment toward trading partners in USTR press releases, 1982–1993 (parenthetical figures are rounded percentages of the total references to each group).

	Paternalistic	Favorable	Unfavorable	Mixed	Neutral	Total
Total	710	234	291	129	98	1,462
Non-OECD	662	92	134	38	40	966
	(69)	(10)	(14)	(4)	(4)	(100)
OECD	19	86	133	58	40	336
	(6)	(26)	(40)	(17)	(12)	(100)
CEES	25	18	8	9	3	63
	(40)	(29)	(13)	(14)	(5)	(100)
All world	4	38	16	24	15	97
	(4)	(39)	(16)	(25)	(15)	(100)

SOURCE: Author's content analysis of U.S. trade representative press releases (1982–1993).

from the United States toward the non-OECD countries were paternalistic, which made up a total of 93 percent of the total paternalistic references that the United States made.[7] However, 40 percent of the total references from the United States toward the OECD countries were unfavorable, whereas only 14 percent toward the non-OECD countries were unfavorable. Only 6 percent of the total references to the OECD countries were paternalistic and were in press statements on issues such as the GSP or regions such as NAFTA in which the OECD countries were also included; thus there are no paternalistic references directed solely at an OECD country. The dominant tone of the trade policy toward major U.S. trading partners is quite aggressive (unfavorable in tone), whereas toward the developing world it was paternalistic or benevolent. It is important to remember that the tone does not mean concessions were received or given.

Most of the references to paternalism toward the developing world pertained to the granting of preferential access, which includes the following in the period covered here: the Generalized System of Preferences, Sugar Rate Quotas, Multi-Fibre Arrangement, Caribbean Basin Initiative, Andean Trade Preferences, and Enterprise of the Americas Initiative. In terms of trade issues that garnered paternalistic references, 18 percent pertained to agricultural issues, 14 percent to investment issues, 8 percent to intellectual property, 5 percent to manufacturing, and 3 percent to services. The highest number of paternalistic press releases was in the "several issues" category, which included GSP. The annual reports on GSP renewal and petitions against issuing GSP, latter mostly from U.S. producers or interest groups, were often the longest press releases.

They list countries and quotas granted in specific products. In the case of petitioners, these press releases list interest groups or firms seeking revocation of GSP usually on the grounds of workers rights or insufficient intellectual property rights laws (latter discussed in Chapter 6). In terms of countries, of the total 710 paternalistic tone references in the data set, high-low paternalism references included countries as follows:

- Twenty or more paternalistic references: Colombia (21), Brazil (20)

- Ten to nineteen paternalistic references: Thailand (19), Mexico (18), Honduras (17), Argentina (15), Costa Rica (15), Malawi (14), India (15), Belize (10)

- Zero to nine paternalistic references: Cote d'Ivoire (9), Chile (6), Egypt (4), Turkey (5), all EC states (0), Japan (0)

The GSP press releases almost always carried a statement of the extent of benevolence from the United States. This statement from the March 31, 1983, press release is a typical instance:

The Generalized System of Preferences is a program of unilateral tariff preferences granted by the United States to developing countries to assist in their economic development. Nineteen other industrialized countries also maintain GSP programs. At present, the United States grants duty-free treatment on approximately 3,000 products from 140 developing countries and territories. Since the program's implementation in 1976, the value of imports receiving GSP treatment has risen from $3.0 billion to $8.4 billion in 1982. GSP imports account for three percent of total U.S. imports.

Compare this with a nonpaternalistic press release, in this case, a statement that is unfavorable in tone, from a February 20, 1987, press release:

Ambassador Clayton Yeutter today initiated an investigation of an alleged unfair trade practice involving restrictions on U.S. almond exports to India, Deputy U.S. Trade Representative Alan Woods announced today. This action is based on a petition filed under Section 301 of the Trade Act of 1974 by the California Almond Growers Exchange.

Finally, this June 4, 1990, press release conveys a favorable tone without being paternalistic:

United States Trade Representative Carla A. Hills today urged the nations of the Americas to form a "new hemispheric partnership" and to "work together to make the decade of the '90s the decade of the Americas, the decade of growth and opportunity.

Addressing the Organization of American States (OAS) General Assembly in Asuncion, Paraguay, Hills hailed the dramatic political and economic changes in Latin America and said the United States stands ready to work with its trading partners in the hemisphere to achieve even more.

Although these excerpts provide a sense of the variation in sentiments and tone, more than two-thirds of the references to the non-OECD countries were paternalistic. Other paternalistic references include those praising the developing world for signing trade and investment agreements with the United States, thereby allowing them to benefit from U.S. foreign direct investment and consumption. The first bilateral investment treaty (BIT) was with Egypt in 1982. As of 2015, the United States had signed forty-eight BITs, almost all of them with developing countries and East European countries. Before the close of the Uruguay Round, Turkey was the only OECD country to sign a BIT with the United States. A typical statement of such paternalism is the following pertaining in this case to the announcement of the signing of BIT with Bangladesh on March 12, 1986, in which USTR Clayton Yeutter is quoted:

Developing countries such as Bangladesh, which recognize the importance of direct investment to their long-term economic development plans, now are taking actions to attract such investment. I hope that more countries follow the leadership Bangladesh has shown.

Another instance is preferential access granted to Andean countries under the Andean Trade Preference Act. A 1992 release admitting Ecuador to ATPA notes:

The ATPA fulfills the U.S. commitment to improve access to the U.S. market for exports from the Andean nations. It is designed to help the beneficiary nations encourage their people to export legitimate products instead of illicit drugs. The United States supports the strong efforts of the Government of Ecuador to combat drug trafficking and to modernize its economy.

At face value, this could be taken as a measure of net benefits from paternalism (access to U.S. markets and investments, curtailing illicit trade). However, as pointed out in the last chapter, the preferential system of GSP diverted from the task of trade liberalization and over time may have contributed to creating systems of dependence among developing countries that were not particularly competitive. Goldstein, Rivers, and Tomz (2007: 54–56) update conclusions similar to those from the *Haberler Report* (GATT 1958) note to show that many nonmultilateral trade measures have expanded trade in the long run. The exception is GSP and nonreciprocal preferential trade arrangements, which have a negative effect on expansion of trade (reciprocal PTAs have a positive effect).[8]

There are three reasons for coding statements about the virtues of markets and investment as paternalistic, despite the fact that, like the earlier quote from USTR Yeutter, they follow a particular logic in economics. First, such statements are directed only at the non-OECD countries. There are no press releases where the United States adopts this language for the OECD countries, even though in many cases the measure in question also follows the same logic in economics. Therefore, these press releases are an instance of the paternalistic lectures that the developing world received on markets and investment. Second, directing such statements at the developing world implicitly assumes that the United States follows market principles in granting access to developing country exports. This book demonstrates otherwise. Therefore, there is a holier-than-thou assumption in press releases that lecture the developing world on the virtues of international trade (see the epigraphs at the beginning of Chapters 1, 3, and 6 for counterpoints). Third, these statements mask the many strategic reasons for which the United States signs a BIT (for example, with East European states in the 1990s after the breakup of the Soviet Union) that have very little to do with economics.

The next issue that the coding can help us address is the number of press releases that addressed particular country groups and trade sector issues. Table 4.2 provides a summary of the number of references based on whether countries were in the OECD, non-OECD, Central and East European States (CEES), and All Trading Partners category. On average, the ratio of press releases dealing with OECD countries versus non-OECD countries was roughly similar (240 for OECD versus 209 for non-OECD). On agricultural and manufacturing issues, the ration was 2:1 in favor of OECD. In services it was 3:1. Press releases dealing more with the non-OECD countries were in investment and intellectual property. In investment, the ratio was 1:7; for intellectual property (IP) issues, the ratio was 1:9. This follows from the pressure that the United States applied on the developing world to comply with its IP norms and to sign BITs. The IP issue will be taken up in Chapter 5. Each press release was coded for only one issue. The "several issues" category captures instances of the GSP (which included agriculture and manufacturing) or those where there was a press release on Section 301 countries, but it dealt equally with intellectual property and GSP.

Table 4.2.   Country groups and trade sector references in USTR press releases.

	OECD	Non-OECD	CEES	All world
Agriculture and minerals	65	32	5	5
Manufacturing	82	40	6	17
Services	24	8	0	4
Intellectual property	4	36	4	7
Investment	2	14	6	3
Currency and finance	1	2	0	2
Several issues	62	77	21	58
Total	240	209	42	96

NOTE: The level of aggregation used in NVivo here tracks the number of press releases that addressed each group (not any particular country).
SOURCE: Author's content analysis of U.S. trade representative press releases (1982–1993).

Table 4.3.   Country groups and trade policy and issue references in USTR press releases.

	Paternalistic	Favorable	Unfavorable	Mixed	Neutral
U.S. trade measures	8	5	**50**	9	2
U.S. trade and investment agreement	16	**57**	29	35	22
U.S. protectionism	1	**25**	16	9	6
Preferential treatment	**52**	14	12	3	1
Foreign restrictions	5	33	**55**	37	11

NOTE: The modal category in each row is in bold.
SOURCE: Author's content analysis of U.S. Trade Representative press releases (1982–1993).

Table 4.3 explains what types of U.S. trade law and measures and trade policy and outcomes tended to carry the most paternalistic references. In this case, each press release was coded more than once if it referenced more than one measure or outcome. For example, a press release containing language about a U.S. Section 301 investigation in the United States could also reference a dispute settlement at GATT or be part of a free trade agreement.[9] Not surprisingly, the highest number of paternalistic references is in preferential trade agreements. In terms of favorable language toward trading partners, press releases announcing trade agreements or maintaining protectionist measures in the United States generated high numbers. Those dealing with the negotiation of

Table 4.4.   U.S. trade sentiment in press releases through the Uruguay Round (percentage of the total in each category).

	Positive	Negative	Paternalistic	Mixed/neutral
1982–1986	36	29	15	20
1987–1990	31	25	15	30
1991–1993	25	32	17	27

SOURCE: Author's content analysis of U.S. trade representative press releases (1982–1993).

trading partners' restrictions also generated favorable press releases, but these were generally after the trading partner had reduced these barriers. The highest number of unfavorable sentiments expressed was also with reference to trading partners' restrictions. U.S. trade measures such as Section 301, Section 304, and Section 305 generated a high number of unfavorable references as well.

Finally, the coding allows an overall assessment of changes in sentiments expressed about the trading partners over the twelve-year period. Overall, the positive sentiments tend to decrease over this period whereas the negative sentiments increase. Paternalistic sentiments stay about the same. In the period from 1982 to 1986, corresponding to the years before the Uruguay Round was launched, press releases with positive sentiments were 36 percent of the total, and those with negative sentiments were 29 percent of the total (the rest were neutral, mixed, or paternalistic). In the next four years (1987–1990), press releases with positive sentiments decreased to 31 percent of the total, and those with negative sentiments were 25 percent of the total. In the last three years, the unfavorable assessments were greater than the favorable ones (32 percent negative, 25 percent positive), reflecting most probably the aggressive stance that the United States assumed in the closing years of the Uruguay Round.

These codings allow a detailed first-order glimpse into paternalistic trade sentiments toward the developing world and the trade issues, trade measures, and a few outcomes in which paternalistic sentiments may be detected in U.S. trade policy and negotiations. However, these codings are not particularly useful for higher levels of analysis. They pertain only to the United States, and thus it is hard to test them against trade concessions given and received in the developing countries from all their trading partners. To put it bluntly, it would be hard to test trade concessions given and received in countries when we have only one observation for one paternalistic state, namely the United States.

Second, the codings here pertain to all trading issues that arose in the United States from 1982 through 1993. They allow a sense of the way the United States characterized its trading partners, but not all the issues pertained to the Uruguay Round negotiations. There were many where the Uruguay Round was referenced explicitly, or where the issue in question had vast implications even if Uruguay Round was not mentioned (for example, intellectual property issues). However, there were many instances of bilateral trade issues that were not directly about the Uruguay Round (BITs, for instance). Thus, there is considerable noise in this data to use it just for the Uruguay Round. Third, I carried out the content analysis myself over a four-month period. Although I developed a codebook and guidelines, the estimates have not been vetted for internal or intercoder reliability.[10] The next section thus turns to developing a measure for paternalism for the developed and developing worlds to allow a test for the degree of paternalism in trade reciprocity.

Merchandise Concessions during the Uruguay Round (1986–1994)

The Uruguay Round ostensibly offered the developing world a Faustian "grand bargain." In return for concessions in services and intellectual property, the developing world received concessions in agriculture and a phase out of the quantitative restrictions for textiles and clothing through the Multi-Fibre Arrangement, dating back to 1961. The deadlock to start the round, and include services and intellectual property in its agenda, was broken with a group of moderate states that included both developing and developed countries and came to be known as the café au lait coalition after its leaders, Switzerland and Colombia (café au lait later evolved into the coalition known as the Friends of Services group with up to forty-four members).

The last section examined the presence of paternalistic and other statements or tone only for the United States and also did not test its effects on measures of trade reciprocity. The remainder of this section presents the quantitative results for tariff concessions the developing world received as a whole in merchandise trade from the Uruguay Round. Two sets of causal factors are examined: degree of paternalism from a trading country and negotiation strength. To do so, a data set was compiled from various sources for the independent and dependent variables. The codebook and data sources are listed in Appendix B. The independent and dependent variables are discussed first before presenting the results. The two hypotheses examined in this chapter on merchandise trade and the next on agriculture trade are:

- *Hypothesis 1*: Paternalism is negatively related to the developing world's trade concessions.

- *Hypothesis 2*: The developing world's negotiation strength is positively related to the trade concessions it receives.

Dependent Variable: Reciprocity Measures

To examine tariff reductions, the following analysis presents two types of dependent variables. At the broadest level, the differentiation is between merchandise tariff concessions received minus those given. However, data for these dyads are limited to forty-five countries in available data. Therefore, this study also provides results from merchandise trade concessions received, which raises the number of observations from eighty to 124, depending on the model, in available data. These data are not paired with concessions given but, it is important to note, with a bigger sample size, they can account better for explanatory factors such as effects of being a former colony or being part of a developing country coalition. The data set creators also note that the "concessions received" data reflect the "concessions given" data as a baseline (Finger et al. 1996: 20). In addition, although concessions received is not a reciprocal measure per se, the countries included here, from the total of 123 countries who signed the Uruguay Round agreement, made up more than 95 percent of the trade among WTO members.[11] Therefore, one can assume that these concessions were informed with some overall notion of "specific reciprocity" (Keohane 1986), implying congruence between concessions received and those given. Furthermore, these concessions do not include preferential schemes such as GSP, which means that the concessions relate to reciprocity rather than nonreciprocal trade measures.

Two sets of independent variables are presented to test for negotiation and paternalism, and other controls are introduced later for robustness checks. Where relevant, the data are for 1990, which served as the midway point of negotiations for the Uruguay Round from 1986 to 1990.[12] Many of the deadlocks in merchandise trade, services, and intellectual property had been overcome by 1990, and the final outcome would be based on the formulas or modalities that were already in place.

Paternalism Measures

For developing a measure of paternalism, this study employs three indices (themselves composites of several variables): cultural distance from the United States, values of the affinity index for the United States in the UN General Assembly (s3un), and a measure of export market concentration, which deals with the export markets and products. Except for the Hofstede's cultural distance scores, the other data are for 1990 (or, if that year is unavailable, the closest year after 1990). A dummy variable on colonies, not included in the paternalism index, is also employed separately for an additional test of paternalism.

The three indices mentioned in the preceding paragraphs allow for a factor analysis—roughly common elements in variables, or statistically the principal components from a correlation matrix of the variables. Factor analysis is also known as latent variable analysis and helps to obtain a measure of phenomena not readily observable in practice for subliminal phenomena such as paternalism and racism (Bartholomew et al. 2011). However, a group of behavioral factors can yield a measure through a search of latent common components to these variables. The paternalism measure developed in this book looks for these common components across political, cultural, and economic indices. The book puts forward a "paternalism strength index" (PSI) as a variable that is derived from a factor analysis of three indices noted earlier that address cultural, political, and economic differences and strength among developed and developing countries. Each index is discussed briefly here. Table 4.6 lists the values of the paternalism strength index, which varies from −0.81 for Albania to 3.17 for the United States. Almost all countries in the developing world have negative values.

One of the central economic relationships of the colonial era was relegation of the colonies to production of a few export commodities (agricultural or more resources). Therefore, the inclusion of the export market concentration here is relevant. The export market concentration index in this case is a better measure of paternalistic relations than the Herfindahl-Hirschman Market Concentration Index. The former examines the dispersion of products across trading partners, whereas the latter examines only the number of trading partners and not products. The Export Market Concentrations Index is also known as the Export Market Diversification Index. The values for these data come from the World Integrated Trade Solutions database of the World Bank.

Table 4.5.   Variables and expected signs of coefficients.

Dependent variables	Independent variables	Expected sign of coefficient	Notes based on my theory	Variable name
(1) Tariff concession received minus given for merchandise trade (2) tariff concession received minus given in agricultural trade (3) merchandise concessions received (4) agriculture concessions received	Cultural distance	Negative	Paternalism toward culturally distant groups	col_cultdist2
	Colonized status	Negative	Former European colonies do not receive reciprocal trade concessions from current paternalistic countries, including the United States.	colony_euro
	Index of export market concentration	Positive	Higher scores indicate better BATNA, allow for tradeoffs and linkages.	xmktcon
	G10	Positive	Coalitional pressures	g10
	Cairns Group	Positive	Coalitional pressures	cairnsgroup
	ASEAN	Positive	Coalitional pressures	asean
	Paternalism strength index (PSI): includes cultural distance, affinity index score for United States, and index of export market concentration	Positive	Countries that score high have diversified export markets, vote with and are culturally contiguous to the United States.	paternalism7

The cultural distance indicator is a composite index calculated from Hofstede's four-part criteria measuring cultural distances of countries from each other from 0 to 100. These indicators are power distance (PD), measuring degree of inequality in society; individualism (IDV), measuring connections of people to each other; degree of masculinity (MAS) in society; and the uncertainty avoidance index (UAI), which measures reactions to the unknown in any society.[13] To measure the cultural distance of a developing country, I first developed a "hybrid colonizer" that provided the value for seven colonizers (Britain, France, Germany, Netherland, Portugal, Spain, and the United States) and then calculated the cultural distance of every country from this hybrid colony.

Table 4.6. Paternalism strength index values.

Albania	−0.8109284	Libya	−0.5820554
Argentina	−0.3223387	Luxembourg	1.052012
Australia	0.4893678	Malawi	−0.1609605
Austria	0.6255863	Malaysia	−0.6184586
Bangladesh	−0.5839211	Malta	−0.0210197
Belgium	1.932742	Mexico	−0.5499941
Bhutan	−0.7720973	Morocco	−0.3670844
Brazil	−0.2480851	Mozambique	−0.7336348
Bulgaria	0.2372405	Namibia	−0.569971
Burkina Faso	−0.6901152	Nepal	−0.4660807
Cabo Verde	−0.73989	Netherlands	1.515262
Canada	0.9359984	New Zealand	0.3072304
Chile	−0.5126343	Nigeria	−0.5884925
China	−0.0829096	Norway	0.5674079
Colombia	−0.6423934	Pakistan	−0.3258992
Costa Rica	−0.3496192	Panama	−0.0779771
Czech Republic	0.7054436	Peru	−0.5733998
Denmark	0.5367373	Philippines	−0.5733998
Dominican Republic	−0.3609271	Poland	0.6356289
Ecuador	−0.690582	Portugal	0.6027461
Egypt, Arab Republic	−0.4937889	Romania	0.1547732
Ethiopia	−0.6743574	Russian Federation	−0.3307148
Fiji	−0.6021034	Saudi Arabia	−0.6708078
Finland	0.5047826	Senegal	−0.5532253
France	2.483069	Sierra Leone	−0.6597261
Germany	1.867206	Singapore	−0.4701186
Ghana	−0.6950196	Spain	0.7712071
Guatemala	−0.797995	Sri Lanka	−0.5704128
Honduras	−0.4982734	Suriname	−0.5871229
Hungary	0.3347276	Sweden	0.4970181
Iceland	0.3765892	Switzerland	1.374652
India	−0.3069715	Syrian Arab Republic	−0.5193524
Indonesia	−0.5714398	Tanzania	−0.5912595
Iran, Islamic Republic	−0.397204	Thailand	−0.333317
Ireland	0.3429839	Trinidad and Tobago	−0.597253
Israel	1.41593	Turkey	0.213421
Italy	2.200504	Ukraine	−0.5985859
Jamaica	−0.6140104	United Arab Emirates	−0.6127051
Japan	1.158722	United Kingdom	2.339722
Jordan	−0.5578369	United States	3.1736
Kenya	−0.5004151	Uruguay	−0.4202677
Korea, Republic of	0.8186827	Venezuela, Bolivarian Republic of	−0.6455445
Kuwait	−0.6885493	Vietnam	−0.5873122
Lebanon	−0.5356991	Zambia	−0.5311572

The cultural distance scores from the hybrid colonizer vary from 12.2 for Luxembourg to 84.6 for Guatemala in the data set. The assumption in Hofstede's scores, based on a survey of 117,000 IBM employees around the world between 1967 and 1973, is that cultures change slowly, and therefore the values remain relevant. They are especially relevant for this chapter, evaluating paternalism in the 1960s and 1970s prior to the Uruguay Round, and for this book's historical perspective ascribing relevance to colonization and subsequent paternalism. Table 4.7 provides the descriptive statistics for the dataset.

The affinity index (s3un) for the United States, taken from Anton Strezhnev and Erik Voeten's "United Nations General Assembly Voting Data," provides values for least similar (–1) to most similar (+1) for voting with the United States in 1990. The United States, as the agenda setter in trade, is used as a proxy for the developed world.

Negotiation Measures

The negotiation variables are tested through measures of export diversity (economic conditions) and coalitional strength. As mentioned in Chapter 2, alternatives are important in negotiations, at the macrolevel as measure of "bargaining power" and during the negotiation process for effecting trade-offs and linkages. The export market concentration index from the World Bank is employed again for export alternatives. The index gives higher values for a reporter country that exports a particular product divided by the number of countries that report importing the product that year.[14] The index takes account of all products exported. Countries exporting a large number of products to a large number of countries earn high scores. Thus the United States earns 21.28, India 6.22, and Trinidad and Tobago earns a 2. The highest value is for France at 26.79, and the lowest is for Palau at 1.1. A score of 100 would be for a hypothetical country that exports all of the products that every country reports importing. The export market concentration index is a good proxy for the economic dependencies between the North and South that affixed the developing world into producing a few primary commodities for export markets, which were limited by the colonial masters at one time. The export market concentration index thus features twice in the variables discussed earlier. First, it appears as part of the paternalism strength index, but the book also tests its independent influence in the models presented in the following discussion, which separately helps to capture its influence as a negotiation variable.

The major coalitions examined in this paper follow from Narlikar (2003), which examines the role of each coalition carefully for the Uruguay Round. The four most important coalitions for the Uruguay Round were G77 and G10 from the developing world; the Cairns Group, which included developed and developing countries to argue for agricultural liberalization; and the café au lait group, which was a group of moderate countries that came forward to move the Uruguay Round forward and was later important for services negotiations. The developing world was opposed to the inclusion of high-tech issues such as intellectual property and services in trade, which delayed the launch of the next multilateral trade round from 1982 to 1986. The G10 coalition, chiefly identified with India and Brazil, led this opposition. G10 had existed as an informal group with G77 but started to coordinate its strategies in trade in the early 1980s. The Big Five were Argentina, Brazil, Egypt, India, and Yugoslavia, and the other countries were Chile, Jamaica, Pakistan, Peru, and Uruguay (Narlikar 2003: 54–55).

G77 was active in the 1960s and 1970s for the GSP, but it is arguable as to whether it played a big role in the Uruguay Round. It is almost synonymous with former European colonies, and thus a dummy is included for countries in the Global South that were colonized by a European power. This also makes sense conceptually; if the North is going to make concessions due to paternalism, then we would expect ex-colonies to receive them. The data also provide a dummy for ASEAN, a regional trade bloc coalition made up of the pre-1993 members of the Association for South East Asian Nations, because of the pressures that the United States applied to this group in particular on intellectual property, and therefore it would be interesting to examine whether the types of concessions they received in agriculture and manufacturing were in lieu of their acquiescence in intellectual property issues. G77, G10, and the Cairns Group are particularly relevant for this book.[15]

There are two major control variables: the log of GDP per capita and the Polity2 index from the Correlates of War data set, which provides values on a 21-point scale from –10 for an absolute autocracy to +10 for an absolute democracy. The GDP per capita allows for a control other than PSI so that the former is not seen just as a proxy of economic strength or prosperity. The Polity2 scores allow for a test of audience costs: As noted in Chapter 2, democracies may find it harder to make concessions than autocracies do because of interest group pressures.

Table 4.7.   Descriptive statistics.

Variable	Obs	Mean	Standard Deviation	Min	Max
merconrece~d	140	1.25375	.9175768	.028	6.999
agconrecei~d	116	1.855534	3.028266	0	17.732
paternalism7	88	2.75e-10	.8684252	−.8109284	3.1736
xmktcon	184	3.668804	4.35814	1.1	26.79
col_cultdi~2	99	51.34343	15.18725	12.2	84.6
s3un	156	−.3686847	.2638561	−.5952381	1
colony_euro	217	.640553	.4809478	0	1
g10	215	.0465116	.2110818	0	1
cairnsgroup	214	.0654206	.2478462	0	1
asean	217	.0322581	.1770932	0	1
gdp_pci_co~s	177	8864.153	14633.94	141.3696	109705

Table 4.5 earlier summarized the expected signs of coefficient for each independent variable. An analysis is now provided for each of the three categories of negotiation analyzed here.

Reciprocity in Merchandise Concessions Received and Given

At the broadest level of reciprocity or percentage of concessions given and received, it is hard to say much with the limited number of observations (forty-five) in the data set. Most important, the relationship between the paternalism strength index and reciprocity is not statistically significant (the p-value is 0.748). However, a scatter plot (Figure 4.1a) allows us a preliminary glimpse into the impact of paternalism on reciprocity. The graph reveals a slightly negative relationship between PSI and reciprocity, implying that paternalistic countries are *not* net beneficiaries of concessions received (minus those given). The negative relationship regarding PSI and reciprocity may mask two important trends. First, many countries in the developing world, such as India and Thailand, made proportionately higher concessions than those they received. Second, the net gains for most countries in the developed world (excepting Canada and Australia) are positive.

Further parsing the data into whether countries received foreign aid or did not receive foreign aid reveals some interesting trends. Recall that foreign aid is often a side payment instead of trade concessions (look again at Table 1.5). Figures 4.1b and 4.1c show that paternalistic countries, which receive no foreign aid, made overall gains whereas nonpaternalistic countries did not. However,

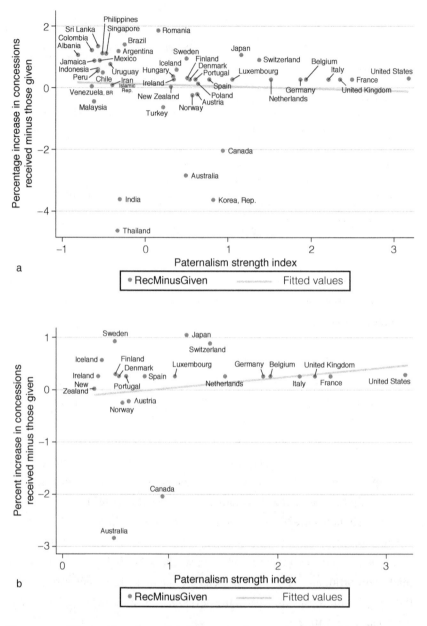

Figure 4.1. Uruguay Round merchandise concessions received minus those given explained with paternalism. (a) All countries' merchandise concessions received minus those given. (b) Merchandise concessions received minus those given for countries receiving no foreign aid. (c) Merchandise concessions received minus those given for countries receiving foreign aid.

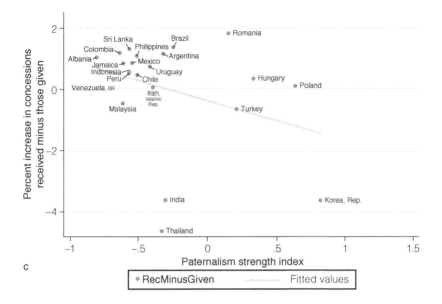

c

the huddle of nonpaternalistic countries with net gains on concessions received minus those given does provide some pause, necessitating further analysis.

Merchandise Concessions Received

Many of the macro findings from the overall reciprocity data are confirmed in the findings for seventy-three to 124 countries (depending on the model) for concessions received in Table 4.8. In the raw data, concessions received vary from 0.208 to 6.999, implying that every country received some concession. The most important finding from Model A in Table 4.8 is that every one unit increase in paternalism (from minimum of −0.77 for Bhutan to a maximum of 3.17 for the United States) results in nearly a one-third percent of an increase in concessions received (the percentage increases to 0.4 in Model C with multiple variables). Model A predicts that United States, with a 3.17 PSI value, received 1.15 percent more concessions than Venezuela with a −0.65 value, and 1.04 percent more than India with a −0.31 value (in actuality Indian concessions were greater than predicted here). These findings are corroborated in the other three models with PSI. The sign for PSI remains significant at 95 percent level in Model B with the Polity2 variable, implying that the presence of democracy does account for some variation. However, the value of Polity2 is not statistically

Table 4.8. Merchandise concessions received explained with paternalism and negotiation indicators.

DV: merchandise concessions received and given	Model A (robust standard errors)	Model B	Model C	Model D (robust standard errors)	Model E	Model F (robust standard errors)
Paternalism strength index	0.309*** (0.056)	0.218** (0.094)	0.396*** (0.1)			
Export market concentration index				0.0271*** (0.010)	0.040** (0.019)	0.039*** (0.012)
Cultural distance				−0.001 (0.006)		
European colony (historical)				−0.283* (0.162)	−0.329 (0.234)	−0.240 (0.238)
G10		−215 (0.216)	−0.174 (0.224)	−0.117 (0.169)	−0.295 (0.315)	−0.279 (0.185)
Cairns Group		0.278 (0.196)	−0.129 (0.194)	−0.162 (0.143)	−0.106 (0.273)	−0.066 (0.158)
ASEAN		0.700** (0.291)	0.584** (0.291)	0.5** (0.25)	0.348 (0.399)	0.172 (0.266)
Polity2		.029** (.012)			.018 (.013)	
GDP per capita constant prices (logged)			−0.074 (0.052)		−0.161** (0.068)	−0.074 (0.083)
Constant	1.263*** (0.064)	1.207*** (0.078)	1.897*** (0.429)	1.345*** (0.345)	2.54*** (0.604)	1.895 (0.748)
R-squared	0.194	0.305	0.261	0.243	0.155	0.07
Number of observations	80	73	77	84	104	124

OLS estimates, standard error in parentheses.
Statistical significance: *$p < 0.10$; **$p < 0.05$; ***$p < 0.01$

significant in Model 5 with more observations and modeled with overall prosperity of the economy (measured via GDP per capita).

Models D through F test the influence of the Export Market Concentration index separately. This index, as mentioned earlier, captures elements of trade diversification and, at higher values, decreasing degrees of paternalistic control in negotiations. During the colonial era, European powers ensured paternalistic control through exclusive trade and extraction in the colonies. This pattern continued in the postcolonial era through practices such as imperial preferences. The degree of export diversification is positive and significant in all three models.[16] Models D through F show that the export market concentration index by itself is a relatively good predictor of concessions received, establishing its importance for negotiations.

Surprisingly, the coalitional variables do not perform so well. Three of the coalitional variables—G10, Cairns Group, and European colony—have negative signs and are not statistically significant, except for the European colony variable in Model D.[17] This could mean any of the following: (1) Developing country coalitions did not matter for concessions received; (2) developing country coalitions were punished for coalescing; or (3) they received negative concessions. The only coalition with a statistically significant result in three models is the ASEAN countries, and the sign is positive, meaning that they received on average almost one-half to more than two-thirds of a percent more than other countries. The United States courted ASEAN heavily during the Uruguay Round. They were the first to come along to U.S. intellectual property and services agendas and therefore might have received more merchandise concessions in return.[18] The next chapter also shows that a few ASEAN nations made high concessions in agriculture.

Table 4.8 models confirm that paternalism matters for receiving concessions, even with additional controls for robustness. This is especially important with controls for GPD per capita because it shows that paternalistic strength predicts concessions over and above those from being prosperous or economically strong. Being a democracy did not matter much. Even in the model where the variable was statistically significant, the coefficient is small. The UN affinity index variable is not tested separately in the models in Chapters 4 and 5. It does well as a predictive variable, especially in manufacturing, showing that voting with the United States is rewarded with trade concessions, but it is collinear with the export market concentration variable. Furthermore, when data are parsed for the developing and developed worlds, only the latter earn concessions. This is an interesting finding and is reported in the conclusion (Chapter 7).

In terms of negotiations, if developing countries diversify their exports, they are able to garner concessions, but coalition building was less effective for obtaining merchandise concessions. The more than average concessions India made in merchandise trade (look again at Figure 4.1) might also indicate that India was "punished" for being a leader of the G10 and other coalitions from the developing world. However, these results also need further context and analysis. Most of the developing country concessions received in manufacturing were in textile and clothing, and many of the concessions that the developing world made in merchandise trade were in agriculture. Agriculture trade is explained in Chapter 5, and the case for textile and clothing is examined in the next section. Finally, the developed world could argue that most of the concessions in manufactured products for the developing world came in the form of GSP concessions.

The Textiles and Apparel Case

Textiles and clothing provide the success story in this book of the developing world's attempts to end a protectionist regime, which restricted their exports for fifty years. They also form the bulk of the merchandise concessions the developing world received.

Since the late 1950s, the developing world had accepted voluntary quota restraints on their products. The politics of this trade protection feature domestic industry mobilization, as expected from import competing defensive interests, but also some fairly colorful protests, especially from the U.S. South as the regime came to a close in 2005. China, the world's biggest textile and apparel exporter, received the brunt of these attacks. The campaign against China included the U.S. labor union AFL-CIO's drive to block Chinese entry to the WTO and apply Section 301 sanctions against its exports. U.S. media and politicians, such as Senator John Edwards of South Carolina, blamed the Chinese for harboring sweatshops, making inferior products, abusing human rights, disregarding market principles, and manipulating their currency to make exports competitive.[19] The story began in the 1950s when the United States prevailed on Japan to accept voluntary export restraints on its textile products, which spiraled into a series of import restriction measures that were never GATT compatible.

A brief history recollects the main points of the protectionist regime in textiles and apparel. Until the mid-1950s, the United States had a net surplus in textile exports, but the surge in Japanese exports made the free-trade Democrats from the U.S. South protectionist: "But if the industry's substantive case for relief was a bit overstated, its power was taken seriously" (Destler 1992: 25). This power included the influence of Southern Democrats in the U.S. Congress, and the emotional appeal of independent small businesses that employed up to 2 million people. The Japanese unilaterally curbed their exports in 1955, and President Eisenhower negotiated "voluntary export restraints" with the Japanese in 1957. The Europeans, starting with the British in 1959, worked out similar

Table 4.9.   Textile and clothing export growth rates for select countries.

	1965–1973	1973–1983	1983–1996
China	13.8	18.5	16.0
Hong Kong	19.4	11.9	5.1
India	3.7	5.7	15.7
Turkey	55.4	25.8	14.7
Japan	8.9	7.9	1.7
Germany	20.8	7.2	7.7
United Kingdom	9.6	5.4	9.7
United States	10.1	7.9	12.8
World	15.8	10.7	9.9

SOURCE: Adapted from Dean Spinanger, "Textiles beyond the MFA Phase-Out." *The World Economy* 22(4, 1999): 455–476.

arrangements on the grounds of "market disruptions" that GATT had to recognize. By the late 1950s, such agreements affected the textile and apparel sectors in Japan, Hong Kong, India, and Pakistan. This laid the seeds of "liberal protectionism" (Aggarwal 1985).

President Kennedy worked out a "Short-Term Arrangement" (STA) in textiles in 1961, which instituted a system of quotas. The "Long-Term Arrangement" (LTA) replaced the STA in 1962. A 5 percent annual growth rate was imposed on international textiles. Although the LTA curbed imports on many categories and instituted high tariffs on others (wool, for instance; look back at Table 3.3), low-cost producers from East and South Asia could still compete effectively against domestic producers in the West. Table 4.9 shows that the growth rates of textile and apparel exports from the developing world were consistently above those from Europe and the United States. India, which concentrated on the Soviet market for its textile and clothing exports until the mid-1980s, was an exception. Developing countries were, for example, easily able to outcompete on wool products, even with the high tariffs. The LTA was multilateralized in 1973 as the Multi-Fibre Arrangement (MFA) and was the cost President Nixon had to pay to win congressional approval for pursuing the Tokyo Round.[20]

The MFA regime applied to textile and apparel exports to Canada, the European Union, Norway, and the United States. The regime "applied widespread and restrictive quotas" that "violated the fundamental GATT principle of non-discrimination" (Kheir-El-Din 2002: 186). Nevertheless, Congress shied away from enacting any legislation against textile imports; instead, the MFA was negotiated, and members of Congress such as Wilber D. Mills of Arkansas, House and Ways Means Committee Chair from 1958 to 1974, were adept at crafting these agreements for the textile industry through pressures on the administration, although they were themselves nominally for free trade (Destler 1992).

As Southern Democrats lost power in the U.S. Congress, there was a window of opportunity to end the MFA (Destler 1992). Second, the developing world was unwilling to proceed in negotiations in new high-technology issues such as intellectual property and services before the Uruguay Round without a significant commitment to inclusion of agriculture and textiles on the agenda. A negotiating group on textiles took up this agenda during the Uruguay Round. During the negotiations, the two most difficult issues were safeguards against surges in imports, and the timetable for the phase out of MFA. GATT has several provisions for safeguards, including voluntary export restraints (VERs): Finger (2002) lists twenty as part of GATT articles. VERs, in general, including those in the MFA, were about power politics. But exporters benefited from high prices for their products, and at times the paternalistic countries compensated them through other means, such as through foreign aid or other nontrade issues (Finger 2012: 422). The developing world feared that safeguards would be invoked for protections and sought to limit their use (Reinert 2000). On the timetable issue, twenty-three developing countries, represented through the International Textile and Clothing Bureau, wanted the MFA phased out in six years at the Brussels ministerial in 1990 (Preeg 1995: 101). ASEAN countries were willing to extend the time period to 2000, whereas the EC and Japan argued variously for ten years. However, the details on the scope of the liberalization during the phase-out period were less clear. Eventually, the United States and the EU agreed to a ten-year phase out after the Uruguay Round, prompting this reaction from the American Textile Manufacturing Institute: "We're bitterly opposed to it" (Preeg 1995: 138). The USTR was on the defensive with its MFA and the attendant measures such as VERs and OMAs (orderly market arrangements). Table 4.10, based on content analysis of USTR press releases, shows that in these issues the favorable assessments were greater than the negative ones, and, in contrast to other issues, the USTR did not assume a paternalistic stance toward its trade partners.

The MFA phase out, therefore, included protectionist hurdles and an unrealistic timetable. Apart from phase outs, the United States, the European Union, and Canada frontloaded many textile and apparel items into the MFA, which would make it easier for them later to argue that they had phased them out. This was simply an Alice in Wonderland logic in reverse: having less from

Table 4.10. Characterization of sentiment toward trading partners in USTR press releases, 1982–1993, on textiles and MFA and VERs and OMAs.*

	Paternalistic	Favorable	Unfavorable	Mixed	Neutral
Textiles and MFA	1	14	7	4	0
VERs or OMAs	0	15	6	6	6

*A few VER and OMA references were not about textiles and covered, for example, U.S. trade with EC on steel.
SOURCE: Author's content analysis of U.S. Trade Representative Press Releases (1982–1993).

more.[21] The phase out entailed four phases from January 1, 1995, to January 1, 2005. The first phase would affect 16 percent of the import volume; the second phase, starting January 1, 1998, would bring in an additional 17 percent; another 18 percent would be brought in on January 1, 2002; and the final 49 percent was to be cut on January 1, 2005. The Textile Monitoring Body, made up of a chair and ten WTO members, would oversee the liberalization and resolve disputes.

Most reports of the MFA phase out during the 1990s were negative, and leaving nearly one-half of the liberalization until 2005 was viewed as unrealistic (Spinanger 1999; Reinert 2000; Kheir-El-Din 2002). China bashing reached a feverish pitch by 2004–2005. China accepted a three-year phase-in period to 2008 after its exports surged in 2005. The fear that China would be the only country to benefit from textile and apparel exports turned out to be unfounded. In practice, countries such as China, Honduras, Mexico, and the territory of Hong Kong have experienced declining market shares, after initial spikes, since 2005. Countries such as Cambodia, Kenya, and Madagascar that initially saw their exports register negative growth rates soon recovered (Asuyama et al. 2010; Fukunishi and Yamagata 2013). Developing countries such as Bangladesh, India, Pakistan, and Vietnam have been able to offset cost advantages in China with their labor cost advantage and policies promoting their exports and reforming domestic sectors (Lopez-Acevedo and Robinson 2012). Wages in the textile and garment sector have gone up, and empirically the expected race to the bottom, including falling wages, in the liberalized post-MFA era has not materialized (Fukunishi and Yamagata 2013).[22]

Conclusion

The developing world did not gain overall in merchandise concessions. The systems of preferences in GSP may have undermined the concessions that the developing world received. Summing up this record, Michael Finger (2008: 31) notes: "My thesis: mercantilist economics was good enough for the GATT, but it is not good enough for the WTO. Failure to notice the difference has stuck us with a North–South bargain that is politically troubling and economically inane."

The apparel and textile agreement left in enough loopholes when negotiated, especially in safeguards and delayed phase-ins, to enable developing countries to benefit immediately. In hindsight, though, the Uruguay Round's Agreement on Textiles and Clothing (ATC) is the developing world's success story, both in breaking trade barriers in the West and also in adjusting to the post-MFA competitive era after 2005.

The inclusion of new issues and the developing world as full-fledged negotiators made the Uruguay Round ponderous, but it ended in an agreement. Subsequent negotiations through the Doha Round were deadlocked after more than a decade. One of the reasons is the inability of the North to manipulate the South. The changing dynamics of the global economy have allowed emerging powers to become export powerhouses, whereas domestic pressures in the developed world have led either to protectionism or to preferential trade agreements where the strong find it easier to coerce the weak.

Chapter 5

An Uneven Playing Field in Agricultural Negotiations

> The very idea of sweetness came to be associated with sugar in European thought and language, though honey continued to play a privileged minor role, particularly in literary imagery. The lack of clarity or specificity in European conceptions of sweetness as a sensation is noticeable.
>
> Sidney Mintz, *Sweetness and Power* (1985: 17)

THE epigraph above conveys the changing conceptions of sweetness in Europe from the times of Elizabethan England, when honey was the chief sweetener, to the nineteenth century, when cane sugar production spread in the colonies. The changing conceptions of sweetness might as well be a metaphor for postcolonial international trade in agriculture: The sweet talk continues, but, like sugar plantations of yore, it provides limited benefits to the developing world. Meanwhile, the former colonial masters guard their own interests. They no longer need the colonies for sugar, cotton, or foodstuffs, and they favor their domestic producers. This regime begins to be cracked open in the twenty-first century but so far to limited effect. This chapter analyzes the evidence at all levels discussed in this book: quantitative, historical, and case studies of sugar and cotton. Former colonies fare worse in agriculture than they did in manufacturing, even after the Uruguay Round, which ostensibly opened up some markets in agriculture. The Uruguay and Doha Rounds are discussed separately. Furthermore, a microanalysis of the causal factors—paternalism and negotiation advocacy—in the sugar and cotton cases helps to examine the underlying cultural intransigence that blocks benefits for the developing world.

Macroquantitative Findings

The content analysis and regressions results confirm, as they did with manufacturing, the presence of paternalism and the limited concessions that the developing world received at the Uruguay Round. As agriculture is of utmost importance to the developing world, the next section discusses the history of agricultural negotiations before and after the Uruguay Round.

The main content analysis results for agriculture were prefaced in the last chapter. Table 4.2 showed that there were twice as many references to agriculture for OECD countries than for the developing world in the USTR press

Table 5.1.   The U.S. trade sentiments toward trading partners in agriculture.

		Paternalistic	Favorable	Unfavorable	Mixed	Neutral
OECD	Overall references	9	9	34	6	7
	In sugar	8	1	1	0	1
Non-OECD	Overall references	19	1	7	3	2
	In sugar	16	0	0	0	1
CEES	Overall references	0	2	0	0	3
	In sugar	0	0	0	0	0

SOURCE: Author's content analysis of U.S. Trade Representative press releases (1982–1993).

releases analyzed for the 1982–1993 period. This foreshadows the fact that, although the developing world was included in the agricultural negotiations, the Uruguay Round Agreement on Agriculture mostly reflected the Blair House accord between the EU and the United States in November 1992. Table 4.3 also showed that preferential treatment, which included the GSP in agriculture and sugar rate quotas, accounted for over 60 percent of the total paternalistic references (investment treaties accounted for another 20 percent).[1] Table 5.1 further divides the numbers from Table 4.2 for country groups and also for sugar to provide a detailed look at U.S. sentiments toward its trading partners in agricultural negotiations. Two-thirds of the paternalistic-sounding references in agriculture are toward the non-OECD countries, and of these sugar makes up nearly all of the sole references to agriculture (there are other references to agriculture in the GSP category, not included here—see Chapter 4 for explanation). Three-fourths of the unfavorable references in agriculture are toward OECD countries.

Turning now to regressions with the second data set, the two sets of models presented in Tables 5.2 and 5.3 do not validate the supposition that the developing world received disproportionate agricultural benefits.[2] In fact, they confirm the opposite: The developed world received most of the concessions. The Uruguay Round bargain was purportedly based on a grand bargain whereby the developing world received concessions in agriculture and textiles in return for signing on to restrictive intellectual property provisions and for liberalizing services markets. This is not a valid supposition.

The first model in Table 5.2 shows how the PSI predicts agricultural concessions received minus those given. With limited observations in the data avail-

Table 5.2. Uruguay Round agricultural concessions received minus those given explained with paternalism.

Source	SS	df	MS			
Model	568.7475	1	568.7475	Number of obs	=	34
Residual	2784.25274	32	87.0078982	F(1, 32)	=	6.54
				Prob > F	=	0.0155
				R-squared	=	0.1696
Total	3353.00024	33	101.606068	Adj R-squared	=	0.1437
				Root MSE	=	9.3278

ag_recminu~n	Coef.	Std. Err.	t	P > |t|	[95% Conf. Interval]	
paternalism7	4.20635	1.645224	2.56	0.016	.8551387	7.557561
_cons	−3.893234	1.933761	−2.01	0.053	−7.832176	.0457088

Table 5.3. Agricultural concessions received explained with paternalism and negotiation indicators.

DV: Agriculture concessions received	Model A	Model B	Model C	Model D (robust standard errors)	Model E (robust standard errors)	Model F (robust standard errors)
Paternalism strength index	1.7*** (0.37)	2.397*** (0.517)	1.387*** (0.52)			
Export market concentratwion index				0.136* (0.078)	0.162** (0.07)	0.165** (0.066)
Cultural distance				−0.001 (0.028)		
European colony (historical)				−2.312** (1.088)		
G10		−0.265 (1.193)	−0.462 (1.104)	−0.292 (0.672)	−0.269 (0.774)	−0.688 (0.599)
Cairns Group		2.336** (1.055)	1.562* (0.886)	1.919** (0.914)	1.483* (0.813)	1.407* (0.841)
ASEAN		−0.476 (1.534)		−1.2 0.999)		
Polity2		−0.118* (0.065)			−0.0813 (0.088)	
GDP per capita constant prices (logged)			0.302 (0.268)		0.8** (0.422)	0.486** (0.189)
Constant	1.96*** (0.332)	2.067*** (0.434)	1.897*** (0.429)	2.373** (1.17)	−5.338** (2.818)	−3.070 (1.123)
R-squared	0.227	0.303	0.284	0.312	0.321	0.291
Number of observations	74	68	74	79	92	106

OLS estimates, standard error in parentheses.
Statistical significance: *$p < 0.10$; ** $p < 0.05$; *** $p < 0.01$
NOTE: As ASEAN is not statistically significant and of less relevance to agricultural negotiations, its effects are tested in only two of the models above to maximize the use of other variables. With high standard errors in models B through D, when European Colony, GDP, and Polity2 variables are introduced the results must be interpreted with caution. However, these models are placed here for consistency with Table 4.8.

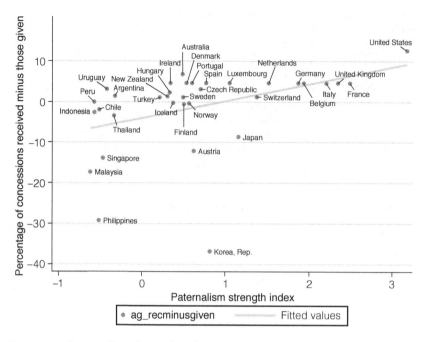

Figure 5.1   Uruguay Round agricultural concessions received minus those given explained with paternalism.

able (only thirty-four in this case), it is hard to evaluate the overall reciprocity (agriculture concessions received minus those given) against the PSI. However, the results confirm that the PSI is positively related to net concessions received (see Table 5.2 and Figure 5.1). Every one-unit increase in the PSI provides 4.21 percent net increase in net concessions received. Interestingly, many East Asian countries (including Korea, Japan, and three countries from ASEAN) made disproportionately higher concessions in agriculture, which also might account for at least ASEAN making net gains in merchandise trade instead. However, as the *r*-square (Table 5.2) and outliers (Figure 5.1) show, the fitted line is not good beyond indicating a weak positive relationship. The fitted line and *r*-square could also be due to the East Asian countries making negative concessions, but, in that case, the upward slope of the line is all the more remarkable.

There are between seventy-four and 106 observations in the data set on agriculture concessions received than on concessions received minus those given, which had only thirty-four observations. Therefore, taking agriculture concessions received as a dependent variable allows analysis with multiple variables.

The six models presented on agricultural concessions received also confirm the supposition that the developing world did not receive disproportionate agricultural benefits during the Uruguay Round.

Taken by itself Model A in Table 5.3 shows that every one-unit increase in the paternalism index accounts for 1.7 percent increase in agricultural concessions received, which vary from zero to 17.7 percent. If this was the only variable in consideration, the United States, with a PSI value of 3.174, received 5.91 percent higher concessions than India, with a PSI value of −0.307 and 6.75 percent higher than Guatemala, with a PSI value of −0.798 because of its paternalistic strength (look back to Table 4.6 for PSI values).

Furthermore, other variables also indicate that the developing world was at a disadvantage in agricultural negotiations. Being a former colony reduces agricultural concessions by 2.31 percent (Table 5.3, Model D). If paternalism was benevolent, we would expect that being a former colony or being a member of G77 would garner trade concessions.[3] G77 is almost coterminous with being a former European colony so that this coalition did not bestow any advantages.[4] The dummy European colony has high multicollinearity with the GDP per capita and Polity2 variables. Therefore, it is employed in only one of the models, but the negative sign and the high value of the coefficient are important.[5] The G10 sign is also negative, though statistically insignificant, as is the one for ASEAN. The latter might be due to ASEAN's overall gains in merchandise trade.[6]

The protrade Cairns Group in agriculture, discussed qualitatively later, did yield positive benefits to its members at the Uruguay Round. Table 5.3 Models B through F demonstrate this positive and statistically significant relationship. In terms of negotiation advantages, the sign for the export market concentration index, showing diversity in products and markets, is also positive and statistically significant. As noted earlier, the export market concentration index suggests a break from paternalistic patterns of dependency and also the ability to indulge in trade-offs and linkages at international negotiations. Model F, with 106 observations, also confirms the main findings for Models D and E for the export market concentration index.

The robustness of the PSI and the export market concentration index through multiple iterations is also important in the context of two other control variables. The Polity2 scores measure high levels of democracy in the positive values, and, arguably, democracies would thwart agricultural concessions. Except for a weak and low coefficient for Polity2 in Model B, democracy is not an encumbrance. The PSI accounts for the lack of concessions to the developing world. Similarly, the GDP per capita makes no difference to concessions in Model C with the PSI, although it is significant for Models E and F when the export market concentration is used. This indicates that the PSI is a better predictor of the lack of economic concessions to the developing world than the economic strength of the developed world. Finally, as Chapter 7 will show, the UN General Assembly affinity index does not predict any concessions to the developing world, as was the case with merchandise trade.[7] Aligning country interests with the United States is not helpful for receiving reciprocal concessions.

The World Bank data used here for agricultural concessions received needs further context. First, these data include the tariff equivalents of nontariff barriers for agriculture (Finger et al. 1996: 6). Therefore, it is a complete measure of the protections in agriculture, which often feature several types of nontariff barriers. Second, the data do not standardize the size of the agricultural concessions to the rule-of-thumb formula that emerged at the Brussels meeting of the GATT in 1990: namely 33 percent cuts for the developed world and 25 percent cuts for the developing world. In other words, they show concessions as made instead of adjusting them on the basis of what was expected from developed or developing countries. If these data were standardized for the formula expectations, the inequity of concessions would be higher.

The story of agricultural trade is full of references to side payments and, of course, nonreciprocal concessions. Although the latter will be analyzed later in the chapter, it is useful to recall Figure 1.1 from Chapter 1 for the finding regarding foreign aid as a side payment. The hyperbola in this figure shows that countries that received foreign aid did not receive agriculture concessions during the Uruguay Round.

The Uruguay Round Agreement on Agriculture

The Uruguay Round Agreement on Agriculture (URAA), despite outcomes analyzed in the previous section, was an exception to the limited role agriculture played in the earlier GATT negotiations. For the first time, GATT dealt with premises such as market access for agricultural goods, internal price support mechanisms, and reduction of domestic and export subsidies. The developing world had in fact pushed for many of these negotiations, though it was soon marginalized in the agriculture negotiations. After 1995, it found agriculture commitments unfulfilled, undone, or delayed. At the beginning of the Doha

Round, many countries in the developing world reverted to advocating forms of special and differential treatment, although there were many different types of coalitions rather than a single bloc advocating different versions of this stance. Furthermore, although countries such as Argentina and Brazil have pushed for agricultural liberalization, others such as India and Indonesia have advocated various forms of agricultural protection.[8] This has, in turn, contributed to the current divide in the WTO between the Global North and the Global South.

It is useful to consider a brief context of GATT and agriculture leading to the outcomes of the Uruguay Round and the agenda of the Doha Round before explaining the negotiation tactics and the sweet and not-so-sweet developed country talk on agriculture.

Throughout the advocacy for lifting the trade barriers for agricultural products from the developing world, the developed countries either provided preferential trade arrangements (discussed in Chapters 3 and 4), or they invoked two GATT articles for its protectionism. GATT Article XI prescribes "elimination of quantitative restrictions," but the United States received a special waiver for agriculture. Article XVI deals with subsidies, including export subsidies, but its wording, again at U.S. behest, includes the right of contracting parties to undertake export subsidies provided that "such subsidy shall not be applied in a manner which results in that contracting party having more than an equitable share of world export trade in that product." The wording on "equitable share" was designed to be ambiguous. A French subsidy on wheat in 1958 was found inequitable, but the same subsidy was found equitable in a GATT panel years later even though the EU's share of global wheat exports went up from 29 percent to 75 percent in the period from 1961 to 1981 (Lanoszka 2009: 88). This was despite the wheat "subsidy wars" when both the United States and the EU increased their domestic wheat subsidies (Coskeran, Kim, and Narlikar 2012: 358). Therefore, Article XXXVI, included in the "Part IV Trade and Development" text that developing countries negotiated in 1965, was essentially ignored until the Uruguay Round (see Chapter 3 for context). This article noted: "Given the continued dependence of many less-developed contracting parties on the exportation of a limited range of primary products, there is need to provide in the largest possible measure more favourable and acceptable conditions of access to world markets for these products."

The United States woke up to subsidies more as a result of the Common Agricultural Policy (CAP) of the European Economic Community than developing country efforts. CAP can be connected to the region's desire to boost its food production in the postcolonial era (Laurent 1983). The CAP budget made up the biggest portion of the EEC's budget, above 70 percent of the budget in 1980, but the shadow of the Cold War allowed for these subsidies to be tolerated rather than reduced.[9] The EEC would not discuss the issue at the Kennedy Round while CAP was still in an incipient stage and also institutionalized its system of imperial preferences through the Lomé Convention in 1975 with African, Caribbean, and Pacific (ACP) countries. At the Tokyo Round, the final deal favored the GSP or quantitative restrictions in lieu of no tariffs on these products. Although Brazil and Mexico participated in a few agricultural negotiations—along with the United States, the EC, Japan, Australia, and Canada—the resulting agreements were weak. During the Uruguay Round, EU states wanted to both maintain ACP preferences and CAP agricultural tariffs and subsidies (van Riesen 2007).

At face value, URAA outcomes were far reaching: Agriculture was negotiated, and tariffs and subsidies were brought down. These were the major outcomes:

- *Market access*: Nontariff measures (NTMs) were converted into tariffs through a process involving the difference in world and domestic prices. This made the process transparent even if the tariffs remained high, though countries also adopted tariff rate quotas (TRQs), which allowed low tariffs only up to a fixed volume of imports (Ingco and Nash 2004: 27–30).

- *Domestic subsidies*: Subsides were classified into three boxes: Green box non–trade-distorting subsidies were allowed; amber box subsides were to be cut but also allowed under particular circumstances; red box or trade-distorting subsidies were to be eliminated or drastically reduced. The EU campaigned for and also instituted a blue box entailing direct income payments to farmers (for its CAP program).

- *Export subsidies*: Twenty-five countries committed to export subsidy reductions, which would be reduced by 21 percent on average (Coskeran, Kim, and Narlikar 2012: 359; Ingco and Nash 2004: 33). Limitations were also placed on introduction of new subsidies.

The URAA introduced tariffication and transparency, but its implementation and consequences roiled the developing world for several reasons (Ingco and Nash 2004: chapters 1–2; World Bank 2008). First, the United States and the EU agreed at the Blair House negotiations in November 1992 that countries could use the higher 1986–1988 prices, which meant that in practice subsidy cuts were lower when compared with what they would have been with 1988–1990 or later price levels. The URAA barely made a dent in export subsidies. Second, peak and high tariffs continued to exist for products of interest to the developing world such as sugar, cotton, oilseeds, and rice (look back to Table 1.2). Third, the emergent regime of subsidies is complex and allows for hidden subsidies and moving products from one box to another with political pressures. Fourth, the URAA imposed high costs on the developing world with agreements on sanitary and phytosanitary (SPS), technical barriers to trade, or customs agreement measures. Finger (2008) notes that large parts of the technical assistance to the developing world went into these programs. He cites an African government official: *"They want us to understand SPS so that we will import more chicken"* (305; italics original).[10]

Given their level of dissatisfaction, the developing world reverted to calls for nonreciprocal trade access before and during the Doha Round, all the while calling attention to URAA implementation issues. Developed country protectionism in export crops such as cotton and sugar received widespread attention, whereas the developing world sought smaller cuts for key sensitive products. Countries such as India also asked for exemptions on "special products" for purposes of food security (World Bank 2008), whereas the LDCs argued for longer transition periods and higher levels of technical assistance.

Negotiations

The run-up to the Uruguay Round was preoccupied with new issues such as services and intellectual property. Agriculture liberalization was brought to the agenda through the creation of the Cairns Group, named after the Australian city where the group was convened, on August 27, 1986, two weeks prior to the launch of the Round at Punta del Este, Uruguay. Eleven of the fourteen members of the Cairns Group were developing countries, and together they accounted for nearly a quarter of global agricultural exports.[11] Its formation was an indication that the developing world was willing to move beyond calls for special and differential treatment, although this issue did not completely go away.

The United States supported the Cairns Group agenda, and sought reduction of tariffs and subsidies, along the lines of the three bulleted points given earlier, while including SDT for a few products. The United States had tolerated the EC's Common Agricultural Policies and Japan's Basic Agricultural Law in the context of the Cold War, but by the 1980s it was openly opposed. This decade also followed that of widespread crop failures in the 1970s. At the end of the Kennedy Round, the United States expressed dissatisfaction with the International Grain Agreement, governing exports of wheat and other grains. The CAP not only comprised a major portion of the EC's budget, but it also did not regulate subsidies for production quotas, though some attempts were made, such as affixing sugar price guarantees to the production volumes of 1968. In 1983, therefore, the EC's overproduction beyond 100 percent for its needs was as high as 144 for sugar and extended to other products such as beef (104), butter (123), poultry (110), and wheat (125) (Higgott and Cooper 1990: 597). The EC agricultural exports increased 156 percent in the period from 1976 through 1982, and it became the largest exporter of sugar and poultry, accounted for three-fifths of the exports in butter and dried milk, was the second-largest exporter after Australia of beef, and was a major exporter in grains (598). The United States was aware that any changes it desired in the EC's agricultural policies would also require changing its own policies, but strategically it aligned itself with the Cairns Group and advocated a zero option for elimination of export subsidies.

Within the Cairns Group, the pressures for changes to EC's CAP were most vocal among the Latin American countries. A meeting among efficient, and mostly non–subsidy-giving agriculture producers—Argentina, Australia, Brazil, New Zealand, and Uruguay—in April 1986 preceded the August 1986 Cairns meeting. In fact, Argentina left the G10 to play a role in the Cairns Group. The developing world was also vocal about "standstill and rollbacks," asking the developed world not to institute further import restrictions while requesting a rollback of GATT-inconsistent nontariff barriers, although many of these provisions governed both agricultural and manufactured goods. The call for SDT provisions addressed concerns of least-developed countries and of members such as Brazil and India who were hesitant to join the Cairns Group coalition for the fear of losing LDC support for other coalitions such as G10.[12] In turn, the Cairns Group included products such as sugar of export interest to Brazil. From the outside, the Cairns Group of developing countries also had to attend to the concern of the Food Importers Group, including countries such as Egypt, Jamaica, Mexico, and Nigeria.

After the launch of the Uruguay Round, the Cairns Group slowly found itself marginalized in the U.S.–EC agricultural negotiations. The Group met in

Thailand in November 1986 to work out its four major reform platforms and over the next two years served as a middle-level (Higgot and Cooper 1990) or bridge building (Narlikar 2003: chapter 6) coalition between the United States, by supporting its proposals for tariffication, and the EC by being sensitive to its rebalancing rather than zero-bindings. Nevertheless, by the 1988 midterm review at Montreal, the Cairns Group was marginalized for three reasons. First, Australia had hardened its position on elimination of subsidies, not always to the liking of other coalition members, especially its de facto coleader Canada. The United States, reflecting support from its heavily subsidized dairy and sugar lobbies, also stuck to its zero-option position as a negotiation strategy—the United States could nominally be seen as protrade, although knowing that the zero option was impossible to implement and, therefore, that it could maintain its subsidies in the long run. Second, developing countries in G10 had hardened their position against the developed world while the LDCs were working with organizations such as FAO and UNCTAD for special and differential treatment. Third, the Montreal meetings produced a deadlock chiefly in agriculture from the EC, which also halted the negotiations to the Round's fourteen other working groups. From then onward, the negotiations became a bilateral exercise between the United States and the EC/EU. The December 1990 Brussels ministerial also ended in a deadlock. Nevertheless, as the quantitative results in Table 5.3 show, the Cairns Group is one of the few coalitions, including developing counties, that received positive returns from its coalitional activities and may have been rewarded for its early work and protrade positions.

In an effort to resolve the Montreal deadlock, Arthur Dunkel forwarded a chair's text that came to be known as the 436-page Dunkel draft in December 1991. It called for tariffication of nontariff barriers, a 20 percent reduction in domestic subsidies, and a 36 percent reduction in export subsidies. The Dunkel draft was denounced in the developing world (for its intellectual property provisions on seeds and medicine) even though the director-general was quite sympathetic to its needs. The draft also did not resolve the U.S.–EC differences, and the Brussels meeting ended in a deadlock. In particular, the French had hardened their position over agriculture, and it seemed unlikely that the Round could be concluded before the April 1993 deadline when the U.S. president's fast track authority was due to expire. On November 5, 1992, EC Agricultural Commissioner Ray MacSharry accused the French of sabotaging the agricultural negotiations at the Blair House in Washington, DC, and resigned. MacSharry had worked tirelessly to convince the Irish to come around to a proagricultural position, which was upheld in an Irish referendum.

The U.S.–EC deadlock was resolved at the Blair House accord in Washington, DC, in 1992, which effectively paved the way for conclusion of the Uruguay Round.[13] The two parties agreed to several measures that formed the basis of the URAA. First, they agreed to reduction in subsidies, but the base period for reductions in export subsides was 1986–1990 and for domestic subsidies 1986–1988, when the prices were high, which later meant that the actual reductions were less than or more than the prices in 1992. Second, the two agreed to a "peace clause," ensuring that no legal challenges to subsidies could be made until 2004. Finally, the two also agreed to a system of amber, blue, and green boxes in subsidies for various products. Although the amber or red box was trade distorting, and not allowed, green box subsidies were the opposite. However, a 5 percent de minimis of the total agricultural product was allowed red box subsidies (10 percent for developing countries). Since the Uruguay Round, both the EU and the United States have played a delicate game of moving products to the ambiguous blue box, which allows some subsidies but also requires production limits.

The URAA was ineffective for agricultural liberalization: The agricultural subsidies went up, and imports of commodities from the developing world may have decreased rather than increased. Even before the final signing, a Blair House II in 1993 allowed the EC to frontload its commitment, which "substantially lightened the EC's reduction commitments" (Hoda and Gulati 2007: 126). Eventually, the total volume of agricultural subsidies in the OECD increased from $271.2 billion in 1986–1988 to $330.6 billion in 1998–2000, and the developed countries continued to export below their cost of production, while receiving revenues that were often one-third above world prices (Clapp 2006: 565). Nevertheless, the inclusion of agricultural trade itself was a feat, and the tariffication of nontariff barriers provided an incentive to continue these negotiations into the Doha Round (Anderson and Martin 2006).

The Doha Round

Fairness and implementation issues, especially in agriculture, held up the start of the new round at the Seattle meetings of the WTO in 1999. Given the record of the URAA, the road to Doha was paved with calls from the developing world to implement agreements and a hardening stance that reverted many countries to calls for special and differential treatment. Jawara and Kwa (2003: 26) note that the URAA was "in effect providing special and differential treatment to developed rather than developing countries." The net effect on the developing world of subsidies and moving products among amber, blue, and green boxes was that the degree of protection for the developing world in agriculture may have increased rather than decreased. The "market" prices for agricultural export products from the developed world were below production costs: 20 percent for corn, 15 percent for cotton, and 46 percent for wheat (Jawara and Kwa 2003: 26; International Cotton Advisory Committee 2006). As noted earlier, subsidies in the OECD countries increased from $271.2 billion in 1986–1988 to $330.6 billion in 1998–2000 as these countries moved their products to blue and green boxes, where these subsidies were allowed, with the latter more than doubling in this period (quoted in Clapp 2007: 40).

With good reason, the developing world argued that the promised agricultural liberalization had not taken place. However, instead of seeking liberalization, many developing countries went back to calls for SDT, whereas others pushed for liberalization. The chief coalition from the developing world calling for SDT before the Doha Round was the Like-Minded Group, initially formed in 1996 to oppose the four "Singapore issues" at the WTO ministerial that the EU and Japan, with some support from the United States, wanted to include in the new round. These issues were transparency in government procurement, trade facilitation or customs issues, trade and investment, and trade and competition policy. The LMG initially included Cuba, Egypt, Indonesia, Malaysia, Pakistan, Tunisia, and Uganda. The Dominican Republic, Honduras, and Zimbabwe joined by the Seattle ministerial, and Sri Lanka and Jamaica joined before the Doha ministerial.[14] Kenya also lent some support. As many countries in this group had benefited from SDT in the past, the shift away from the Cairns Group liberalization agenda is not hard to infer. The Doha declaration affirmed that SDT would be incorporated in the negotiations.

The new Round was termed the Doha Development Agenda. The first two years of agricultural negotiations belied this appellation. The United States and the EU proceeded to negotiate among themselves, but a North–South showdown at the 2003 Cancun ministerial changed the politics of the negotiations. First, at the multilateral level, these politics could not overlook or exclude North–South issues. Second, the South's inclusion in agriculture made the Round complex and difficult, resulting in deadlocks that cannot be overcome.

Although the politics are chiefly North–South, the divisions among ranks in both hemispheres has made agreements elusive, although there were moments, such as after the 2005 ministerial in Hong Kong and the July 2008 negotiations in Geneva, when the parties came close to agreement.

The September 2003 Cancun WTO ministerial broke down over a number of issues: The North–South confrontation over agriculture was paramount. In May 2003, the so-called Cotton Four—Benin, Burkina Faso, Chad, and Mali—called attention to U.S. cotton subsidies, which they argued depressed world prices and affected 10 million cotton farmers in these countries (see the next subsection). At the September meeting, the C4 gave an emotional press conference. Meanwhile, the exclusion of the developing world, and the latter's realization that the URAA did not liberalize agriculture for them, led to the formation of a G20 coalition at Cancun that revived calls for agriculture liberalization in the developed world while at the same time seeking special and differential treatment for the developing world. Its ranks included Brazil, India, and China, which joined the WTO in 1999, and over time more than half the countries have also been members of the Cairns Group.[15]

In response to particular needs of the developing world, apart from the G20 and C4, several other coalitions reflected the pressures. The G33 countries, which had forty-six members in 2014, argued for special safeguard mechanisms for food security and crises and special products that would be exempt from tariff cuts. The G90 coalition that dated back to UNCTAD was most closely aligned with maintaining the system of preferences, which had evolved in the EU with the Cotonou Agreement that became effective in 2003.

The responses from the developed world were both deflective and constructive. USTR Zoellick responded to the South's new insurgency, such as in cotton, by speaking of diffuse reciprocity in the final package. The United States and the EU also responded to SSM by seeking similar exemptions for their own products. The European Union initially sought to tie reductions in subsidies and export credits to other measures, such as in manufacturing. In 2006, it agreed to an end date of 2013 for export subsidies because the internal reforms in CAP envisaged the cuts by that date. Meanwhile the politics of box shifting and delicate rebalancing continued. The United States and the EU argued over the reductions to the blue box de minimis (2.5 percent at the Hong Kong ministerial), and both wanted extensions to the Peace Clause. The closest the North–South got to an agreement was the July 2008 Framework negotiations, where the United States offered to cap its subsidies at $14.5 billion. India and China rejected this move, whereas Brazil supported it. The breakdown of the July 2008 framework is now regarded as the breakdown of the Doha Round itself.

Problems of unity and cohesion have plagued the developing country proposals, both as a result of pressures from the developed world and from divisions within their own ranks. Shortly after the Cancun ministerial five countries—Colombia, Peru, Guatemala, El Salvador, and Costa Rica—dropped out to either sign or begin preferential trade agreements with the United States. This may have been strategic on their part, to extract concessions from the United States, but there were also specific pressures from the United States to make them defect.[16] China and India were inducted into the Five Interested Parties (FIP) in 2004 to break the agricultural deadlock in a small group, which included Australia, Brazil, EU, India, and the United States. Later, the G4 (excluding Australia) came out of this group. Whereas India and Brazil sought to represent the various coalitions from the Global South, they were also frequently blamed for abandoning them in pursuit of their own goals. These charges became especially vociferous after India defected from the July 2008 accord. In 2006, the G20, G33, and G90 came together briefly to coordinate their positions and were called the G110 (Clapp 2007: 50).

Brazil and India did pursue a couple of issues individually. For Brazil, this issue was cotton, described in detail later, and it successfully challenged U.S. cotton subsidies at the WTO dispute settlement. In India's case, the issue of food security continued to gain importance in its domestic politics. India signed on to the WTO Bali accord, signed at its December 2013 ministerial, on the reduction of customs tariffs, which were to produce nearly $10 billion in trade gains, but in exchange for progress on food security issues. After India's new Modi government came to power in May 2014, it initially refused to sign on to the Bali accord, citing lack of progress on food security issues. India did approve the Bali accord in November 2014.

By 2015, there were slim chances of any progress on the Doha Round, and it was de facto called off at the December 2015 WTO Ministerial in Nairobi, Kenya. The United States, after signing a spate of PTAs with small trading partners, moved toward negotiating regional pacts: the Transatlantic Trade and Investment Partnership (TTIP) with the EU, begun in February 2013, and the Trans-Pacific Partnership (TPP)Agreement with East Asia, begun in 2005. Both were to be concluded in 2015 after President Obama received fast track authority from the U.S. Congress in June 2015. However, only TPP was signed in February 2016, and TTIP negotiations are ongoing.

Sugar and Cotton

The chapter now discusses two tropical agricultural products, sugar and cotton, in which many developing countries can claim a comparative advantage. In both cases, the patterns of trade and existing outcomes can be traced back to colonial days, further supporting the cultural preferences argument in this book. In both cases, subsidies allowed the United States and the EU to protect their own agriculture while providing preferential access in the margins to the developing world. Recent challenges from the developing world have exposed, but not quite broken, the discriminatory logic and injustice inherent in the paternalistic regime. The global regime in sugar is examined historically, but, for brevity and focus, only recent challenges to cotton at the WTO are discussed.

Sugar

All historical and political economy accounts of sugar start with its importance in the making of the modern colonial world and the ways it strengthened instruments of oppression including slavery, indentured labor, and racism. Stanley Mintz (1985: 35) vividly captures the patterns in *Sweetness and Power*:

> England fought the most, conquered the most colonies, imported the most slaves (to her own colonies and, in absolute numbers, in her own bottoms), and went furthest and fastest in creating the plantation system. The most important product of the system was sugar.[17]

Most accounts that are critical of the colonial antecedents of capitalism also outline the importance of sugar: "Legions of slaves came from Africa to provide King Sugar with the prodigal, wageless labor he required: human fuel for the burning" (Galeano 1997: 59). As Chapter 2 notes, 300,000 slaves were shipped from Africa to the Caribbean in the sixteenth century, 1.35 million in the seventeenth century, and 6 million in the eighteenth century. Richardson (2009: 2) notes that sugar embodies "a complex social relation and a penetrating capitalist metaphor." Brennan's (2006) account for sugar seeks to establish a case for reparations to be paid to the developing world for the human rights abuses and racist oppression that occurred as a result of the colonial sugar cultivation and industry.

Almost every political economy account of sugar protectionism recounts this commodity's colonial origins, but subsequently these explanations defer to the strength of domestic producer interests in the United States and the EU to explain protectionism. This historical elide misses an important part of the puzzle of the sugar story dealing with the shape and scope of global trade rules in sugar, specifically (1) the historical antecedents of the producer interests and the strength and the clout of the sugar lobby, and (2) the presence of country-specific preferences and quotas despite "domestic" opposition. These factors are described in the following discussion in terms of paternalism, to explain why benevolence or nonreciprocal trade access in sugar trade, albeit in limited mounts, continued to exist. The opposition to this paternalism has arisen mostly from developing world's challenges to the old regime. Therefore, the sugar story is important to counter the possible critique that global rules for sugar can be explained with great power domestic interests alone.

Historical Antecedents and Political Clout   The sugar trade epitomizes closed and preferential relationships. Despite the tripartite trade—slaves from Africa and plantation owners from Europe, raw sugar from the metropoles, and refined sugar to the colonies—sugar remained mercantilist, and the plantation owners became adept at guarding their privileges over the long run.[18] In the nineteenth century, as antislavery movements began in Britain and the Parliament abolished this practice in 1833, the state subsidized the sugar barons in the Caribbean to bring cheap indentured labor from South Asia. Sugar extraction from beets also changed the scope of sugar industry in starting production in the metropoles and facilitated the end of slavery and of reliance on the colonies for this commodity. Historically, there was no respite from indentured labor in the Caribbean colonies, and farm workers recorded lower wages than for other agricultural crops (Lewis 1954). Persaud (2015) focuses on the lack of indentured female labor in Guiana, which led to various forms of gender violence, exacerbated through race relations that constructed the identity of these women in immoral terms. Persaud notes:

The history of sugar is also associated with slavery and some of the worst forms of colonial domination, racial oppression, predatory sexual relations, labor exploitation, civilizational marginalization, paternalism, and various forms and levels of violence. (118)

There are virtually no accounts of the sugar industry arguing for humanitarian norms in the twentieth century: The industry emerged in the postwar era disregarding the comparative advantage of sugar workers and their plight in the developing world. One exception might be the U.S. farm lobby, including sugar, presenting powerful testimonies in favor of Philippine independence in the U.S. Congress in the 1940s. These testimonies disguised the fact that U.S. sugar barons in Hawaii and Puerto Rico (and their allies in Cuba) competed against low-priced sugar from the Philippines, owned by local sugar barons, and thus the real interest of the farm lobby was to grant Philippine independence and then advocate for protectionist tariffs against its sugar in order to bring up the price in the United States (Friend 1963; Pepinsky 2015). Sugar policies, therefore, historically evolved through the industry's "carefully staged decisions" (Richardson 2009: 43).

Preferences are shaped historically through institutions, and this explains their stickiness through time—and sugar is no exception (Krueger 1988). Later examples of the sugar industry guarding its privilege ruthlessly are not hard to find. The shape of the postwar sugar protections in the United States reflected the 1930 Chadbourne Agreement between the United States and Cuba, under which Cuba "voluntarily" restricted its exports to 2.8 million tons and the United States restricted domestic production to keep prices high. The Jones-Costigan Act of 1934 institutionalized this arrangement, and the postwar agreements such as the 1948 Sugar Act also reflected the earlier patterns. The developing world's inability to argue against protections in the North met with the historic prowess of the sugar barons in the North to maintain their privilege. Thus, the sugar industry obtained the equivalent of "infant industry" protections for its sugar cultivations and refining, protections that the developing world was hardly able to obtain through GATT for its fledgling manufacturing industries (see Chapter 3). Agriculture, as noted earlier, was excluded from GATT until the Uruguay Round: Sugar imports along with cotton epitomized the protectionist barriers that the developed world erected against tropical products from the developing world.

Extreme concentration of wealth in a few hands resolved the collective action problems for the sugar industry in the North, but the barons also logrolled the few small farmers to their cause. The political clout in the United States developed from traditionally high expenditures on political campaigns of both parties. The story in the European Community is slightly more complicated but similar. The sugar industry in Europe was also concentrated and was provided protection through high tariffs and subsidies for production and export. These politics are now explained.

Protections and Quotas   Domestic interests in the United States and the EU explain mercantilism, but they do not explain the continuation of the system of preferences in the North. In the United States, the sugar industry did not want quotas for any country. The 1930 Chadbourne agreement might have restricted Cuban exports, but the sugar industry wanted all quotas abolished:

Ironically in 1948, it was a perceived obligation to Cuba, rather than any motivation of domestic producers that led to the reinstatement of the program. During the years 1948 to 1960, Congressmen dealing with the sugar program were regarded virtually as foreign agents—their interests appear to have been primarily in allocating import quotas rather than benefitting domestic interests. (Krueger 1988: 53)

The United States continued a system of quotas for Cuba and Philippines despite opposition from its industry. In 1948–1949 the world production of sugar was 29.2 million tons, of which 21.1 million were cane sugar. Cuba was the largest producer with 5.1 million tons, and the United States was second with 3.6 million tons (including sugar from its protectorates Hawaii and Puerto Rico). Britain, France, and Portugal, along with their colonies, accounted for another 14.2 million tons. The total free and preferential "trade" in sugar was 12.7 million tons, or 43 percent of global production. The chief exporters were Cuba (5.8 million tons), Europe (1.7 million tons), Asia and Oceania (1.9 million tons), Africa (0.6 million tons), and the British West Indies (0.4 million tons) (all data from White 1952). Krueger (1988) asks an important question: Why did the U.S. sugar industry agree to country-level quotas for sugar in the postwar era when a global quota to be auctioned would have been more efficient? Again, institutional stickiness, in this case that of paternalism, is the answer. To this day, the sugar rate quotas, as they are known in the United States, are awarded to the country's "friends," mostly in the Latin American region, although the Philippines has also been a historical beneficiary. The quotas are frequently amended and changed to conform to various pressures. Interestingly, the United States maintained these preferences while arguing against imperial preferences in the GATT negotiations.

After postrevolution Cuba faced the U.S. embargo for its products, the country diverted its exports to the USSR and, along with crop failures, the price of sugar climbed to record highs in 1974. At that time the United States lifted its sugar quotas: Artificial policies to keep sugar prices high or keep out imports were no longer necessary, as sugar producers could sell at high prices anywhere in the world. However, the quotas were restored in 1977 when world sugar prices fell. In the 1980s, the sugar industry was also hit with the production of artificial sweeteners, and by the mid-1980s they accounted for over 15 to 16 percent of the total sweetener market in the United States (Krueger 1988: 60). The sugar industry, including this time in coalition with the artificial sweetener producers, again lobbied against sugar quotas, and the Reagan administration obliged, cutting sugar quotas from 2.7 million tons to 1.0 million tons in 1987. As Chapter 1 noted, the Caribbean was especially hard hit with a loss of 350,000 jobs and scarcity of foreign exchange (Richardson 2009: 83). Interestingly, in 1984 President Reagan launched the Caribbean Basin Initiative (CBI), which among other things included quotas for agricultural products from the region.[19]

The United States often uses domestic support in the EC as an excuse for maintaining its own agricultural support schemes, all the while "appearing" to be free trade oriented in public statements. In general, the EC ignored the developing world, and a GATT Working Party in 1983 found that the United States had not fulfilled its obligations in sugar.[20] Just as the Reagan administration responded to protectionist calls from its sugar lobby to reduce import quotas and increase domestic support, a press release from the USTR noted in 1986:

"The United States is under increasing criticism for having sugar price support levels that are far higher than the prevailing world market price," Yeutter said. "This is a practice we have condemned for years when other countries do it, and we simply cannot defend it as U.S. policy."

"As a consequence," Yeutter said, "Agriculture Secretary Dick Lyng intends to propose legislation next year which will reduce our sugar price supports to a more rational and defensible level, while also giving income support to our own producers through transition payments to be phased out over a five-year period." (USTR, 1986c)

Meanwhile, the European Community matured through its own system of protections with a system known as the Common Market Organization (CMO) for sugar, which was created in 1958 and persisted until 2005. It relied on price supports for domestic producers, import quotas for foreign producers, and subsidies for exports. Imperial preferences were initially accorded to sugar, but, under the Common Agricultural Policy as the EC processed its own sugar through beet production, the case for imperial preferences began to erode. The quotas were extensively negotiated during the 1975 Lomé Convention between the EC and the group of countries that came to be known as African, Caribbean, and Pacific (ACP) countries, which were provided sugar quotas for up to 1.3 million tons. Britain had insisted on continuing the Commonwealth Sugar Agreement (CSA) as a price for joining the EEC. Interestingly, the total sugar exports from the Commonwealth countries to the UK was also 1.3 million tons. Britain was not a major sugar producer, and its motivation included keeping the price of sugar low while also reducing the need for high subsidies in the Common Market. The total production of sugar in the EC in 1975–1976 was 9.7 million tons, and the ACP share of the total EC sugar was less than 13 percent of the total (calculated from Ravenhill 1985: 234). ACP countries, with help from Britain, therefore overcame the opposition from CAP producers of allowing no imports if they could produce the commodity themselves. Further, the Sugar Protocol was to be of indefinite duration, and the prices that the EC provided to ACP countries were higher than world prices. Sugar accounted for nearly 70 percent of total ACP exports to the EEC in 1977 (Ravenhill 1985: 225).

The EC began to export sugar through a complicated arrangement that ultimately undermined the Sugar Protocol in 2005. The EC was producing more sugar than it consumed, and initially the CAP farmers accused the UK of undermining EC production with its imperial preferences. This challenge included full-page advertisements from the French beet producers in the *Financial Times*. Eventually, the EC began to dispose of the surpluses at considerable cost on world markets at lower prices. As a whole, the sugar subsidies accounted for 10 percent of CAP and 4.5 percent of the EC budget (Ravenhill 1985: 233–234). A challenge to the Sugar Protocol at the WTO in 2002 led to its dismantlement in 2005. The change in U.S. and EU regimes, beginning with the Uruguay Round, is discussed next.

Tinkerings since the Uruguay Round   The breakdown of the paternalistic sugar regime features internationally negotiated and adjudicated challenges. First, the Uruguay Round resulted in a limited amount of "free trade" in sugar. The United States, for example, had to admit a minimum of 1.139 million tons of sugar, although this figure also includes the nearly forty TRQ countries. Total U.S. imports actually declined in the post–Uruguay Round era to an average of 1.573 million tons from the amounts that existed before 1980: They accounted for only 12.5 percent of U.S. sugar consumption from a high of 33.5 percent or nearly 3 million tons in 1981–1985 (Haley and Ali 2007: 26).

More significantly, the United States allowed some trade in sugar through NAFTA and subsequent regional and bilateral trade agreements. The reaction from the sugar industry was to keep sugar off the table, failing which it whittled down the import provisions. NAFTA allowed free trade in sugar from Mexico above its domestic production. The sugar lobby forced a side agreement through a separate letter, which made Mexico include its consumption of artificial sweeteners in calculating its surplus. The Dominican Republic–Central American Free Trade Agreement (DR-CAFTA) also included provisions for sugar that would allow free trade in sugar up to 1.2 percent of the total U.S. consumption, which amounted to a spoonful of sugar per person per day. The amounts were negligible, allowing up to 151,00 metric tons in TRQs from all signatories except Costa Rica, which was allowed 200,000 metric tons. The DR-CAFTA vote in Congress was 217–215 and almost did not pass in 2005 due to pressures from the sugar lobby.

The sugar lobby in the United States chiefly relies on a two-pronged strategy to maintain its position. First, it argues that preferential trade agreements are not about free trade because of the "preferred" trading partners. Meanwhile, it keeps its eyes on efficient producers such as Thailand and Brazil to point out their distortionary subsidies. Although sugar production the world over is subsidized, nothing compares to the calculated $3.5 billion it costs the U.S. taxpayer annually for the sugar program, from direct subsidies as well as the high price of sugar for consumption (*Bloomberg View* 2013). The sugar industry provides employment to only 142,000 people in the United States, of whom around 80,000 are in sugarcane, and sugar contributed 2.39 percent of total crop value in 2004 (Haley and Ali 2007: 3). Total agricultural employment in the United States is about 2.2 million, and thus sugar jobs are about 6.45 percent of the total. As such, the employment and value numbers are much lower than those for wheat, cotton, corn, and soybeans, while the total federal support is much higher. Second, the sugar industry spends upward of $3 billion per election cycle in the United States and provides high donations to both parties for congressional and Senate races (Forrer et al. 2005). It is, therefore, no surprise that, despite opposition to the latest farm bill of 2013–2014, the bill kept intact the U.S. sugar program providing domestic support for price and import quotas. Total U.S. support for agriculture was calculated to be $195 billion over a ten-year period.

In July 2015, one of the last rounds for the Trans-Pacific Partnership talks between the United States and twelve Asia and Pacific nations also stalled over three issues, including sugar (dairy and intellectual property were others).

In the EU, a legal challenge from efficient sugar producers led to the dismantling of the Sugar Protocol. Australia, Brazil, and Thailand challenged the Sugar Protocol at the WTO in 2002. The EU adopted the decision against itself in May 2005 when the WTO Appellate Body upheld the panel report from 2004. The case involved EU providing subsidies for the 4 million tons of sugar, known as C sugar, that it sold on world markets (A sugar deals with productions quotas, and B sugar is a surplus for shortages). The Appellate Body ruled against the below-market price of C sugar and the cross-subsidization that operated in the EU sugar regime (which ostensibly produced the sugar surpluses). The WTO case was about export subsidies and not import quotas. However, the EU's response to the ruling was to cancel the Sugar Protocol in 2009 that had existed since the 1975 Lomé Convention and had been renewed through the Everything but Arms initiative in 2001, which had provided duty-free and quota-free access to forty-eight least-developed countries. The sugar quotas were later renewed through the EU's Economic Partnership Arrangements but with a plan to phase out agricultural quotas for ACP countries. The EU has also provided incentives since 2006 to member states to reduce their domestic quotas with no promise of renewal in 2017 when the current CMO expires. In 2015, nineteen member states produced 13.5 million tons of sugar and allowed 2.5 million tons in imports.

The developing world coalitions have hedged their protrade and food security concerns at the Doha Round through multiple coalitions. The G20, which includes low-cost sugar producers such as Brazil, China, India, the Philippines, and Thailand, is inclined toward a cautious protrade position on sugar. Many of the G20 members are also in the proagricultural Cairns Group. This includes Brazil, Indonesia, the Philippines, and Thailand. Nevertheless, the G33 group has sought to exclude sugar from trade on the grounds that it is a "special product" (SP). Many of the G33 members include the ACP and the G20 group countries, including India, Indonesia, the Philippines, and sugar producers in Africa and the Caribbean. G33 also supports a special safeguards mechanism (SSM) for food security or employment concerns. In India, for example, there are 50 million sugarcane farmers who make up 8 percent of the rural population (Richardson 2009: 149).

As with agriculture in general, the divisions in developing world coalitions have produced several deadlocks in the Doha Round but also played into the hands of great-power sugar interests. The EU mobilized the ACP to argue that sugar should be included as a sensitive product (SSP). In the 2008 negotiations, developed countries sought exceptions to include 4 to 6 percent of all tariff lines in the SSP category. Although most countries provide domestic support for their sugar industry (including Brazil, India, and Thailand), the arithmetic at the WTO has served to disguise the divisions between low-cost producers such as Brazil, Guatemala, and Thailand, and those that could not survive in the market without quotas.

Cotton and Brazil

Brazil and the United States reached a political compromise on October 1, 2014, over a prominent trade dispute in cotton after a decade of successive Brazilian legal victories at the World Trade Organization.[21,22] The outcome lets the United States maintain its domestic subsidies in exchange for a $300 million payment to Brazil. However, in 2009, the WTO had authorized Brazil to impose $830 million of sanctions in the form of retaliatory tariffs on key products, including pharmaceuticals, if the United States did not eliminate its subsidies.

The October 2014 deal looks good on paper, but a closer look demonstrates persistent problems with North–South trade issues. The cotton deal is an example of how hard-fought concessions from the developing world, this time through WTO's dispute settlement, often result in disappointing outcomes in the long run for the developing world. The outcomes also fit the pattern of trade policy in the United States and the EU described earlier: Instead of providing real trade concessions through reduction of their tariffs or subsidies, they provide quantitative carve outs such as lump sum payments or preferential quotas for developing country products.

There are three main provisions in the U.S.–Brazil cotton agreement:

- The $300 million will go to the Brazil Cotton Institute for technical assistance to its farmers and those who trade with Brazil and Mercosur countries. This includes countries in West Africa who were also advocating for elimination of U.S. subsidies.

- The United States will eliminate the small amount of export subsidies for cotton, related to long-term export credit guarantees.

· Brazil has agreed not to challenge the domestic subsidies for cotton in the 2014 farm bill for its duration of five years.

The United States discovered a political opportunity in Brazil's 2014 election cycle to affect a political compromise that made the struggling incumbent President Dilma Rousseff look good and contributed to her victory in the presidential elections in October. But the $300 million payment is in return for a Brazilian agreement not to challenge the 2014 U.S. Farm Bill, which doles out generous subsidies to its farmers over the next five years. In February and March 2014, Brazil threatened its preapproved retaliatory legal action when the Farm Bill was announced. The deal struck was prompted in this context. Leaked documents showed that the United States was willing to pay up to $460 million to Brazil (Reuters 2014).

Despite the WTO rulings, the powerful cotton lobby in the United States has managed to preserve its subsidies, most of which go to rich cotton farms in states such as Texas, Mississippi, Arizona, and California. Ten percent of U.S. cotton farms receive 79 percent of the total domestic subsidies (Pfeifer, Kripke, and Alpert 2004). There is bipartisan support for overall farm subsidies—$20 billion in direct payments alone.

Cotton subsidies in the United States deflate global prices, which benefits U.S. exports. In 2002, when developing country advocacy against cotton subsidies reached maturity, the International Cotton Advisory Committee (2006) calculated that prices would be 15 percent higher if all cotton subsidies were eliminated. Subsidies in the United States account for nearly half of that 15 percent. This affects farmers in West Africa, for example, who are among the most cost effective globally but cannot compete against artificially depressed prices. Interestingly, China is one of the biggest markets for U.S. cotton exports, even though the United States railed against Chinese garment exports when the ATC became effective (see the last chapter; also, Rivoli 2014). Oxfam calculated that the U.S. cotton subsidies paid to its 25,000 farmers were $3.9 billion in 2002 ($4.2 billion in 2004), nearly twice the official development assistance from the United States to Sub-Saharan Africa (Pfeifer et al. 2004). The United States accounted for 41 percent of the world exports, which made up 76 percent of the country's total production.

Cotton is symbolic of the developing world's efforts to pry open developed world agricultural markets and play by free trade rules. At the 2003 WTO ministerial at Cancun, Mexico, trade ministers from the so-called Cotton Four (C4) countries—Benin, Burkina Faso, Mali, and Chad—gave an emotional press conference calling for an elimination of trade subsidies in the United States. The latter responded with vague promises of reciprocity and eventually gave foreign aid instead, none of which was for cotton, and that was definitely less than what these countries would have earned from cotton exports. Cotton made up 40 percent of C4 exports for 10 million of its farmers. The C4 argued that U.S. subsides accounted for $400 million in losses for their farmers (Williams 2005).

Brazil began to challenge the U.S. position in 2002 at the WTO, which found these subsidies to be non–trade compliant in 2004. Despite condemnations from the WTO, the United States kept its subsidies intact in successive farm bills. In March 2010, Brazil moved toward retaliation by releasing a list of fifty products, narrowed from an initial 200, for which it is legally allowed to impose retaliatory tariffs of $560 million. Furthermore, Brazil planned another $270 million worth of "cross-retaliation" that allows Brazil restrictions in nontariff barriers. Then-U.S. Secretary of State Hillary Clinton rushed to Brazil and held off retaliation by subsidizing Brazilian cotton farmers for $147.3 million each year and also agreed to cut subsidies in the next farm bill. The United States was now subsidizing cotton farmers in the United States and in Brazil!

The cotton deal preserves liberal protectionism, which does not destroy the overall fabric of the liberal regime that envelops it (Aggarwal 1985). Brazil's own farm groups praised the deal. The Peterson Institute for International Economics in Washington, DC, noted that the $300 billion benefits Brazil's farmers, whereas counterretaliatory tariffs would not (Hufbauer 2014). The political compromise could also be indicative of the strength and flexibility of the WTO, which allows countries to suspend their trade provisions temporarily or pay compensation for not changing a trade policy (Rosendorf 2005). Certainly Brazil's legal victory and U.S. capitulation can be understood in this context.

The long-run implications go further. The 2014 Farm Bill is not a temporary suspension of trade policy but the continuation of an enduring policy since the Great Depression. Second, the compromise fits into another historical pattern: Pay off the developing world rather than provide real trade concessions. The total payoff of $300 million (even when combined with past annual payments of $143 million) is much less than the $830 million annually that was authorized. Meanwhile, U.S. cotton farmers will continue to reap billions of dollars in domestic subsidies and earned incomes from world markets by selling cotton at discounted prices. For the developing world, the status quo continues in agriculture, although the WTO system provides a few opportunities. In this case, both the $300 million and the elimination of the export guarantee credits resulted from the moral, legal, and coalitional negotiation strategies used by Brazil (with support from others such as the C4).

Conclusion: Paternalism in Agriculture

This chapter has examined North–South negotiations in agriculture since the beginnings of the Uruguay Round in the 1980s. The context of the so-called Washington Consensus is also important as it provided the backdrop for the Uruguay Round. The term *Washington Consensus* referred to a set of policies from the Bretton Woods institutions and the U.S. Treasury to push for market liberalization in the developing world. U.S. President Ronald Reagan and British Prime Minister Margaret Thatcher personally chaperoned these policies. At the start of the Uruguay Round, the acting U.S. Secretary of the Treasury Peter McPherson noted that the import substitution industrialization policies of the developing world were "built on false assumptions" and went on to condemn the developing world's push for SDT policies that were merely a "cover for protectionism" (quoted in Preeg 1995: 73). There is breathtaking dissonance between pushing for liberalization in the developing world while maintaining protectionist barriers on agricultural products from the developing world.

There are three paternalistic strategies the developed world has employed in the Doha Round period. First, there are many forms of side payments, to diffuse demands from the developing world rather than meaningful liberalization. Brazil was unable to move the United States to decrease its cotton subsidies, but the dispute was settled in late September 2014 with a $300 million payment to the Brazil Cotton Institute. Side payments were also used to break up coalitional pressures. The Central American countries defected from the G20 soon after its formation after the Cancun ministerial in response to U.S. overtures for preferential treatment. Look back again at Figure 1.1 to see evidence of this for the developing world as a whole.

Second, the politics of shifting boxes and the successive legislations to ensure agriculture subsidies, such as in the U.S. Farm Bills, do not show subsidy reductions. In fact, the subsidies increased in the post–Uruguay Round period. Third, developing countries have been quickly singled out either for blocking trade agreements or for purported economic harm in the Western world. India was blamed twice, once for the failure to accept the deal offered in July

2008 on agriculture and then subsequently after India refused to ratify the 2013 Bali accord.

There are also a few features of the negotiations in the Doha Round that are not easily understood as paternalism. Briefly, more than the Uruguay Round, the Doha Round is the North–South Round. The inclusion of Brazil and India in FIP or G4 or the diversity of coalitions from the developing world may be understood in this regard. There may be instances of learning in the developed world. The developing world is no longer portrayed in the developed world as the bastion of protectionism. Recently, India's rejection of the Bali accord was understood as a response to its domestic politics rather than merely as a protectionist stance (Singh 2014a). The extension of the peace clause to India's food security program in November 2014 was an acknowledgment of these domestic politics. In prior negotiations, developed country negotiators often acted as if domestic politics was something that happened in their countries but not in the Global South. Third, North–South agricultural negotiations do not feature unified developing country interests. As shown earlier, although many countries favor liberalization, others push for protection. India wants to preserve domestic protections for its food security program while becoming one of the biggest agricultural exporters in the world.[23]

Even the colonial regime in sugar is beginning to crack open. The regime began to be dismantled in the EU following a dispute settlement challenge in 2002 from Australia, Brazil, and Thailand in which the WTO Panel found the EU's export subsidies to be non–WTO compliant. In the United States, the Uruguay Round and bilateral and regional trade agreements, starting with NAFTA in 1993, opened the door slightly for limited sugar imports through free trade as opposed to preferential quotas. However, the change in trade rules cannot be exaggerated—as explained earlier, it amounts to great-power manipulations in the margins. The limited paternalistic behavior is a sop: The small and almost meaningless preferences in sugar disguise the underbelly of historical practices that benefited colonial and postcolonial sugar barons.

Chapter 6

Big Disparities in Services and Intellectual Property

> Where there are no rules to protect inventors in their commercial transactions,
> the legitimately aggrieved parties must necessarily take action. While waiting
> for appropriate rules—and dispute settlement procedures—for such vital
> areas as intellectual property protection, we cannot in the meantime abandon
> these vital areas of commerce to robbery by ruling out trade-restrictive
> measures that may be necessary to respond to the robbery.
>
> US Trade Representative Press Release, February 21, 1989

> I should mention the strange controversies that have been generated on what
> is called "business process outsourcing." The very process of liberalization, on
> which we have been lectured for so many years, has created competitive skills,
> which are available for utilization by businesses everywhere. We should not
> now drive a reverse process.
>
> Former Indian Prime Minister Atal Bihari Vajpayee, March 2004

WHILE the developing world fought to include two old issues, agriculture and textiles, at the Uruguay Round, the United States introduced two gigantic issues on the trade agenda several years before the launch of the round. One contentious issue was trade in services, the "intangible" flows across borders of "products" such as airlines, banking, and telecommunications. It resulted in the General Agreement for Trade in Services (GATS) at the end of the Round. The other issue arose from U.S. business concerns starting in the 1970s about trade in counterfeit products and led to the agreement known as Trade-Related Aspects of Intellectual Property Rights (TRIPS).

Developing countries signed on to the GATS and the TRIPS agreements after immense pressure from the developed world but did manage to gain a few concessions through coalition building and, as in agriculture and manufacturing, through possessing better alternatives at negotiations with their trade diversity (or export market concentration). In GATS, many developing countries even discovered new sources of economic growth through tourism or foreign direct investment, but the TRIPS agreement remains contentious to the present day. Michael Finger (2008) notes that the regulatory provisions and enforcement in both agreements entail net costs for the developing world, whereas forms of liberalization in merchandise and agricultural trade that the developed world was asked to undertake would result in net welfare gains for consumers through reduced prices.

GATS and TRIPS also allow an analysis of the increasing number of preferential trade agreements that the United States and the EU have signed with the developing world. The gains in GATS and TRIPS that the developing world made in multilateral negotiations at GATT or the WTO have often been lost in the bilateral and regional preferential trade agreements, where the odds for a developing country to effect concessions from a great power across the table are greatly reduced. Therefore, the stringent services and intellectual property agreements resulting from bilateral and preferential trade agreements are often termed TRIPS+ and GATS+.

Intellectual property (IP) is examined first in this chapter. It has evolved from maneuvers, starting in the late 1970s, on the part of the United States to restrict production of counterfeit goods to one of the most coercive, and often secretive, trade negotiations issues on the U.S. and EU agendas. Through its evolution, the developing world has been accused of piracy and stealing and manipulated into signing preferential trade agreements whose provisions are far more restrictive than the WTO agreements. Concerted advocacy from the developing world led to the Doha Health Declaration at the launch of the tenth GATT/WTO trade round in November 2001, to allow relaxed IP provisions for health emergencies, but since 2001 these provisions have been diluted, although TRIPS+ pressures have increased. Any exceptions to TRIPS provisions have resulted from the developing world's advocacy.

GATS has turned out to be a beneficial agreement for many parts of the developing world although, like intellectual property, it has made more commitments in services at PTAs than their developed country counterparts.[1] This runs contrary to the perceived wisdom that the developing world caved into unfettered services liberalization (Kelsey 2008; Raghavan 2002). GATS has even enabled many developing countries—ranging from India as an outsourcing hub to developing country island states as tourism corridors—to "discover" their comparative advantage in services products. A closer examination reveals another story: Through coalition building, the developing world assured for itself a slow approach toward GATS liberalization at the Uruguay Round. The GATS+ bilateral and preferential agreements have not obeyed this slow logic and have opened up developing world markets for foreign direct investment (FDI) and liberalization in several sectors. Along the way, the developing world has also been singled out in policy and media accounts in the United States and the EU for "stealing" high-tech jobs, and fairly explicit racism has been directed at countries like India, targeting its outsourcing practices.

Intellectual Property

North–South negotiations in intellectual property can be analyzed in three phases starting with TRIPS negotiations at the Uruguay Round, leading on to the Doha Health Declaration in 2001 acknowledging public health concerns at the WTO ministerial and the TRIPS+ agreements negotiated in the last decade.[2] In the first two cases, the developing world extracted meager concessions to allow for national emergencies, despite coercive threats from the United States; in the latter case, the developing world signed on to costly intellectual property enforcement provisions. The chief framing device from the United States and the EU has referred to any intellectual property infringement as "piracy," "robbery," and "stealing."

TRIPS Article 31 and the Uruguay Round

The Uruguay Round ended with the developed world obtaining most of what it wanted in intellectual property negotiations (Drahos 1995; Sell 1998, 2003).[3] The biggest victory at the beginning of the Uruguay Round was that intellectual property became a trade issue. At the end of the round, GATT/WTO provisions began to be applied to TRIPS, and IP infringement became subject to WTO trade arbitration and dispute settlement. In 1982, the EEC did not agree with the U.S. position that trade in counterfeit products was subject to trade rules. By the time TRIPS was signed, the EU and Japan were on board, and the agreement included protections for patents, trademarks, copyright, and industrial designs not just as protections against counterfeits but also for "pipeline" protection for the time spent to invent and create and for varying periods of protection thereafter including provisions known as exclusive marketing rights for patented products.

The developed world's IP position evolved slowly but, by the late 1980s, it presented a concerted coalition to the developing world along with trade pressures that were hard to side step. The U.S. trade act in 1974 set up the Advisory Committee on Trade Policy and Negotiations (ACTPN), headed by Pfizer CEO Edmund T. Pratt, who took on the cause of making IP a trade-related issue.

An anticounterfeiting coalition developed in the later 1970s, including brand names such as Samsonite, Izod, and Gucci and headed by Levi-Strauss.

The U.S. government mostly worked "behind the scenes" to unify the developed world on intellectual property. Although the ACTPN and the USTR began prioritizing trade issues, the first mention of intellectual property issue in a USTR press release was not until 1986 (U.S. Trade Representative 1986a). In 1985, the USTR appointed an assistant USTR for International Investment and Intellectual Property but, unlike other top-level appointments, the USTR did not have a press release for this position. The developing world had not paid sufficient attention to the domestic politics within the United States on the burgeoning intellectual property rights agenda and was caught unaware (Watal 2001; Singh 2008; and interviews with negotiators).[4]

At the start of the Uruguay Round, ACTPN's efforts culminated in the creation of the Intellectual Property Committee (IPC), which varied from thirteen to fifteen Multinational Corporations (MNC) members, who began to bring together the varied IP interests and also to persuade counterparts in the EC and Japan. The IPC worked directly with the European Union of Industrial and Employers' Confederation (UNICE) and Keidenran, the Japanese federation of businesses. The work of the IPC was directly responsible for the hardening of the IP position in the developed world. Jacques Gorlin (1985) articulated the industry's position in a paper commissioned by IBM that served as the basis of the U.S. position at the Uruguay Round. The IPC presented a 100-page position paper known as "Basic Framework of GATT Provisions on Intellectual Property" in 1988.

Beginning with the Tariff and Trade Act of 1984, the United States began to apply Section 301 of the 1974 trade act to apply to intellectual property, which meant that the United States could abrogate the GSP and other trade privileges to the developing world if any country was found to infringe intellectual property provisions. For example, Mexico lost $500 million of GSP benefits in 1987, Brazil amended its copyright law in 1987 and patent law in 1988 to such threats, and Thailand lost GSP benefits in 1989. The U.S. Congress also passed the Omnibus Trade and Competitiveness Act of 1988, which authorized the USTR to prepare "priority watch lists" of countries infringing IP and to investigate them. The inaugural list included Korea, Brazil, India, Mexico, China, Saudi Arabia, Taiwan, and Thailand. These and other countries regularly feature in the most unfavorable terms in the USTR press releases analyzed in Chapter 4.

Table 6.1.   U.S. trade sentiments toward trading partners in intellectual property.

	Praise	Mixed	Threats and sanctions
OECD	0	1	12
Non-OECD	0	2	57
CEES	6	9	2
Total	6	12	69

SOURCE: Author's content analysis of U.S. Trade Representative press releases (1982–1993).

Table 6.1 provides a summary of the intellectual property issues covered in the USTR press releases during the period from 1982 through 1993. Of the eighty-seven total mentions of countries, fifty-nine are in the developing world. In addition, fifty-seven of the sixty-nine threats and sanctions are also toward the developing world, almost all of them related to Section 301 or the priority watch list. The countries that receive the most mentions are Thailand (ten), Brazil (eight), China (five), India (six), and three mentions each for Argentina, Korea, Saudi Arabia, and Taiwan. The unfavorable language used against the developing world is remarkable. Here are a few examples:

1986: The pirating of U.S.-financed research and development discourages innovation, denies markets to American exports, and threatens technological progress. Protection of intellectual property rights preserves America's technological edge, which is a key to our continued international competitiveness. (USTR April 7, 1986b)

1988: "Despite some recent improvements, international respect for American intellectual property rights is deplorable," Yeutter said. "That is why the Uruguay Round negotiation on the trade-related aspects of intellectual property rights is such a high priority for us. We have already submitted a proposal on intellectual property in the round. Other countries must also treat this issue with the urgency it deserves." (USTR February 26, 1988)

1989: Declaring that Thailand fails to safeguard U.S. intellectual property rights in a satisfactory manner, Ambassador Clayton Yeutter today announced President Reagan's decision to deny duty-free benefits on approximately $165 million in imports from Thailand. In taking this action, the President indicated that future requests for flexibility for Thai products under the Generalized System of Preferences (GSP) would not be looked upon favorably until Thailand provides appropriate intellectual property protection. (USTR January 19, 1989)

1991: The Government of the Mongolian People's Republic has agreed to adhere to the Berne Convention for the Protection of Literary and Artistic Works and to the Geneva Phonogram convention, which protect intellectual property. It will introduce legislation in the areas of patents, copyrights, proprietary information (trade secrets), and integrated circuit layout designs, and provide effective enforcement of these rights. (USTR January 23, 1991)

1992: Following a nine-month investigation under the "Special 301" provisions of the Trade Act of 1974, as amended (the Act), United States Trade Representative Carla A. Hills today determined that India's denial of adequate and effective patent protection is unreasonable and burdens or restricts U.S. commerce. Ambassador Hills said that she is leaving the door open for trade action and has asked an interagency group to develop options for consideration. "We will continue to urge changes in India's position in bilateral negotiations and in the Uruguay Round," she said, "and will assess whether trade action is appropriate." (USTR February 26, 1992)

The developing world was caught off guard with the developed world's closure on intellectual property. Since the late 1960s, the developing world had been pushing for a dilution of the Paris Convention on patents to manufacture cheap drugs through compulsory licensing that would allow its manufacturers to break patents and manufacture cheap drugs for public health purposes (Gallagher 2000: 282–283). Later, the developing world was somewhat complacent in believing that the burgeoning IP agenda in the developed world applied only to counterfeit brands. The appointment of the moderate Swedish Ambassador to GATT, Lars Annel, may have also signaled moderation in the developed world's position to the developing world. The expansion of the 1974 trade act in 1984 and the passage of the 1988 omnibus act caught it unawares. Many developing countries caved in to U.S. pressures, especially those in ASEAN and Latin America (Croome 1999: 114). The agricultural and manufacturing concessions that the ASEAN coalition received (see Chapter 4) may also be directly linked to the Section 301 pressures and their acquiescence to the U.S. IP agenda.

The developing world argued that the IP agenda set in Punta del Este was misleading. The Punta del Este declaration referred mostly to counterfeit goods and not intellectual property. However, the developing world could not find any support in the North. Intellectual property was a particularly important issue for India, which faced violent protests from farmers fearing restrictions on patented seeds and from its pharmaceutical firms, which were competent at manufacturing generics.[5] In India, farmers groups led a "Seed Satyagraha" (civil resistance) against the evolving intellectual property provisions and argued against relinquishing the control of seed banks to MNCs such as Cargill (Sharma 1994: 24–26). By 1988, though, both Brazil and India had come around. President George Bush personally lobbied Prime Minister Rajiv Gandhi, who instructed Indian negotiators to move forward. India's TRIPS negotiator notes that India did not ask for any concessions in return, further limiting the notion of a trade-off.[6]

India was able to extract a concession by the time of the Brussels ministerial in 1990. This was the famous Article 31 of TRIPS, which would serve as a basis for the Doha Health Declaration, allowing for limited forms of compulsory licensing. Article 31 developed out of India's request to merge government use and compulsory licensing and reflected knowledge of similar laws in the United States for national security emergencies. The EC and Japan supported this move, as did Canada, which suggested it to India. After the Brussels meeting, the TRIPS text moved forward, and the next big confrontation was in November 2001 in Doha.

Doha Health Declaration

The start of the Doha trade round in November 2001 was held up with pressures from the developing world for a health declaration, which would allow them to procure medicine from countries where the drug is cheaper or to break the patents themselves. The former process is known as parallel imports, whereas the latter is known as compulsory licensing. Parallel imports arise when a firm sells a drug to country X cheaper than to county Y, allowing country Y to import the drug from country X.

The pharmaceutical industry was vehemently opposed to the moves toward compulsory licensing, but there were several important exceptions. One was that the United States softened its threats on compulsory licensing despite pressures from its powerful Pharmaceutical Research and Manufacturers Association (PhRMA). AIDS/HIV activists in South Africa propelled transnational advocacy and sympathetic media framing toward President Mandela's South African Medicines and Medical Devices Regulatory Authority Act of 1997, which allowed for limited forms of compulsory licensing. The U.S. government withdrew its opposition in 1999 to this act, but only after South Africa was named on the 301 Priority Watch List and its GSP privileges were revoked in 1998 at

PhRMA's behest. The medicines crisis in South Africa was counterframed as "death," as opposed to the "piracy" and "stealing" framing the United States had employed (Odell and Sell 2006). A second notable exception was that the U.S. and Canadian governments moved toward compulsory licensing of the drug Cipro after the anthrax scare following the 9/11 attacks when a poisonous powder containing the virus, mailed to media and congressional offices, killed five people and afflicted another fifteen, including postal workers. No compulsory licenses were issued, but the U.S. government negotiated steep price discounts from Cipro's manufacturer, Bayer. The U.S. hypocrisy was obvious. Odell and Sell (2006: 103) cite a Latin American negotiator who noted: "Why are ten lives sufficient [to break a patent in your country] but one million lives in developing countries are not sufficient?"[7]

At Doha, the Global South stood vehemently opposed to the North's IP agenda. The opening of the Round was held up until the member-states agreed to issue a document that came to be known as the Doha Health Declaration (World Trade Organization, November 14, 2001). Para 6 instructed the TRIPS council to "find solutions for countries experiencing public health emergencies." This task was completed in August 2003 ("the paragraph 6 decision") after the United States (a) sought assurances that the drugs being manufactured for public health emergencies will not be reexported and (b) limited the list of diseases that would constitute a public health emergency. The net result of these moves was that very few compulsory licenses have been issued at all, making the Doha Health Declaration a hard-fought but weak maneuver in the long run. Knowledge Ecology International, a leading advocacy organization, noted in a recent submission to the U.S. International Trade Commission that the United States "is leading the world in the use of compulsory licenses, and is hypocritical in voicing indignance when developing countries issue compulsory licenses for essential drugs" (quoted in *The Economic Times*, May 20, 2014).

Bilateral and Regional Trade Agreements
The thrust of the U.S. and EU pressures for restricting IP has now moved toward bilateral and multilateral preferential trade agreements where the United States can apply several forms of direct pressures, and the developing countries have less recourse to coalition building. A few negotiations, including the Anti-Counterfeiting Trade Agreement, have also been held in secret in the name of national security.

In bilateral and regional trade agreements involving two or more parties, developing countries have recourse to fewer bargaining tactics.[8] RTAs have proliferated in practice since the 1990s, and WTO members are required to notify the organization of RTAs because in principle they grant exceptional rather than MFN privileges to those that sign them. By April 2015, GATT/WTO had received 612 notifications, of which 406 were still in force. Although the dynamics governing the growth of RTAs are varied, it is no coincidence that the RTAs have proliferated during a period when the developing world has begun to play a greater role in multilateral negotiations.

Drahos (2001) notes that TRIPS was always understood in the United States as a minimum standard, and thus TRIPS+ rules, following a prepared text that other countries are asked to sign, have proliferated in bilateral trade and investment treaties. IP protections also underlie many of the preferential trading schemes such as the Caribbean Basin Initiative from 1983, the African Growth and Opportunity Act from 2000, and almost all the PTAs and BITs that the United States has signed with other countries. "Preferential trading arrangements, in short, create dependencies by weak States on the strong States that may be subsequently exploited by negotiators from the strong States" (Drahos 2001: 801). Sell (2013) calls attention to forum shifting, where the United States moved to a forum such the World Intellectual Property Organization (WIPO) or the OECD (horizontal forum shifting) or bilateral agreements (vertical forum shirting) for TRIPS+ provisions.

The secrecy surrounding the multilateral agreement known as the Anti-Counterfeiting Trade Agreement (ACTA), negotiated between 2008 and 2010, produced heated debates.[9] The negotiations were between 2006 and 2011 and were kept mostly secret until a draft leaked out in 2010 through Wikileaks and subsequently successive drafts from other sources. It was signed in 2011 by Australia, Canada, Japan, Morocco, New Zealand, Singapore, South Korea, and the United States. Mexico and the EU signed in 2012. Kader Arif, the European rapporteur for ACTA, resigned in protest after the EU signed the agreement in January 2012. The European Parliament is unlikely to ratify the agreement, and similar developments are noticeable in other states that signed the agreement, including the Mexican Parliament. Only Japan has ratified the agreement. Similarly, the intellectual property provisions in the Trans-Pacific Partnership agreement signed in February 2016 among twelve countries are known to be quite restrictive. Sell (2013) calls the TPP provisions to be ACTA-plus, which would include "ex-officio" power to customs officials for drug seizures of generics, like those mentioned earlier. At one of the final rounds of the TPP negotiations at the end of July 2015 in Hawaii, the agreement was held up with opposition to the IP provisions from East Asian countries.

IP advocates in the developed world argue their case for protections on the basis of links between economic prosperity and intellectual property enforcement. In doing so, they overlook an obvious factor. Property rights in the Western world historically developed as a tug-of-war between concentrated and dispersed interests (Greif 2006; North 1990; Olson 1982; North and Thomas 1973). Prosperity and good governance furthered property rights and, in turn, created conditions that facilitated the creation and legitimacy of these rights. In the long run, though, consent between the governors and the population has been especially important for the legitimization of property rights (Acemoglu and Robinson 2012). So far, TRIPS+ has been more about forced consent rather than voluntary legitimacy given to treaties.

There is another problem with data positing a relationship between IP enforcement and prosperity: the problem of endogeneity. Figure 6.1 shows the rela-

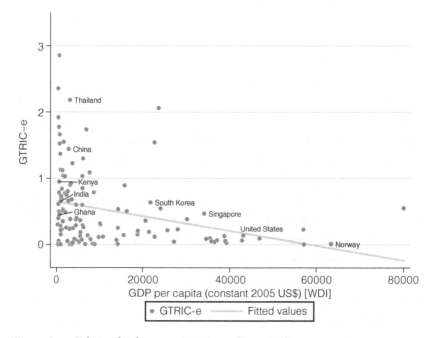

Figure 6.1.   Relationship between GTRIC-e and 2010 GDP per capita.

tionship between the General Trade-Related Index of Counterfeiting and Piracy of Economies (GTRIC-e) from the Organisation for Economic Co-Operation and Development (2008) and the 2010 GDP per capita income (at 2005 constant prices). The GTRIC-e is based on a survey sent to the 169 World Customs Organization (WCO) members and covers infringements of TRIPS provisions on trademarks, copyrights, patents, and industrial designs. The GTRIC-e scores vary from low infringement of 0.000372 to high infringement score of 2.849408. The relationship between GDP per capita and IP enforcement implicit in the GTRIC-e is fairly straightforward. However, in actuality, the fitted line shown in Figure 6.1 is an inverted U-shaped curve. Economies with very low PCI also have low rates of infringement because they may not have the resources to replicate commodities.

The logic of IP enforcement can be inverted. Instead of showing how prosperity and IP enforcement are linked, one may ask if a certain minimum amount of prosperity is not a precondition for IP enforcement. In such a case, the logic of IP enforcement from the developed world comes unraveled. The degree to which poor states can implement policies based on international pressures is questionable, although there may be plausible reasons for the efficacy of business pressures for states such as China that have low PCIs but do not lack resources in general. In practice, the Section 301 watch lists from the United States are carefully calibrated to include big states such as India and Brazil but also a few smaller states. Chile, China, India, Indonesia, Thailand, and Turkey have been listed on the watch list since this list began in 1989 (Froman 2014).

Services

The General Agreement on Trade in Services (GATS) pertains to sectors that account on average for a majority of the total national income in most economies. The 2012 share of services in the GDP of the United States was 77.7 percent, India 50.0 percent, and Tanzania 43.7 percent.[10] In old parlance, they were known as the tertiary sectors and included services such as telephones, water, electricity, and banking and insurance, which were public monopoly utilities in most parts of the developing and developed world. The GATS agreement opened these sectors for trade and thereby addressed the inefficiencies in public- or private-sector monopolies. Services and liberalization of market entry and regulation, rather than tariff reduction, are the relevant criteria for negotiation and became the basis of trade negotiation. Therefore, countries make "commitments" to market access and national treatment.

The GATS Agreement and the Uruguay Round

The GATS agreement is flexible, allowing countries to list the sectors or subsectors (positive list) that are included for liberalization. The United States, which led the way for trade in services to be on the GATT/WTO agenda, had wanted every sector to be liberalized unless countries listed exceptions. This was known as the "negative list" approach. The positive list approach resulted from coalition building, this time from a coalition that included both the developed and the developing world. Since its inception, the GATS agreement has propelled "autonomous liberalization," which means that countries have liberalized their sectors more than their commitment in GATS.

The chief coalitions influencing services were the G10 and a moderate coalition known as café au lait after the Swiss and Colombian efforts that created it. The G10 came about in 1982 to oppose the services agenda. Café au lait was formed in 1986 and included both developing (G20) and developed world (G9) countries. The coalitions responded to the moves from the United States to include services on the trade agenda and those from G10 to prevent it from moving forward. As with intellectual property, the United States pushed the services agenda, though in this case with service industries in banking, software, and finance in the 1970s. The issue came up in the Tokyo Round, and the OECD's Trade Committee began to look into services trade in 1979. At this time, momentum gathered in Washington: The government established an Interagency Taskforce on Services and the Multilateral Trade Negotiations at the White House. A number of think tanks in Washington and London began to conduct studies on services trade and frame services as an important form of comparative advantage for the developed world (Drake and Nicolaides 1992). The planned start for a new trade round at the 1982 GATT ministerial in Geneva was delayed after the aggressive U.S. moves to push a services agenda. The European Economic Community favored a go-slow approach, and the G77, led by India and Brazil, voiced its opposition. Developing world unity soon collapsed on this issue. In 1983, the Colombian ambassador to GATT began to convene the "Jaramillo Group" to informally push the services agenda: A few Asian Newly Industrializing Countries began to come around to the U.S. position. In May 1985, the Swedish ambassador convened twenty-four trade ministers in Stockholm along with GATT Director-General Arthur Dunkel to break the North–South impasse. The idea for a two-track approach for trade negotiations in GATT developed, one for goods and the other "separate but parallel" one for services (Croome 1999: 17). India countered in July 1985 with a paper on services that received the support of another twenty-four developing countries. The developed world proposed a series of preparatory or Prepcom meetings at the GATT, starting in November 1985, for a new trade round, but the impasse over services continued. As the stalemate at Prepcom ran on, the Swiss Ambassador Pierre-Louis Girard convinced a group of nine (G9) moderate developed countries (Australia, Austria, Canada, Finland, Iceland, New Zealand, Norway, Sweden, and Switzerland) to draft an agenda that the G9 presented as a draft to Prepcom on June 11, 1986.[11]

Brazil and India, with the support of the G10, struck back immediately with a proposal. They asked for a complete rollback and standstill of protectionist measures as a precondition for including services and other new issues in the Round. The move backfired; it was seen as extremist, and the G10 support itself showed dwindling of developing country ranks.

A direct result of the Brazilian proposal was the explicit defection of twenty moderate developing countries (the G20, including Colombia, Chile, Jamaica, and Korea) that joined ranks with the G9. The Korean ambassador, who hosted a dinner for the moderates at his house in Geneva, led the G20 defection.[12] Switzerland's Girard and Colombia's Jaramillo led the G9 and G20—along with the United States, Japan, and the EC, who played mostly observer roles—in meetings at the European Free Trade Association (EFTA) offices in Geneva. The Swiss–Colombian draft was the clear winner at Prepcom although a proposal from the G10 hardliners (nine after Argentina's defection) was also discussed at Prepcom. However, on the last day of Prepcom meetings (July 31), the EC broke ranks and sided with the hard-liners (its motives may have been its protectionist agricultural interests). The EC suggested the two-track approach that would allow India and Brazil to save face. Felipé Jaramillo also proposed this approach to the EC after Ambassador Dubey of India suggested that they would go along with it.[13]

Eventually, Jaramillo proposed a procedural solution, albeit one favoring two tracks: The services talks would be separate as in the EC proposal but conducted by the same officials and the GATT secretariat. In other words, the two tracks, in the language of GATT, would be "a single-undertaking" although it did not really apply to services. The United States accepted this proposal, and the Uruguay Round was launched and expected to be concluded in four years.

The procedural distinction agreed to at Punta del Este led to the constitution of the Group of Negotiations of Goods (GNG) and the Group of Negotiations on Services (GNS). The Trade Negotiations Committee (TNC) directed the whole round. Arthur Dunkel and his successor Peter Sutherland after July 1993 headed the GNG and the TNC while Felipe Jaramillo headed the GNS. In keeping with the Punta del Este declaration, fourteen negotiating groups were appointed for goods and one for services in January 1987.

The GNS included several developing countries and was headed by a developing country ambassador. By 1988, the basic framework for GATS was ready: The GNS agreed that services could be supplied through several modes, such as movement of consumers, suppliers, commercial organizations, and cross-border flows.[14] With the framework of modes of supply and principles in place, the GNS moved toward sectoral testing exercises, involving microagendas, in 1989. The sectors were telecommunications, construction, transportation, tourism, professional services, and financial services. This list was pared down from thirteen sectors and over 100 subsectors. In general, these exercises revealed the limits of applying many of the GATS principles carte blanche to sectors covered. Second, specialists from these sectors got involved. In telecommunications, the support of the International Telecommunication Union (ITU) helped to resolve many technical matters, but its involvement also might have allowed developing countries to resist moves toward cost-based pricing that the United States wanted (the ITU supported the old pricing regime).

Coalition building with developed countries provided a few benefits to developing countries. One of the debates that arose from sectoral exercises, and the fifteen papers that were submitted by countries during autumn 1989, was the scope of sectoral coverage.[15] Here, the United States wanted a top-down approach of a negative list requiring countries to list sectors and subsectors that were not covered. This position was viewed as extreme by most of the developing world and parts of the developed one, mainly within the EC. The EC and the developing world wanted a bottom-up positive list covering only the sectors listed (Preeg 1995: 104). As it became clear that the evolving services framework would favor a positive list approach, the powerful Coalition of Service Industries in the United States, formed in 1982, changed its position and denounced the services framework coming out of the GNS. In July 1990, the USTR announced that the United States would need to derogate from MFN in shipping, civil aviation, and basic telecommunications (Drake and Nicolaides 1992: 87). Subsequently, USTR Carla Hills announced in November that the United States was not agreeing to unconditional MFN in services. The EC and developing countries were outraged. Ironic, given that a little over three years earlier, developing countries did not even want to negotiate services.

The positive list approach in the GATS agreement ensured that countries did not undertake trade liberalizations that were difficult politically. For signing on to GATS, countries were asked to undertake a token commitment: Tiny Belize committed to opening its neurosurgery market.[16] The lack of liberalization, along with the degree of autonomous liberalization, runs contrary to the belief that the services agreement was a form of neocolonialism or imperialism, which only served the interests of services firms from the United States and other countries in the Global North (Kelsey 2008; Raghavan 2002).

Most of the GATS concessions in the Uruguay Round and thereafter have come from the developed world. Roy (2011), Marchetti and Roy (2008), and Roy, Marchetti, and Lim (2008) provide a standardized measure for gauging the depth of GATS commitments across countries. These scores range from 0 for no commitment to 100 for full commitment and include commitments undertaken at the Uruguay Round and thereafter. The post–Uruguay Round negotiations include sectoral negotiations in telecommunications and financial services and those for accession negotiations for China. Therefore, any results from using Marchetti and Roy's data, one of the only data sets available for services negotiations, must be used with caution. Despite the inclusion of post–Uruguay Round commitments in the Marchetti and Roy data set, the developing countries do not seem to have made overly burdensome GATS liberalization commitments. The lowest figure is for St. Kitts and Nevis at 5.1, and the highest score is for Chinese Taipei at 61.6. The United States has a score of 55.4 and the EU12 a score of 55.3. Brazil scores 19.6, and India scores 32.5. These data and overall regressions (see later) confirm that liberalization commitments are positively related with countries that score high on the paternalism strength index (look back to Table 4.5). The PSI's positive correlation is borne out in both binary and multiple regression contexts.

The "macro" results for GATS commitments, including all sectors, are summarized in Table 6.2. The PSI is statistically significant and positively related to GATS liberalization commitments in all the models presented. In the binary

Table 6.2. GATS commitments explained with paternalism and negotiation indicators.

DV: GATS commitments	Model 1	Model 2	Model 3 (robust standard errors)	Model 4 (robust standard errors)	Model 5 (robust standard errors)
Paternalism strength index	12.696*** (1.753)	12.968*** (2.158)	8.566*** (2.607)		
Export market concentration index				1.195*** (0.254)	1.194*** (0.256)
G10					0.423 (5.03)
Cafe au lait		3.036 (4.027)	1.556 (3.286)	6.239** (3.052)	6.202** (3.051)
Polity2		−.027 (.385)			
GDP per capita constant prices (logged)			5.144097*** (1.636)	6.246*** (1.461)	6.275*** (1.523)
Constant	34.048*** (1.833)	32.552*** (3.353)	33.15979*** (3.204995)	19.70677*** (3.773544)	20.53018*** (3.241038)
R-squared	0.544	0.534	0.654	0.561	0.561
Number of observations	44	43	45	61	61

OLS estimates, standard error in parentheses.
Statistical significance: *p < 0.10; **p < 0.05; ***p < 0.01
NOTE: Due to the limited number of observations in the data set, Models 2 and 3 are limited to three independent variables. When the regressions are run with just two variables (PSI and either café au lait or G10), the results obtained are similar, with neither of the coalitions being statistically significant, but the G10 coefficient is negative and the café au lait coefficient is positive.

model, every one percent increase in PSI is related to nearly 13 percent increase in GATS liberalization commitments. In Models 4 and 5, the coefficient for the index of export market diversification is also statistically significant and positively related to GATS commitments and shows that every one-unit increase in the index of export market concentration leads to a 1.2 percent increase in GATS liberalization. The PSI and index of export market concentration are not exactly comparable because the former ranges from −0.81 to 3.17, while the latter ranges from 1.1 to 26.79, but, even with the difference in ranges, both seem to show roughly equivalent increases in GATS liberalizations.

There is no statistically significant relationship between G10 or the café au lait group and GATS commitments in most models, but this is not surprising. The most impact these coalitions had in the services negotiations was toward the GATS framework itself and not specific commitments that were undertaken. However, the café au lait members do well in services when their influence is considered separately from paternalism indicators and in conjunction with export market concentration. This is hard to interpret but may indicate the willingness of states to undertake reciprocal commitments, when not in the shadow of the paternalistic states.

The models stay robust through additional controls, but they yield interesting insight. First, the level of democracy in any country (Polity2) is not a deterrent to commitments. Richer states with high per capita incomes also make more commitments than poor ones, but this is over and above the paternalism indicators, providing further proof that paternalism is different from being a rich state.[17]

The statistically significant constant terms reflects that every country undertook a minimum level of GATS commitments, on average starting at 34 in Model 1 to 20 in Models 4 and 5. However, only modest commitments were actually made in services at the Uruguay Round: GATS was mostly a framework agreement, but GATS article XIX committed countries to ongoing negotiations even if a new multilateral round had not been launched.

The content analysis of USTR press releases from 1982 through 1993 confirms that the United States used much more favorable language in services and that most of its efforts were directed at the OECD countries. Seventy-five percent of the press releases targeted OECD countries (look back again to Table 4.2). Further, of the total of thirty-one press releases coding sentiments toward a trading partner in services, eight were favorable, nine unfavorable, eight mixed, four neutral, and two paternalistic. The almost equality of favorable and unfavorable sentiments and the low number of paternalistic sentiments are in contrast to the high numbers of negative and benevolent press releases in agriculture, manufacturing, and intellectual property.

Post–Uruguay Round Negotiations

GATS sectoral negotiations on financial services, maritime transport, and telecommunications continued after the Uruguay Round closed. Of these, telecommunications is the most important for liberalization, and it is described in the next subsection. GATS is relatively marginal to global finance rules, and there was no agreement in maritime transport.

Three developments explain North–South issues in post–Uruguay Round negotiations. First, the interest of the developing world in services liberalization reveals a protrade stance. To put it simply, the developing world has not been interested in SDT and the GSPs in services. The opposite is true: Many countries have undertaken unilateral or "autonomous liberalizations" that go beyond their GATS commitments. The protrade stance is important and reveals the developing world's interest in this Pareto-superior outcome. Second, the flexibility in GATS provisions and coalitions at the multilateral level allowed the developing world to tailor the liberalization schedules. This was the case at the Uruguay Round with the positive list approach. Third, the thrust of the developed world's approach to effect concessions in its favor has been to push for GATS+ provisions, negotiating further concessions in preferential trade agreements and specifically in investments. Mode 3 of GATS on "commercial presence" is the investment part of the agreement and key to developed country firms for "trading" services in foreign territories. The United States began to push for bilateral investment treaties (BITs) starting with the first agreement in 1982 with Egypt. Although BITs are broader than services, they do include services trade.[18] By 2015, there were forty-eight BITs in place, and almost all of them were with non-OECD countries, except for Turkey and those East European countries that signed BITs before joining the EU.[19]

A number of preferential trade agreements now offer a patchwork of investment rules governing services trade with one thing in common; most of them go beyond GATS commitments in Mode 3. The "gains" that the developing world made through a multilateral framework such as GATS must, therefore, be evaluated alongside the "losses" incurred through BITs, PTAs and GATS+. Marchetti, Roy, and Zoratto's (2012) analysis of forty services PTAs among thirty-six trading partners covering seventy-one bilateral relationships found that there was indeed reciprocity in these agreements but that North–North bilaterals exhibited reciprocity more than the North–South bilaterals. They found that, in North–South PTAs, developing countries give more concessions, especially in Mode 3, which deals with investment. Their data also analyze Mode 1, and they find that concessions in Mode 1 and Mode 3 are positively related, meaning that countries make concessions across sectors and not within them.

I can confirm Marchetti, Roy and Zoratto's results with the paternalism strength indicator using their data for increases in PTAs over GATS commitments and also specifically for Mode 3 commitments. Table 6.3 presents these findings. Unlike the results from Table 6.2, here the PSI sign is reversed, mean-

Table 6.3.   Difference in GATS and PTA commitments explained with paternalism and negotiation indicators.

	Model 1 DV: Increase in PTA commitment above GATS commitment	Model 2 Increase in PTA commitment in Mode 3 above GATS commitment
	(robust standard errors)	(robust standard errors)
Paternalism strength index	−10.12575*** 2.295037	−9.780209*** 2.243987
Constant	27.49973 3.096643	27.14154*** 2.981074
R-square	0.2517	0.2542
Number of observations	46	46

OLS estimates, standard error in parentheses.
Statistical significance: $*p < 0.10$; $**p < 0.05$; $***p < 0.01$

ing that the developing world made most of the concessions, although every country made some minimal concessions, as revealed in the constant.

Although the services agenda has chiefly evolved outside of GATS, a few developments at the Doha Round, which subsumed the GATS 2000 negotiations, are important.[20] First, many countries have undertaken autonomous liberalizations providing a paradox for negotiations that the offers they made at the Doha Round, at least until 2008, were less than the de facto liberalization in the country. Trade accounts reveal that the countries were holding off for concessions in agricultural and NAMA (nonagricultural market access) before conceding on services. A "signaling conference" was held in July 2008 to determine how much the members might be willing to offer in revised concession or offers. As Table 6.4 shows, most WTO members already have existing liberalization commitments in prominent sectors: business services, banking and insurance, telecommunication, and tourism. Audiovisual (or entertainment industries) is an exception with low commitments due to opposition from domestic cultural industries and their ability to frame the issue as a loss to cultural identity (Singh 2011).

Sweet Talk and Secrecy   Despite the willingness of developing countries to liberalize their services sectors through reciprocal concessions, the developed world continues to introduce nonreciprocal concessions for least-developed countries and to exclude emerging powers such as India and China by design.

The recent rhetoric of an MFN waiver for LDCs in services may be another instance of sweet talk and possibly a strategy to isolate and divide services

Table 6.4.   Existing WTO and GATS commitments in services sectors.

Sector (services classification list)	Subsector	Number of countries making commitments
1. Business services	Professional services	104
	Real estate	31
2. Communication services	Telecommunications	105
	Audiovisual	36
3. Construction and engineering	General construction work for buildings	
		76
Distribution services	Wholesale trade	62
	Retailing	61
5. Education services	Higher education	50
6. Environmental services	At least one subsector	66
7. Financial services	Insurance	110
	Banking	112
8. Health-related and social services	At least one subsector	57
9. Tourism and travel-related services	Hotels and restaurants	141
	Travel agencies and tour operated services	118
10. Recreational, cultural, and sporting services	Entertainment services	49
	Libraries, archives, museums	23
	Sporting and recreational	49
11. Transportation services	Maritime	56
	Air transport	66
	Space	3
	Rail	39
	Road	57

The sectoral and subsector classifications follow the Services Sectoral Classification List (World Trade Organization 1991).
SOURCE: World Trade Organization (2015) Services Database. Available at http://tsdb.wto.org.

exporters from the developing world from least developed countries. Although there has been no progress in services liberalization in GATS, in 2011 developed countries accorded an MFN waiver to services and services suppliers from the thirty-two least developed countries in the WTO. This continues the tradition of nonreciprocity for least developed countries and is understood in trade terms as the equivalent of the "enabling clause" for services granting nonpreferential access to LDCs. The rationale for the waiver is unclear: Services exports from LDCs are limited, and service suppliers in banking, telecommunication, construction, or transportation do not exist. Two years after the 2011 ministerial, no waivers or requests for waivers were submitted, and at the December 2013 Bali ministerial members decided that they would move toward "expeditious and effective operationalisation" of the waiver; LDCs made a joint request in July 2014 (*Bridges*, July 24, 2014). The February 2015 meeting of the WTO Services Council announced some preliminary steps for operationalizing the services waiver. Many LDCs could ostensibly take advantage of Mode 4 or movement of natural persons but earlier advocacy from countries like India on this issue were not successful in opening this market in developed countries, where de facto Mode 4 is treated as an immigration rather than a trade issue. Nevertheless, the October 2015 ministerial in Nairobi instituted this waiver at the WTO.

Meanwhile, an ongoing plurilateral in services was shrouded in secrecy and excluded emerging powers. Since 2011, at the behest of Australia and the United States, twenty-three countries and the European Union have been negotiating the Trade in Services Agreement (TiSA) at Geneva but outside the WTO framework. This "plurilateral" negotiation follows the attempts in the Doha Round since 2006 to work out agreements among interested members on services sectors. Developing countries such as India and Brazil and many others resisted these plurilaterals to move forward a services agenda without concessions in agriculture and NAMA. TiSA negotiations, like those of ACTA and TPP, have also been held in secret, though Wikileaks began to reveal parts of the negotiating text in June 2014, which led the EU to publish its "offer" on financial services on its website in July 2014. TiSA provisions also govern telecommunications and data transfers and provide for limitations on government support open source software. The latter issue is important for Brazil. The BRICs are excluded from TiSA negotiations. An analysis of the Wikileaks from the GATS scholar Jane Kelsey notes: "The secrecy of negotiating documents exceeds even the Trans-Pacific Partnership Agreement (TPPA) and runs counter to moves in the WTO towards greater openness" (Kelsey 2014). The clearest lesson for developing countries may be that TiSA forces them to grant concessions in services without receiving reciprocal concessions in other sectors (Raghavan 2015).

Two Cases: Telecommunication and Business Processes Outsourcing in India

We now turn to two cases within GATS. The first case on telecommunications illustrates the confidence of the developing world in services liberalization. This is different from textiles, sugar, and cotton, where the developing world was either excluded or provided quotas. Not excluding the developing world in services makes sense: Liberalization also means access for service providers from the North. Therefore, the second case is important: It describes exports from India, a developing country services powerhouse, which has faced a racist backlash and restrictions in Mode 4 from providing business processes outsourcing (BPO) services to developed country markets. India, along with other BRICs, is excluded from TiSA negotiations.

Telecommunications

The WTO telecommunications accord signed on February 15, 1997, formalized the emerging liberalization in telecommunications worldwide. The accord is known as the Fourth Protocol after the legal protocol used to attach it to the GATS agreement. Originally signed by sixty-nine countries, including forty less-developed countries, it accounted for 95 percent of world trade in telecommunications at an estimated $650 billion (WTO, February 17, 1997). One hundred and five WTO members were signatories in 2015.

Historically, telecommunications sectors were controlled or operated according to national priorities. Since January 1, 1998, global rules underlying the WTO processes now govern the new regime. In accordance with the GATS framework, MFN now applies to commitments made for market access and national treatment in the telecommunications sectors. These commitments allow for cross-national investments in telecommunications (or hasten them given that this process precedes 1997), and trade in basic and many value-added telecommunications services are governed by liberalization norms, both features backed by WTO rules of transparency and MFN.[21] Most significantly, sixty-three of the sixty-nine governments also agreed to introduce "regulatory disciplines" to observe the WTO rules by signing on to a "Reference Paper" in telecommunications that governs regulatory aspects of the sector. Negotiators realized early on that the credibility of the telecommunications liberalization will rest in the hands of the regulatory authorities; the reference paper seeks to ensure such safeguards through transparency, regulatory independence, and safeguards against anticompetitive practices of incumbent monopoly providers, be they state run or private carriers. The U.S. industry was "wildly enthusiastic" about this agreement when it was signed (Sherman 1999: 62).

GATT's Marrakesh agreement in 1994 contained commitments from fifty-seven members to liberalize their value-added or enhanced services in the

Annex on Telecommunications, which was a watered-down version of the original intent. Telecommunications carried the importance of being the "information highway" for the service economy. Telecommunications was thus by far the most important sector in services for imminent liberalization: These commitments were the first test of the evolving GATS principles.[22]

The 1997 agreement concluded nearly three years of efforts that began in May 1994 on liberalizing basic telecommunication under the auspices of NGBT (Negotiation Group on Basic Telecommunications), which was constituted in April 1994 when it was clear that Uruguay Round would not be able to deal with basic service issues. The Council on Services reconstituted NGBT as GBT (Group on Basic Telecommunications) when the April 1996 deadline had to be extended.

Developing countries played an important role in crafting the technical and regulatory provisions of the 1997 agreement. Telecommunications "trade" entails suitable regulations to ensure market access and national treatment, and thus the most important element of the 1997 agreement pertained to the regulatory annex to the agreement, known as the Reference Paper. The negotiations on the Reference Paper best illustrate developing country participation and problem solving in the negotiations. From December 1994 onward, the United States began to convene a small group of regulatory officials, called the Room A group after the WTO room in which they first met. Chaired by the Japanese, whose hospitality and leadership are often acknowledged as crucial to the success in drafting the Reference Paper, the Room A group also included Australia, European Union, Korea, and New Zealand. Brazil, Chile, Mexico, the Philippines, and Singapore also later joined Group A. The process began with the United States distributing its own paper, titled "Procompetitive Regulatory and Other Measures for Effective Market Access in Basic Telecommunications Services" (WTO, NGBT, February 9, 1995). Although the language reflected the evolving provisions of the U.S. Telecommunications Act of 1996, the negotiation process as it proceeded began to incorporate provisions from other member states, including those from the developing world. The EU directive on interconnections requirements for providers was important, as was India's inclusion of language that allowed developing countries to decide their universal service obligations to underprovided areas along with its cost-sharing mechanisms themselves (Sherman 1999: 84).

Developing countries also featured prominently in the negotiations as market players. Although the United States, Japan, and the EU accounted for nearly three-fourths of the world's total revenue, many developing countries did account for significant portion of revenues and traffic.[23] The top ten telecommunications revenue states in 1997 included Korea, Brazil, Mexico, and Argentina (in that order) followed by Hong Kong, India, South Africa, and Indonesia (in the eleventh, twelfth, thirteenth and fifteenth positions respectively). Hong Kong, Mexico, and Singapore ranked among the top ten countries for international telephone traffic; Korea, Argentina, and India were among the top for telecommunication investment; Korea, Turkey, Brazil, and India ranked among the top ten in terms of total number of telephone main lines. Furthermore, in terms of total main lines, the rate of growth in the developing world tended to be higher, 13.8 percent annual average growth rate during the 1990–1995 period in the developing world as opposed to 3.5 percent in the developed world at that time. Similarly, telecommunication revenues grew at an average annual rate of 9.7 percent during the period from 1990 to 1995 in the developing world as opposed to 4.2 percent in the developed world.

Developing countries also employed legalistic and technocratic tactics arguments to influence the negotiation process. Many developing countries played a leadership role, in turn, convincing others to join in the process. In Peter Cowhey's words they became "living-breathing points of reference."[24] Singapore would become a leader in persuading other ASEAN nations whereas countries like Korea and Hong Kong led the efforts in terms of designing or accepting regulatory principles. Hong Kong's Alex Arena was instrumental in designing several regulatory features that developing countries found acceptable. In Latin America, Peru was an early leader, whereas Brazil was quite forthcoming even though its domestic legislative battles were not settled as yet. Earlier, by April 1996, Venezuela had already made a full offer to open its markets by 2000 while Mexico had come close to offering what its national laws would permit (Petrazzini 1996: 13). With Mexico, Venezuela, and Peru on board, other Latin American countries joined in.

Developing countries fared well—both in their technical savvy, in presenting their country schedules and in designing the rules themselves but also in practicing negotiating tactics to advance their mostly proliberalization telecommunication interests. Many of these countries were involved in domestic liberalization and regulatory exercises, and this experience would help them at the international level. At the other end of the spectrum of development were weak offers from poor Caribbean countries: Dominica, the Dominican Republic, Grenada, Jamaica, and Trinidad and Tobago. Together they account for less than 0.15 percent of world's telecommunication revenues, but all of them, with the exception of the Dominican Republic, were able to delay phasing in their market opening after 2007.

Coalitional tactics were also obvious. Countries like Singapore played a key role in convincing major Asian powers. Venezuela, Mexico, Brazil, and Peru may have had a similar affect on other developing countries. In an indirect way, these countries could also hide behind coalitions in the developed world, the EU in particular, when many contentious issues affecting them both came up.

Developing countries' participation in crafting the rules for global telecommunication is sometimes characterized as acquiescence to global MNCs and large users from the developed world (Kelsey 2008; Raghavan 2002). However, it is easy to show that developing country interests in liberalization reflected bottom-up pressures from their domestic constituencies. Developing countries made telecommunications a development priority in the 1980s for a number of reasons and adopted promarket policies because of the resource constraints that they faced. Two powerful coalitions, one opposing liberalization (including domestic monopolies and their employees, government agencies, and protected businesses) and the other favoring it (business, large users, MNCs, and international organizations), defined the particular resolution of these battles in these countries. It is hard to find a case where a developing country merely acquiesced to international demands in defining the terms of their liberalization domestically.

The state of liberalization underway in each country is a good proxy variable for the trajectory taken by telecommunication coalitions of each country. Table 6.5 correlates the strength or weakness of offers from thirty-one developing countries with the state of liberalization in each of these countries in the mid-1990s. The summary of offers available at the WTO website on the World Wide Web were used. *Strong offers* were taken to be those that were going to open up their markets in a considerable number of market segments (including voice telephony) within two years of the 1998 implementation date and observe the regulatory principles fully or partially. *Reasonably strong offers* were those seeking to adopt market-opening measures in several segments within two to four years and a commitment to observe regulatory principles in the future. *Weak offers* delay implementation until after four years with a weak commitment in the future toward regulatory principles. For the purposes of domestic liberalization,

Table 6.5.   Comparison between the WTO telecommunication liberalization offers and domestic telecommunication liberalization programs of developing countries.

	WTO liberalization offers		
Domestic liberalization	Strong offer	Reasonably strong offer	Weak offer
Strong program in place	Argentina Chile Dominican Republic Korea Peru		
Reasonably strong program in place	Colombia Malaysia Mexico Philippines Singapore Venezuela	Bolivia Brazil Hong Kong Sri Lanka	Indonesia India
Weak program in place			Antigua and Barbuda Bangladesh Belize Brunei Cote d'Ivoire Dominica Ghana Grenada Jamaica Morocco Pakistan Thailand Trinidad and Tobago

the description of individual countries as presented in an important study by the World Bank published in 1994 was used (nine of the WTO signatories are not described in this book and therefore not included here) (Wellenius and Stern 1994). Although the book was published in 1994, future predictions are included throughout, allowing us to make reasonable estimates of telecommunication markets in these countries in 1996–1997 when they made offers at the WTO.[25]

The correlations in the table provide significant comparisons. Countries that had undertaken significant liberalizations of their domestic markets also made strong offers for liberalization. Similar correlations can be observed between reasonably strong offers and reasonably strong liberalizations, and weak offers and weak liberalizations. The deviant cases (shown in the middle row) are easily explained. Elections constrained India's liberalization program; a fragile coalition in power after June 1996 further restricted the government's hand in making even a reasonably strong offer. India's de facto telecommunication liberalization began after 1999. Indonesia was on its way to a reasonably strong

Table 6.6. GATS commitments in telecommunications explained with paternalism and negotiation indicators.

DV: Telecom liberalization commitments	Model 1 (robust standard errors)	Model 2 (robust standard errors)	Model 3 (robust standard errors)	Model 4 (robust standard errors)	Model 5 (robust standard errors)
Paternalism strength index	17.5354*** (2.849973	17.02695*** (3.898301)	9.142852*** (3.65232)		
Export market concentration index				0.8619478** 0.3616064	0.8709918** 0.3663825
G10					−6.352534 (13.94293)
Café au lait		3.036 (4.027)	−1.483532 (7.307424)	−3.233979 (6.314905)	−2.670483 (6.154516)
Polity2		−0.027 (0.385)			
GDP per capita constant prices (logged)			8.435503*** 2.102768	10.3551*** (2.148766)	9.915899*** (2.420699)
Constant	57.66988*** (4.100124)	55.33711*** (7.159284)	−14.1351 (18.00519)	−33.90682* 18.60653	−29.57624 (21.29396)
R-squared	0.3551	0.3319	0.4726	0.3505	0.3547
Number of observations	46	43	45	61	61

OLS estimates, standard error in parentheses.
Statistical significance: $*p < 0.10$; $**p < 0.05$; $***p < 0.01$

liberalization program, but it had not really taken off as yet, and, although making a weak offer, it committed itself to the possibility of allowing additional suppliers in the future.

These results also hold when compared with multiple regressions on telecommunication commitments using Marchetti and Roy's data. The statistically significant constant term in Table 6.6 implies that all countries on average made some commitments, but, as can be seen from Models 1 through 5, those who were paternalistic or had high per capita incomes made more commitments than those who were not. Former members of the café au lait coalition, including developing countries, may have made slightly fewer concessions; although the café au lait sign is negative, it is not statistically significant.

The telecommunication case discussed so far shows that developing countries can undertake reciprocal liberalization commitments with technical savvy. Further, large developing countries such as Brazil, China, and India have not only liberalized but have used their information infrastructure and skilled human resources to export information service exports and enter other markets. This may have been reason enough for developed countries to exclude them from TiSA negotiations.

India and Outsourcing

In 2013, India was the sixth-biggest service exporter in the world, and its service exports grew 14 percent annually between 2005 and 2013. Commercial services, other than transportation and travel, made up 75.3 percent of India's total commercial service exports of $151 billion in 2013 (World Trade Organization September 2014). These "Other Commercial Service Exports" are made of several categories (look again at Table 6.4), but in India's case information- and communication technology–based business and professional services, or business process outsourcing (BPO), made up a majority share. Computer services made up 80 percent of total business services in India (Goswami, Gupta, and Mattoo 2011: 89).

India's success as a service exporter, in general, or as a BPO hub is counterintuitive and could not be predicted from the stance it took at the beginning of the Uruguay Round in services. Along with Brazil, as a leader of the G10, India tried to block the services agenda. By 1989, India had come a long way in giving in to a U.S-led agenda and began not only to support the GATS agenda but also to envision a future for itself as a services exporter. The combination of large numbers of skilled workers and an IT infrastructure that grew exponentially in the late 1990s allowed India to start providing BPO services.

A number of factors accounted for services sector and service export growth in India. Goswami et al. (2011) present a quantitative model, which predicts that service growth was fueled by the liberalization of service sectors, the availability of skilled personal, and a services-led growth in sectors that initially accounted for small percentages of GNP (a catch-up effect). When disaggregated at the provincial level, those provinces (or states) with higher shares of service sectors were also the ones with higher levels of literacy.

The other counterintuition follows from the backlash India experienced from its major importers in the EU and the United States. Canada and the United States imported nearly two-thirds of India's service exports and Europe another one-quarter (Goswami et al. 2011: 98). India's case is emblematic of the general debate on high-tech outsourcing in the United States and the EU. The anxiety in the United States began with a number of consulting firms who provided extremely high numbers for jobs that would be outsourced, resulting in millions of layoffs, with growth rates of outsourced jobs between 30 and 40 percent (Drezner 2004: 24; Ahmed, Hertel, and Walmsley 2011: 193). Greg Mankiw, serving on President George W. Bush's Council of Economic Advisors, ignited a political controversy in 2004 in noting that outsourcing was a "good thing" and merely the latest aspect of the gains from trade that economists since Adam Smith had hypothesized. Interestingly, the academic side of this debate took place in widely circulated publications such as *Foreign Affairs* and research papers from think tanks such as Brookings, which are all meant to influence policy. Alan Blinder (2006), a Princeton economist and former member of President Clinton's Council of Economic Advisors, put forward a provocative thesis first in *The Wall Street Journal* and then in *Foreign Affairs* arguing that, although current job losses in the United States were less than a million, in the future these would grow to between 28 and 42 million. He argued that Adam Smith's lessons did not apply to the information age, which needed a new vocabulary for international trade. Blinder concluded (127):

Contrary to current thinking, Americans, and residents of other English-speaking countries, should be less concerned about the challenge from China, which comes largely in manufacturing, and more concerned about the challenge from India, which comes in services.

The key to the job loss would be in the types of services that would be outsourced. Alan Blinder and his critics (Drezner 2004, for example) brought up the need for geographical proximity in delivering services and also the distinction between personal versus impersonal services. Based on over 450 job description classifications from the U.S. Department of Labor, Jensen and Kletzer (2006, 2007) distinguish between tradable and nontradable services and measures of geographic concentration. Although they estimated that 38 million jobs were potentially "offshorable," they also called attention to the U.S. sources of comparative advantage in highly skilled service occupations.

For the purposes of this book, the most important aspect of this controversy was the highly politicized debate in the United States, which took on explicitly racist and xenophobic tones in society, popular culture, and policy measures. Many of the outsourcing articles appeared in the midst of the 2004 U.S. presidential elections. Democratic candidate John Kerry called firms that outsourced "Benedict Arnolds." *The New York Times* wrote:

In recent weeks, the outsourcing of white-collar service jobs to places like this financial capital on the Arabian Sea [Mumbai] has become the focus of the American presidential campaign, the brunt of jokes on late-night shows, the subject of angry Web sites, and the target of legislation in more than 20 states and Washington. (Waldman 2004)

The San Francisco Chronicle reported the human angle: "Many Indian call-center workers say they regularly face particular abuse from Americans, whose tantrums are sometimes racist and often inspired by anger over outsourcing" (McPhate 2005). The National Broadcasting Corporation's sitcom *Outsourced* stands as a prime example of American popular culture's depictions, in this case an American business manager who locates to India to manage a call center. The show was widely critiqued in India as being racist. Oh and Banjo (2012) write that shows like NBC's *Outsourced* dealt with anxieties about job losses in the United States with overly paternalistic overtones: "The show does this by presenting U.S. businesses as performing global good in its promotion of personal liberty and of the United States as a racially meritocratic beacon, both of which are tied together with the prevailing racial logic of postracialism."[26]

The political controversy over outsourcing led to the introduction of several bills in the U.S. Congress and in state legislatures to limit outsourcing (Pomeranz 2006). Most of these measures contradicted recently negotiated U.S. international trade deals. The first legislation was Section 233 of the Consolidated Appropriations Act of 2004, which required that any funds that had been appropriated through this act given to a firm could not be used to send jobs outside the country. All U.S. states, with Ohio as frontrunner, have some kind of legislation addressing issues of government appropriations and outsourcing. Subsequent proposed legislations have raised concerns about data privacy and financial information flows to India, and existing data protection laws were often cited to try to restrict financial and health information flows to databases in India. This came after the decade-long U.S. challenges to the EU's 1995 Data Protection Directive, where U.S negotiators argued that the data firms collected about individuals belonged to the collecting agency and was, therefore, freely transferable, while the EU argued its position from European human rights perspectives.[27] Another political tactic was to introduce legislation limiting outsourcing for government procurement. This contradicted the long U.S. history of advocacy for free trade in government procurement and was the subject of highly publicized (and somewhat xenophobic) attacks on the Japanese government procurement practices in the late 1980s. Currently, the TiSA negotiations have again featured the United States pushing for free trade in government procurement.

The main lesson that emerges from the story about outsourcing is the end of *Sweet Talk*. However, this end is a happy story. As evidenced by the data from 2005 to 2013 presented earlier on the growth of BPO exports from India, the nasty paternalistic and racist talk has not dented Indian exports much. If anything, sweet talk, the opposite of the nasty talk in the BPO case, entailed more restricted exports for those who are paternalized. This is a happy ending but with a sad conclusion that exposes the racist underbelly of paternalism.

Conclusion

This chapter has confirmed two things. First, the North bullied the South in intellectual property. Through manipulation, coercion, charges of being labeled a thief, and restrictive TRIPS+ agreements, the developing world caved in to the U.S. and EU's intellectual property proposals. There was no benevolence in the Global North's rhetoric; in this case, the developing world needed to be taught a lesson in respecting the paternal powers' property. The pushback from developing countries, even though limited, came from joining ranks with the EU for narrowing the scope of a few TRIPS provisions at the Uruguay Round. This is similar to the Cairns Group story in agriculture. The developing world also received some respite at the beginning of the Doha Round from its collective advocacy for pubic health provisions, again not an entirely different story from its advocacy leading into the Uruguay Round. The developed world, nevertheless, whittled down the public health provisions. In the end, both agriculture and intellectual property feature the might of the Global North's against the Global South.

Second, the developing world viewed opportunities on the services agenda. It even won crucial concessions at the Uruguay Round, which enabled it to make commitments at a reasonable pace, followed with a pace of "autonomous" liberalizations that went farther than the liberalization offers developing countries made at the Doha Round. In other words, the services case was opposite of intellectual property: Countries did more than they were expected to do.

In many cases, the liberalization commitments followed domestic imperatives. A powerful example of current domestic imperatives is the use of participatory information technologies for development purposes and information "hubs" all over the developing world (Singh forthcoming; Singh and Flyverbom

2016). In a few cases, developing countries have also sought to take advantage of services liberalization to boost their exports. India's case in outsourcing is one of them. However, services exports also include small-island tourism, utility providers in Latin America, and exports of entertainment content from many developing countries. The story of services liberalization is not simply one of lacking comparative advantage.

Old service habits die hard. Concurrent with the developing world's enthusiasm, the United States and the EU pursued GATS+ agreements outside the WTO, came with a GSP-like deal for LDCs within the WTO that divides the developing world, and excluded the BRICs from many regional agreements. The BPO case discussed earlier demonstrates that open racism resulted in a success story in services from the developing world. Nevertheless, this chapter refutes the contention that the developing world would rather play outside of the WTO rules. It also confirms the contention that even when it does so, it has a tough act to play.

Chapter 7

Conclusion

The End of Sweet Talk

To speak means being able to use a certain syntax and possessing the
morphology of such and such a language, but it also means above all assuming
a culture and bearing the weight of a civilization.

Frantz Fanon, *Black Skin, White Masks* (2008/1952: 1–2)

THIS book has analyzed the morphology of sweet talk. It has puzzled about
the consequences of this sweet talk, which arrives cloaked in the meta-
phors of benevolence and seldom responds to international norms of reciprocity but often marginalizes and punishes the weak, not only when they do not
conform to norms but even when they do. It is wretched to be different on
earth. Contrary to the expectations from a benevolent paternalism, this book
finds scant evidence of sustainable material benefits from paternalism in international trade relations. Negotiated alternatives, especially multilateral ones,
provide the weak some advantage. Strategic collective action from the weak
fares well, but strategic economic diversification translates best into negotiation advantages.

This chapter provides a summary of the lessons learned, attends to counterarguments, and conjectures on ways forward for the developing world.

Cultural Lessons

From colonial sugar to information age exports, the developing world has experienced the consequences of preponderant cultural preferences and norms
arrayed against its interests from the West. In the colonial instance, it is being
civilized as it produces sugar, and in the information age it steals digital secrets and outsourced jobs. Literatures dating back to Enlightenment political
thought to current tabloids of foreign affairs support these stark conclusions.

This book presents evidence from mixed methods and multiple streams
of evidence. Table 7.1 summarizes the evidence and empirical findings of
this book.

The evidence presented is at several levels, from microcases, to macrodata-
based conclusions, and the in-between of historical and qualitative materials
and process tracing. In doing so, the book tries to draw on the strength of each

Table 7.1.   An empirical summary of sweet talk.

Issue area	Time period	Paternalistic position	Negotiation processes	Negotiated outcomes
Agriculture	1948–1986	Agriculture excluded; sweet talk about helping postcolonial word	Comparative advantage in tropical products; UNCTAD and G77 advocacy	Limited quotas and imperial preferences (1948–1971); system of SDT preferences thereafter
	1986–2015	Agriculture included; sweet talk on how most developing world benefits from preferences and quotas	Multiple coalitions with defensive and offensive interests (G20, G33, and Cairns Group); WTO dispute settlement challenges	Preferential trade continued; marginal changes in tariffication formulas; Doha Round at a standstill; proliferation of protectionist SPS measures and PTAs
Manufacturing	1948–1986	Biases against infant industry protection; tariffs favor non–value-added exports	Advocacy for acknowledging development needs, including infant-industry and SDT	GSP and MFA
	1986–2015	Willingness to negotiate but also push for FDI	Division between proexport and SDT groups	End of MFA regime, proliferation of PTAs and BITs
Intellectual property	1986–2015	Cohesive coalition of intellectual property interests; accuse developing world of stealing and piracy; sanctions	Coalitional action at the multilateral talks; immense pressures at PTAs	*1986–2001:* Multilateral solutions such as TRIPs and Doha Health Declaration *1995–2015:* Increasing proliferation of TRIPS+ through PTAs
Services	1986–2015	Push for services liberalization	Resistance and then autonomous liberalization	GATS followed with GATS+ through PTAs; also exclusion and racist critiques of developing countries' exports

method while employing another to address the weaknesses. For example, for those concerned that sugar is an isolated case, the book presents other similar cases and then follows up with a large-*n* data set and a qualitative and historical case study of sugar as a whole. In reverse, for those concerned that quantitative indicators do not provide contextual knowledge, the book provides "process tracing," showing that the inference from the independent variables in the quantitative variables must be historically located and understood (George and McKeown 1985; Brady and Collier 2004). Overall, such historical and institutional process tracing is very important for making the cultural claim presented in this book.[1]

The collected evidence points to the conclusions summarized in Table 7.1. Paternalism seldom accords benefits and remains resentful of developing country success in areas where they are supposed to be obedient and accept paternalistic handouts. This is as valid in ancient agricultural products such as sugar as it is in current high-technology information-age products. Bhikhu Parekh (1995: 97) has argued that Western liberalism is opposed to people with different values. In contrast, this book has detailed cases where Western liberalism may be opposed to people with similar values. Paternalism is about patronizing a set of people regardless of the values they hold or holding them to be so inferior that you cannot imagine that the other has the same values as you.

Looking across the several issue areas, the Western world has sweet-talked in issue areas where developing countries have a comparative advantage (agriculture, textiles) but has been verbally abusive in areas where the developed world seeks concessions but the developing world does not comply. The prime examples are words such as *stealing* and *piracy* backed with punitive sanctions in intellectual property. An in-between case is that of services, which was another sector where the developed world pushed for concessions. As the developing world opened its markets to services and foreign direct investment (FDI), the developed world applauded, even if the United States was unhappy with the positive list outcome of GATS. Subsequently, the developed world pushed for GATS+ agreements through PTAs but also excluded BRICs who resisted these moves. However, when India "came of age" as a services powerhouse, the sweet talk gave away to openly racist conversations in the West.

The theoretical stance in this book is that trade preferences have a cultural stickiness. There is no grand meta-theoretical finding in this book that unsettles optimal equations of revealed comparative or policy-induced competitive advantage. The book also does not argue against the importance of political economy in understanding domestic interests. The theoretical takeaway from the evidence is that trade preferences are not just about interests understood through political economy but also pushed in with cultural lenses, which in the North–South case has resulted in paternalistic behavior. Following Hiscox

(2002), we can show that the preferences in textiles were industry based because of lack of mobility in wage labor or that agriculture protectionism might speak to a class-based alliance among farm owners. However, this explanation misses the ties that bound the culture of farm protectionism in the United States in the 1945–1962 or the 1970–1994 era that Hiscox analyzes. Hiscox is also not concerned with the complete lack of empathy among the farmers or politicians for any kind of trade ideals (or broader global norms) about fairness or justice for the postcolonial world.

This theoretical stance about culturally defined preferences supports many burgeoning and older contentions in political economy. Economists now detail meta-preferences to account for the origins of wants (Hausman 2012; Cowen 1993; George 1984).[2] Moravcsik (1997: 513), in introducing this language of liberal preferences to the study of international relations, puts it simply: "Societal ideas, interests, and institutions influence state behavior." Since the time of David Hume and Adam Smith, political economists have spoken to the importance of moral sentiments and empathy in the formation of interests and preferences. These moral sentiments or empathy are important for the functioning of markets and society. In the nineteenth century these sentiments were translated into tastes and institutions and began to be held constant in the ceteris paribus conditions. Recent exhumations in economics and the weight of economic sociology has brought to fore the importance of understanding the origins and shifts in preferences, and the ways that they explain economic change and its limitations. This has entailed a return to ethics: "Choices in economics are often enmeshed in social relations, governed by ethical frameworks and expectations" (Wight 2015: 19).

There is a bias in a liberal theory of preferences. One of the critiques of international liberal approaches in economics and international relations has been that they are predicated toward noticing benevolent outcomes that move toward Pareto optimality or foster cooperation. Degree of reciprocity, this book's dependent variable, is situated in these received notions of benevolence. However, *Sweet Talk*'s explanatory factors or theory are situated in something else: Instead of assuming the benevolence of the butcher or the brewer, to make us all better off, this book also takes account of their cultural biases and blinders that make the world worse off. Akerlof and Kranton (2010) has moved toward this worldview in economics in showing how cultural identity influences biases in preferences. So have Mansfield and Mutz (2009) in international relations.

Hobson (2012: 15) calls the racist and paternalistic genealogy of the Eurocentric bias to be "the dark side of the discipline." The recently released World Development Report (World Bank 2015) summarizes this scholarship, taking a broader view of preferences than mere economic ones and moving beyond utility maximization and degrees of optimality.[3] As noted in Chapter 2, my cultural theory of preferences is also consistent with "sociotropic" preferences that Mansfield and Mutz outline.[4]

Paternalistic cultural preferences explain the distributive consequences and the challenges to the legitimacy of the international liberal regime. Puzzling about the sustenance of cooperation and order has produced important insights for the sustenance of international regimes but also raised important questions. The international regime for textiles and apparel was strongly protectionist but managed to exist within an international liberal regime (Aggarwal 1985). The "reparation" payments to Brazil after the judgments against the United States at the WTO were inadequate but exist within the broad contours of a trade regime that both Brazil and the United States accept (Rosendorff 2005). However, there are serious fissures in this regime, the most important being the Global North–South impasse at the Doha Round. Whether these deadlocks can be resolved will depend on the ability of a trade agreement to overcome the cultural baggage of casting the South in an inferior position. This book differs from Lake's (2009) top-down systemic thesis of hierarchies with authority-subordinate relations: Instead, I posit a bottom-up understanding of racism and paternalism that influences the workings of global liberal order. For the global liberal order to have legitimacy, a trade deal in the future will need to deliver on the aspirations of the developing world in the long run.[5] From the evidence presented in this book, the agreements in textiles and services, despite the China and India bashing, are broadly accepted in the developing world now but not the ones in agriculture and intellectual property. The pursuit of advantage through bilateral agreements in which developing countries are consistently made worse off is also "illegitimate" in the same sense.

The book has borrowed from insights from social constructivist literatures, but empirically it has stayed within liberal zones to test its propositions. Marovcsik (1997) notes that a liberal theory of international politics must be general, parsimonious, and predictive. However, the preferences of actors are always culturally situated, and, as recent advances in economics and elsewhere outlined above note, they need not result in optimal outcomes.

In other words, without their sociological origins, merely studying preferences is a sanitized activity.[6] Nevertheless, once we do account for the cultural embeddedness of preferences, a careful empirical strategy is necessary to account for not only the stickiness of preferences but also their erosion. One of the reasons this book moved toward quantitative and qualitative reasoning as part of its methodological strategy was to avoid the partiality of gathering evidence that points in only one direction. Paternalism or racism, its more evil twin, is too important a matter to be argued against with pieces of evidence gathered here and there. As an illustration, I argue against the scope of benevolent theories of paternalism, which have established their case with a considerable body of historical and experimental evidence. The multiple billions of humanitarian aid and the millions who support these endeavors seem to confirm this benevolence. Social constructivist theories circumscribe to some extent the scope of these endeavors in the historical ways in which such paternalism emerges and expands. Nevertheless, these analyses do not specify the conditions under which paternalism does not yield beneficial results for the paternalized or venture into areas beyond humanitarian and foreign aid efforts where the scope and consequences of paternalism may be more problematic.[7]

One must tread carefully when accounting for the scope and consequences of culturally situated preferences. This book has opted for mixed methods, including falsifiable hypotheses, to provide nuanced results. It parts company with Hobson's (2012) knee-jerk reaction against, versus Lake's (2009) chest thumping in favor of, hypothesis testing and empirical substantiation to highlight patterns of domination in global politics. Lake's book lacks social meanings, and Hobson provides no empirical evidence. We need to employ mixed methods, not because they exist but because they are suitable for particular purposes. Without empirical process tracing, for example, paternalism would be devoid of any social facts.[8]

Instead of merely arguing that global advocacy militates against an inimical paternalism, this book seeks to show what type of advocacy is most or least likely to do so. A point of entry, as Marxist scholars argue, is important for the puzzles generated and results obtained. This book's point of entry is the paternalized. This point of entry enables me to quantify the advocacy strategies from below for a better world. More important, it also helps me measure the opposition to this advocacy in the powerful psychological and cultural frames and the political clout that these oppositions wield in restricting reciprocity toward the developing world.

The results: The book finds very little evidence of humanitarian actors who are deeply empathic to the needs of the postcolonial world at the creation of GATT, and it does not find any deep pockets of humanitarianism that speak against the interest of their domestic actors, who would make worse off the cotton farmers in West Africa, sugarcane growers in Thailand, garment manufacturers in Bangladesh, or software workers in India. At the much-celebrated Seattle protest rallies and marches at the 1999 WTO ministerial, the AFL-CIO sought to marginalize workers' groups from the developing world in various ways, including asking these groups to march farther away from the AFL-CIO. For developing countries, even calls for workers' rights from the AFL-CIO, the U.S. President William Clinton, or the developed world arrived "reeking of protectionism" (Shah 2001).[9]

Counterarguments

The opening pages of this volume responded to a few specific counterarguments. The findings in this volume could also be reinterpreted as the consequence of three other causal perspectives: results of empire, irreconcilable domestic interests, or consequences of power politics. To some extent, each of these perspectives has value, but each falls short in fully explaining the outcomes. An examination of these perspectives also leads to some curious conceptual results, pointing to the willful drive among scholars to overlook paternalism and racism.

Radical scholars of empire and imperialism place class, either as ownership of means of production or unequal exchange, as central to their analysis of international trade. Marxian scholars dating back to Lenin and Hilferding predict that national capital with the assistance of the state (monopoly capital) produces the kinds of trade conflict about reciprocity examined in this book, but the root of these conflicts must be located in the capitalist mode of production (for overview, see Brewer 1990). World system and dependency scholars would predict these outcomes from the working of core–periphery exchange relations that overlay the means of production. Systemic unequal exchange connotes imperialism (Chase-Dunn 1998; Chase-Dunn and Hall 1997; Wallerstein 2004). Semiautonomous states can thus sever the exchange relations and allow production to benefit the periphery (Evans 1995). The problem with these analyses is that race and paternalism are secondary categories, understood as articles of faith, rather than empirical substantiation. Everything becomes an instrument for the management of the interests of the bourgeoisie—state, class, race, ideology, sexuality, and gender. Sidney Mintz (1985), whose analysis of the sugar trade was quoted earlier in this book, notes Marx's own silence on slavery and race in the nineteenth-century sugar plantations. More recently these silences have informed neo-Marxian analyses, dependency theory, and world system paradigms. The question of race is also beyond the grand analysis of empire offered in Hardt and Negri's (2000) description of empire in which the monarchy of nation-states and international organizations (the WTO in our case), along with the oligarchy of global corporations, perform their imperial tasks. An explanation that relegates race and paternalism—or more broadly, the everyday habits of culture—to an afterthought and the outcome of a single grand variable does not take it seriously in the first place.

I am aware that many people I have cited in this book who do explain race—Frantz, for example—also view race as a manifestation of capitalist exploitation. In fact, most analyses in world politics that attend to race are also critiques of the so-called neoliberal project. Chowdhry and Nair (2002: 1) begin their text on international relations of race, gender and class with the following second sentence in the book: "With the ascendance of a neo-liberal paradigm, one that shapes not only the field but also international and national politics and policy, we find an increasing dissimulation around questions concerning equity, poverty, and powerlessness." A thorough examination of this challenge is beyond the scope of this book, but the lining up of all ducks—race, class, gender, homophobia, and patriarchy—to the service of neoliberalism, which is always a little ill defined in these analyses, must be questioned. Nevertheless, one must be grateful to these analyses for caring about race, class, elitism, gender, homophobia, patriarchy, and many other forms of oppression—and the occasional insight that makes one stop and think.[10] Lily Ling (2004), for example, contributes an essay to the Chowdhry and Nair volume on the Asian financial crisis in which her characterization of the Western cultural chauvinism could stand for the paternalism described in this book: "I lead, you follow" (118–121).

Coming down a notch from the grand "variable" of class and empire, a scholar might argue that a political economy of international trade and rent seeking, discussed extensively in Chapters 1 and 2, can explain the lack of reciprocity toward the developing world. These explanations would predict results in favor of powerful domestic groups and politics backing Western agricultural, manufacturing, intellectual property, and service sectors. The empirical evidence in this book suggests that extant explanations need to explain the cultural stickiness of domestic preferences that underlie many of the outcomes that result from paternalism. At the microlevel, they cannot explain specific outcomes (for example, paternalistic preferential quotas for specific countries). They do not go deep enough to examine the origins of preferences beyond a quantitative political economy. My explanation is not, therefore, incompatible with one based in domestic political economy but accounts better for specific outcomes ranging from GSPs to backlash against outsourcing, or the cultural standoffs at the WTO, with a paternalism variable. Rubens Ricupero, the former Secretary-General of UNCTAD (1994–2004), described this standoff as "a legitimacy gap" before the beginning of the Doha Round (Ricupero 2001).

A version of the domestic rents argument can be that the developing world receives preferences from many developed countries, and these make up a sizable chunk of its exports. This argument is often made in trade policy circles in places such as Washington, DC; Brussels; and Geneva. However, an addition of all paternalistic quotas is not helpful unless we also count up everything else that the preferences bring: trade distortions, manipulations, sweet talk, exclusion from negotiation forums, and divide and rule among developing countries. Carnegie (2015) notes that powerful countries manipulate weak countries with instruments of diplomatic coercion such as foreign aid after making trade concessions, which lead to a hostage situation for the weak. I find that they also use these instruments instead of trade concessions to appease the weak.

Finally, one might ask if the lack of reciprocity and the presence of paternalism, as a causal factor, are not both outcomes of power politics in which, as Thucydides pointed out, the great do what they can and the weak suffer. Dealing with the world system as a unit, theories of structural realism predict the behavior of nation-states from their relative position in the hierarchy of power (Waltz 1979). The clearest enunciation of this for North–South relations remains Krasner's (1985) thesis on the structural conflict, where the developing world stands opposed to the international liberal order and tries to define the rules of international engagement in its favor. The policy prescription is that the developing world will not succeed in upsetting the international liberal order; therefore, it can be ignored. Such affinity with the amorality of power politics qualifies it for fairly extreme denunciations in the halls of academia. The

Table 7.2.   Effects of UNGA voting alignment with the United States on manufacturing and agricultural concessions received for poor countries.

	Effects of voting alignment with the United States	DV: Merchandise concessions received		DV: Agricultural concessions received	
		Coefficient/ standard error	Observations/ R-square	Coefficient/ standard error	Observations/ R-square
Poorer economies	For GDP PCI < 2,000	3.299377 (2.985725)	54/ 0.0229	−1.823628 (3.600862)	44/ 0.0061
	For GDP PCI < 5,000	0.6245644 (0.8746402)	78/ 0.0067	−0.6980398 (1.623626 −0.43)	65/ 0.0029
Richer economies	For GDP PCI > 2,000	0.778004** (0.3130273)	74/ 0.0790	3.858718*** 1.222154	60/ 0.1467
	For GDP PCI > 5,000	0.7588224* (0.4016951)	50/ 0.0692	(3.957169)*** 1.683145	39/ 0.13

complete disengagement with questions of oppressions and justice indeed do warrant such a denunciation. More important, like the theories of class and interests discussed earlier, these theories cannot explain the exact shape of rules and do not care particularly about the consequences of those rules. The fact remains that the weak do have strategies, especially in multilateral contexts, but that point is made quite forcefully in the entire social science scholarship.[11]

It is important to reiterate that, in the case of the developing world, it gets punished even when it goes along with liberal norms. The theories and conceptualization in this book do not offer any evidence for the claim that the developing world wanted to defect from the global liberal order. One of the central insights of creating the cultural "other" is our intellectual blindness to seeing our own image in the "other," especially if we believe the other to be inferior (Boulding 1961).[11] Therefore, one finding in this book is that the great powers cannot and will not see the "other" in their own image. Imagine the world of Thucydides, where Malenesians choose to play with Athenian rules but the latter still beat them up. Great powers can be dysfunctional bullies.

The evidence in this book does not support the claim that great powers will support allies from the developing world in international trade, in the form of trade reciprocity. Table 7.2 presents the results of the UNGA affinity index, in this case voting alignment with the United States. After parsing the data for countries with less than or more than US$2,000 as per capita income, and then with less than or more than US$5,000 as per capita income, the effects of the

UNGA affinity index are reported for concessions in agriculture and manufacturing. Only the coefficient and standard errors for the s3un index in binary regressions is reported here. The index also does not perform well in multiple regressions (not reported here) using variables from Chapters 4 and 5 when data are parsed for the developing or developed world: s3un predicts trade concession only for prosperous allies. In no case does voting alignment with the United States beget statistically significant reciprocal concessions for the least developed countries. However, this does not mean that the poor did not get paternalistic handouts and side payments. From the GSP to foreign aid, this book has documented the evidence. The content analysis documents the sweet talk.

A scholar might argue that the results found in this book could be predicted from notions of benevolent hegemony and empathic self-interest (Mearsheimer 1991; Keohane 1984). Bowen, Georgiadis, and Lambert (2016) develop a public goods explanation in which even the efficient hegemon's narrow self-interest is maximized if small countries join the agreement. The developing world fares better under multilateral rules and is provided benevolent preferential handouts for its obedience. To some extent this explanation is powerful, if one ignores the paternalism and racism that accompany these handouts and the extremely small size of the handouts. What emerges with a fuller explanation is a hegemony that is more sweet talk than benevolent in the way its theoretical supporters implied it.[12]

My exposé of major theoretical explanations has named an elephant in the room—paternalism—that most fashions of Northern global political economy analysis have ignored, in turn overlooking the exact shape and consequences of the global trade regime governing North–South relations. This raises questions of the short-run and long-run future of weak-strong interactions to which I now turn.

Moving Forward

I offer two scenarios for moving forward. In the short run, the developing world is better off tethering its fortunes to export diversification. Both the quantitative results and the case studies in this book predicate that economic diversification best explains a strategy to bolster the effectiveness of negotiation tactics and counter the effects of paternalism.[13] Studies also confirm that product diversification allows for best long-run growth and export advantages for the developing world (Newman et al. 2016). Coalition building is successful but

Table 7.3. Effects of export market diversification on agricultural concessions received for poor countries.

(a) regress agconreceived xmktcon if gdp_pci_con2005us<2000

Source	SS	df	MS			
Model	23.2422912	1	23.2422912	Number of obs	=	43
Residual	24.7886585	41	.604601427	F(1, 41)	=	38.44
				Prob > F	=	0.0000
				R-squared	=	0.4839
Total	48.0309498	42	1.14359404	Adj R-squared	=	0.4713
				Root MSE	=	.77756

agconrecei~d	Coef.	Std. Err.	t	P >|t|	[95% Conf. Interval]	
xmktcon	.3788576	.0611042	6.20	0.000	.2554552	.5022601
_cons	−.5859421	.2136651	−2.74	0.009	−1.017448	−.1544366

(b) regress agconreceived xmktcon if gdp_pci_con2005us>2000

Source	SS	df	MS			
Model	63.2303662	1	63.2303662	Number of obs	=	67
Residual	789.469562	65	12.1456856	F(1, 65)	=	5.21
				Prob > F	=	0.0258
				R-squared	=	0.0742
Total	852.699928	66	12.9196959	Adj R-squared	=	0.0599
				Root MSE	=	3.4851

agconrecei~d	Coef.	Std. Err.	t	P >|t|	[95% Conf. Interval]	
xmktcon	.1581719	.069323	2.28	0.026	.0197243	.2966196
_cons	1.833238	.6095834	3.01	0.004	.6158161	3.05066

not as unquestionably successful as economic diversification. A binary regression explains the logic in a simple manner. Table 7.3a shows that export market diversification is positively related to agricultural concessions received during the Uruguay Round for countries with a GDP per capita less than $2,000. Recall that in prior analysis we found that export market diversification had this positive correlation with concessions received, but Table 5.3, Models D through F, pointed this out for all countries in the sample. Its effects remain positive even for poor countries in the sample, those earning less than $2,000 per capita that may be termed least developed. Interestingly, the coefficient for export market diversification is weaker for countries earning more than $2,000 per capita (Table 7.3b) implying that the payoff for concessions received from export diversification for poor countries is greater than for those with higher incomes. This may be an instance of WTO fatigue that Bagwell and Staiger (2013) note that in rich WTO members may have much less to offer each other. For every one-point increase in the Export Market Concentration Index, poor countries receive over one-third of a percent more in agricultural concessions on average, whereas those with higher incomes receive only one-sixth of a percent in concessions from export diversification.[14]

In the long run, social meanings will evolve. Paternalism will continue to change. Berger and Luckmann (1967) note that socialization underlies the social construction of meaning, which leads to objectification. Economic sociologists point out that, although economists might understand the conditioning effect of social institutions, their economic agents are presented as undersocialized (Granovetter 1985). Therefore, change must be examined as the work of agents in embedded structures or networks (Giddens 1984; Kahler 1998, 2009). In other words, change can come through contestation and not only slow transformations of the structure.

This volume's index of paternalism operationalizes several economic, political, and cultural indices to measure the subliminality of paternalistic influences. As developing countries diversify their exports and their voting patterns at the United Nations, the paternalistic index will also change.[15] The long-run legitimacy of the international liberal order lies in reciprocity understood in fairness and justice terms. There is some fairness to any kind of a negotiated agreement (Albin 2001), but if the underlying cultural preferences are distorted, the legitimacy gets withered rather than supported. The MFA regime in the past, and the dispute settlement for cotton in the present, both legitimate and maintain the international liberal order. The questions are: For whom, for how long, and to what ends? Viewing the international liberal regime as liberal without attention to its distributional consequences undermines the notions of justice inherent in this regime. Empirical evidence shows that the durability of negotiated agreements lies in adhering to the embedded notions of justice in the agreements (Druckman and Albin 2011). Moving beyond classical political economy and current political philosophy, Sen (2009) notes that any notion of justice must be global and informed with public reasoning. Pointing out the injustice is the first step (Gotoh and Dumouchel 2009). I suggest that understanding the scope of transnational fairness and justice entails donning cultural-historical lenses, which specify the limits of global deliberations.

The vaunted humanitarian norms and cultures of empathy celebrated in constructivist scholarship have not quite arrived in the corridors of international trade. These norms can be forced through the slow drudgery of collective action and economic change or the enlightening transformational task of slowly changing collective consciousness.[16] The tasks are not mutually exclusive. Many scholars have demonstrated the power of ethical ideas in changing notions of slavery, human rights, and other forms of oppression at the global level over long periods of time. Finnemore and Sikkink (1998: 981) also note that norms are "a standard of behavior for actors with a given identity." There are no bad norms: Slavery was a norm, but justified with a moral claim about civilization. Similarly, it is a liberal norm to characterize the consequences of the global liberal regime in terms of its stability. Nevertheless, in thinking of the long run we are forced to return to the cultural contexts in which norms are embedded.[17]

Humanitarian norms and cultures of empathy are hard to locate in the anarchical world of strategic negotiations where tariffs and monies are up for horse trading. This is when it makes sense to "return" to the philosophical and cultural antecedents to reciprocity that undergirded the foundation of the international trade regime. Many of the people who founded these institutions were racist, but the principles they embedded in these institutions can have universal applications. A return to such universality will mean locating preferences in cultural contexts and framing outcomes and norms accordingly. For now the materialistic world of international trade remains the cultural and civilizational "other."

7-8-17

_jw_

Reference Matter

Appendix A

Node Classification Descriptions for the U.S. Tone/ Sentiment toward Trading Partners

Paternalistic

Moralistic, preachy, or patronizing statements toward the trade partner, often pointing out or providing benefit of nonreciprocal market access, or FDI from the United States. Offers of assistance and measures that are also beneficial to the United States but announced as if they help the other country only (including GSP, BITs). Most GSP press releases contain language of "help" to the developing world. Also includes patronizing and manipulative statements such as telling countries like China and India to be willing to bring their laws in tune with international rules.

Favorable

Praise for the trading partner (often after signing a treaty), lists benefits for the United States, withdrawal of trade sanctions with praise. Praises partner for U.S. trade restrictions such as VERs, OMAs, and MFA, and the like.

Unfavorable

Critiques foreign trade policies and positions, lists costs imposed on the United States, threatens sanctions, full of "asks" from trading partner, points out distortions in the trading partner's policy but omits that of the United States in the same issue, initiates investigations such as Section 301, points out something is lacking in the trade partner's policies or something that the United States is withholding (for example, MFN withheld to Romania in 1990), points out trade barriers in partner and is often critical of them.

Mixed

Mix of favorable and unfavorable nodal classifications. Also includes press releases that delay favorable or unfavorable assessments of the trading partner.

Does not include paternalistic statements.

Neutral

None of the other classifications. Neither praising nor critiquing trade partners.

Appendix B
Codebook and Data Sources

Reciprocity

Applies to all variables for merchandise and agriculture concessions received minus given, and merchandise and agriculture concessions received.

Variables calculate Percentage tariff reduction. Change is weighted as $dT/(1 + T_{avg})^*100$, where T is the average tariff change before and after the Uruguay Round.

EU12 data values for all countries are the same.

Czech and Slovak are given as combined in the original data set; here the same value is assigned to each, taken separately.

Percentage tariff reduction in agriculture incorporates tariff equivalent of NTBs.

Data taken from: Finger et al. (1996).

Trade Diversification Indicators
1990 or Earliest Year Available after 1990

xmktcon: "Index of Export Market Concentration: It is calculated as the number of countries to which the reporter exports a particular product divided by the number of countries that report importing the product that year."

Data available from WITS (2015) database: http://wits.worldbank.org/.

UNGA Voting Record

s3un merged from Erik Voeten's (2015) data set. Inserted 1.0 for United States. Missing values for Switzerland are calculated from the average of France, Germany, and Italy. The South Korea value was taken from 1993.

Data available from Voeten (2015): http://faculty.georgetown.edu/ev42/UNVoting.htm.

Cultural Distance
Variable Name: col_cultdist2.

Cultural distance is from a hypothetical colonial power. The average for all four categories was generated for Britain, France, Germany, the Netherlands, Portugal, Spain, and the United States. Then cultural distance was calculated for each country from this hypothetical colonial power.

Using four of Hofstede's dimensions (PDI, power distance; UAI, uncertainty avoidance; IDV, individualism; MAS, masculinity).

Individual values for each country are preferred in Hofstede's data over regional values (where provided) unless country values are missing.

The value for the European Union is calculated by averaging across EU12 EU in 1992 (Founders: Belgium, France, Germany, Italy, Luxembourg, Netherlands. Joined later: Denmark, Greece, Ireland, Portugal, Spain, UK).

Original data available from Hofstede (2010 and 2015): www.geerthofstede.nl/dimension-data-matrix.

Paternalism Indices
paternalism7: calculated from a factor analysis of s3un, xmktcon, and col_cultdist2.

Variable Name: colony_euro
1   if colonized by Western Europe or the United States. Excludes Japanese or Chinese colonies. Also excludes developed countries: Hong Kong, Singapore, Israel. Includes U.S. colonies.
0   if not colonized by Western Europe or the United States.

Data available from CEPII (2014) GeoDist database: www.cepii.fr/CEPII/en/bdd_modele/bdd.asp.

Coalitions
Taken from Narlikar (2003: 45–47) except for G77.

ASEAN	1 for member, 0 for nonmember
G10	1 for member, 0 for nonmember
Cafe au lait	1 for member, 0 for nonmember
Cairns Group	1 for member, 0 for nonmember

Polity2
Score scale of 21 from −10 (autocracy) to 10 (democracy) from Correlates of War Dataset (2015).

GATS and PTA

Data from World Trade Organization (2014), "Dataset of Services Commitments in Regional Trade Agreements (RTAs)." Available at: www.wto.org/english/tratop_e/serv_e/dataset_e/dataset_e.htm.

Detailed description in Roy (2011), "Services Commitments in Preferential Trade Agreements: An Expanded Dataset." Geneva: Economic Research and Statistics Division, World Trade Organization. Available at: www.wto.org/english/res_e/reser_e/ersd201118_e.pdf.

Notes

Chapter 1

1. The use of the term *Global South* follows the academic convention in referencing developing countries in the Southern Hemisphere. Unless otherwise mentioned, the terms *West* and *Global North*, used interchangeably, reference Western Europe, the United States, and Canada. This particular usage is peculiar to this book because of its subject of study—the postcolonial history of North–South trade.

2. The explanations provided here are consistent with Carnegie (2015), Lake (2009), Gowa and Mansfield (2004), Milner and Yoffie (1989), and Krasner (1985). Most, but not all, of them, fall within the purview of strategic trade theory, whereas the exceptions deal with use of trade policy to maximize other national interests.

3. Exemplars include Krugman 1987, Milner 1988, Amsden 1992, and a review in Bagwell and Staiger 2002.

4. Morocco signed a bilateral trade agreement with the United States in 2004, and trade negotiations are ongoing with the EU. Costa Rica was part of the Dominican Republic–Central America Free Trade Agreement (DR-CAFTA) with the United States ratified in 2005. Brunei is part of the TransPacific Partnership agreement signed in 2015.

5. David Lake (2009: 2–9, 58) narrates a different story about international hierarchies: In his hypothesis, the United States has clearly defined interests in the Caribbean to prevent communism. If Lake is correct, then Reagan protected the authoritarian elite rather than the farmers in the Dominican Republic to thwart communism, surely a costly action. It also does not meet Lake's own criteria of informal empire in the Caribbean and benign rule and the fact that the preferences were revoked three years after the invasion of Grenada to depose a popular leftist government. Throwing 350,000 farmers out of work is not a recipe for containing communism. Lake notes: "Rulers do not command their subordinates to undertake tasks the latter are unwilling to perform for fear of exciting challenges that may reveal the fragile nature of their legitimacy" (66).

6. This book agrees with Lake's (2009) postpositivist stance that reality can be observed, although our knowledge of it will always be imperfect (63n1).

7. The NTB figures are slightly higher for low- and middle-income countries taken together (not reported here) but much less than the OECD.

8. See, for example, Carothers and de Gramont (2013) and Milner and Tingley (2010). Carnegie (2015) shows that resource rich countries provide foreign aid *after* making trade concessions to make demands and meet strategic goals. Figure 1.1 provides a counterpoint.

9. Latent variable analysis, originating in psychology, is also known as factor analysis and measures the behavioral effect of latent influences. Statistically, it examines the principal components from the correlation matrix of several variables (see Bartholomew, Knoll, and Moustaki 2011). In this paper, I extract these "factors" from several international indices that might measure some latent paternalism.

10. Instead of taking a position on the qualitative–quantitative divide in social science (see King, Keohane, and Verba 1994 versus Brady and Collier 2004), this book borrows from their critiques of each other to create a mixed-methods strategy. The statistical variables make sense in the context of process tracing that its cases lend to these variables (see George and McKeown 1985 for process tracing). In situating trade theory in a cultural context, the book also traces a Popperian methodology (Popper 2002). Karl Popper notes that, as each stage of history informs the next, it is difficult to predict all future history with grand variables such as class struggles. Therefore he advises piecemeal and historically specific inferential analysis.

Chapter 2

1. Another possibility, concessions following distributive justice, which addresses past wrongs or outcomes, will be discussed later.

2. The idea that market exchange rests on underlying ethics can be traced back to Adam Smith and early moral political economy (Sen 1987).

3. A few least developed countries (LDCs) who grew up with preferential tariffs and access continue to support "paternalism," but it is arguable whether they do it because the alternatives are worse, because habits are hard to break, or because they could not compete in global markets without them. As subsequent chapters will show, the United States and the EU often quote this "dependence" to continue this system.

4. Preferential trade arrangements and preferential tariffs are different. The terms *preferential access* or *tariffs* usually refer to access for developing country products to the Global North at low tariffs but usually with quantitative restrictions. The term *preferential trade arrangements* refers to exclusive treaties among trade partners, and they may or may not include preferential schemes.

5. Playing by trade rules is benevolent if great powers could choose not to do so. However, this book finds later that great powers have not been benevolent.

6. I do not make a distinction between a positive (as is) versus a normative (ought to be) notion of ethics. From the early economics of Adam Smith to the present, what ought to be follows from what is (White 2011).

7. www.wto.org/english/docs_e/legal_e/gatt47_02_e.htm.

8. On the other hand, Bagwell and Staiger (2001) do accord that GATT Article XXVIII imposes balanced or "substantially equivalent tariff concession" if a government renegotiates a tariff.

9. According to Krasner (1983), international regimes are "principles, norms, rules and decision-making procedures around which actor expectation converge in a given issue area." Social reality, however, is often constructed. In the context of international negotiations, the convergence of expectations may arise out of preexisting collective understandings among actors.

10. There is another meaning of diffuse reciprocity, which implies that unilateral concessions or mutual benefits may be hard to measure (Albin 2001: 39). However, this definition does not a priori rule out strategic conduct or states' preference for an overall balance in concessions.

11. There are many studies on reciprocity in international relations (*International Negotiation* 1998; Goldstein and Freeman 1990), and also a tradition to examine reciprocity with international cooperation. Rhodes (1989) shows how reciprocity in trade relations can foster cooperation in the long run. She pays special attention to the retaliation clauses in GATT for nonconformance with reciprocity.

12. Sylvia Ostry (2001: 7) herself revised her "grand bargain" idea fairly quickly, admitting a "bum deal."

13. The Uruguay Round established guidelines for tariffs and also for converting or calculating nontariff rates in tariff terms. In interviews with Uruguay Round trade negotiators, Finger and Winters (2002: 55–56) note that diplomats did not carefully check reciprocity calculations at the Uruguay Round, allowing for "dirty tariffication," wherein actual tariffs exceeded what the guidelines established.

14. Given the WTO's most favored nation principle, the concessions a country makes to another country apply to all countries, with a few exceptions, such as in case of preferential access. With conditional MFN, all parties might be required to make a concession if they export a major share of the commodity. In services, a minimum commitment was required for countries to be signatories to the General Agreement on Trade in Services that emerged from the Uruguay Round.

15. In response, Bagwell and Staiger (2011) provide the first empirical test of their chiefly economic terms-of-trade theory, which predicts tariff cuts from the ratio of prenegotiation import volumes and world prices.

16. See Hurrell (2007) for a discussion of pluralist versus solidarist norms.

17. For this reason, the book avoids survey data and experiments documenting xenophobic societal preferences in trade because it is unclear how they translate into state-level trade policies. The interplay between preferences and culture tries to get beyond a somewhat unhelpful dichotomy between what came first: preferences (Moravcsik 1997) or social construction/culture (Wendt 1999). Following Hausman (2012), this book notes that the cultural origins of preferences are important and can point to distortions. Hausman specifically addresses the distortionary affects of paternalism and racism (80–81, 100). He concludes that satisfaction of preferences by itself may not be welfare maximizing, but their satisfaction can tell us how to, or how not to, maximize welfare.

18. James N. Rosenau (1990: chapter 2) refers to conceptual jails of international relations paradigms for not being able to understand the turbulence in world politics in

the 1980s, which witnessed phenomena such as the end of the Cold War, the rise of new collectivities and authorities, and new technologies. However, racism is not a new turbulence. Its neglect in scholarship is different. In general, Thomas Kuhn (2012) writes that science follows a sociology, in which "progress" is often within the epistemic boundaries of a paradigm. One could, therefore, argue that the liberal political economy paradigms and the technocrats trained within them had no place for racism. Instead of examining the anomaly of no trade concessions to the developing world, liberal political economy blamed the "victim" for not seeking liberal concessions (even though the developing world did). In doing so, liberal political economy neglected the blinding glasses these officials wore to the two centuries of preceding history (or the civil rights struggles outside the departments of economics in the 1950s and 1960s, at least in the United States).

19. Although Hobson (2012) understands paternalism to be subliminal, he rejects what he terms positivist methods for their study. Hobson (2013: 1078–1079) does move toward "inclusive holism" that combines econometrics with social analysis. I model paternalism using latent variable analysis, which originated in psychology and is well suited for studying subliminal influences. However, other techniques are also suitable. Hughey (2012) employs ethnographic techniques to study the subliminal biases among racist and antiracist groups. Williamson, Skocpol, and Coggin (2011) use mixed methods, including interviews and field research, to explain the rise of the Tea Party and racism in American politics after 2008.

20. Henderson's (2013) careful genealogy of this thought starts with the context within which Hobbesian anarchy, the state of nature, and the famous "warre of all against all" was understood and underscored. He cites Mill: "The literal state of nature is reserved for nonwhites; for whites the state of nature is hypothetical" (80). Crawford (1994) counters the European claims to show that the perpetual peace Kant imagined existed among the Iroquois nations before the European conquest. Hobson (2012) rejects Muthu's (2003) claim that Kant's writing on cultural tolerance and agency made him antiracist, to note that Kant's vision of cosmopolitan citizenship was itself Eurocentric.

21. One of the chief architects of the United Nations was Jan Smuts from South Africa, who wrote the organization's "stirring preamble" but was an "exponent of racial superiority" (Mazower 2009: 19).

22. Mansfield, Milner, and Rosendorff (2000) empirically demonstrate that pairs of democratic countries liberalize trade more than pairs involving an autocratic country.

23. Ignoring agency and resistance of the Global South can also smack of paternalism and can be traced back to William Du Bois's claim that "the Negro Question" in the American South had much to do with black revolt to the oppression of the plantation economy.

24. Kenneth Boulding's (1961) work on societal images, including the national image, rests on similar dynamics.

25. This is consistent with new work in preference formation. Hausman (2012), for example, argues that utility maximization does not take into account the origins of preferences that would show what it is that agents maximize.

26. Goldstein (1993) attributes this to the training of the technocrats who make trade policy.

27. There is also plentiful qualitative and quantitative evidence that charts the influence of cultural identity factors in electoral politics in general (Skocpol and Williamson 2012; Frank 2005). In general, most American electoral politics breaks down voter preferences along many cultural dimensions including ethnicity, region, and religion.

28. There are few studies of cultural identity and trade policy; thus the explicit shift here to referencing the United States rather than the North.

29. Barnett (2011, 2012) establishes a case for humanitarian assistance based on universal rather than ethnocentric values and one rooted in competence and results. He admits, though, that humanitarian organizations are always on a slippery slope: "Some humanitarian organizations slide faster than others, and some do not even realize the ground beneath them is uneven" (2011: 233).

30. Within Marxian scholarship, important works include Amin (1976), Arrighi (1994), and Emmanuel (1972). Within dependency theory, Frank (1966), Cardoso and Faletto (1979), Evans (1979). For world systems, see Wallerstein (2004) and Chase-Dunn (1998).

31. The next chapter examines this advocacy and the economists who influenced it.

32. In agriculture, the data used incorporate tariffs and the tariff equivalents of non-tariff barriers.

33. This is similar to the politics of "resentful paternalism" that Baker (2015) analyzes in the context of welfare and redistributive policies internal to developed states such as the United States with mixed ethnicities.

34. Bargaining power is a tautological concept. A priori it is hard to show what it means before the effect on the dependent variable (negotiation gains). Examining alternatives offers a way out of this tautology.

35. Krasner (1985) does acknowledge that developing countries might have some negotiation advantage with multinational firms as host countries.

36. A most likely case is also the theory-infirming case of the "if not here then nowhere" type (George and Bennett 2005).

37. This essay provides an overview of the coalition formation literature in trade negotiations.

38. Hampson (1995: 5) writes that "the hallmark of multilateral diplomacy is that it occurs between groups or coalitions."

Chapter 3

1. The twenty-three founding members were Australia, Belgium, Brazil, Burma, Canada, Ceylon, Chile, Republic of China, Cuba, Czechoslovakia, France, India, Lebanon, Luxembourg, Netherlands, New Zealand, Norway, Pakistan, Southern Rhodesia, Syria, South Africa, the United Kingdom, and the United States of America.

2. The Truman administration believed that Congress would not ratify the ITO Charter and thus GATT became the de facto trade organization.

3. Hull's memoirs are explicit in honoring self-determination of "dependent people" in the colonies and the support for this objective in the Atlantic Charter. Hull is also acutely aware of international conflict if self-determination is not granted and realizes, as in the case of India, that a promise of self-determination is necessary to enlist Indian support for the war. But he notes: "We could not alienate them [British] in the Orient and expect to work with them in Europe" (Hull 1948: 1599). Hull is also forthright in stating the loyalty that must follow. The last chapter, "What of the Future?," notes that the U.S. Constitution protects its minorities but then lumps them with communists and left-wingers to assert the following: "These interfering minorities are generally composed of or influenced by left-wing or reactionary extremists and also by persons who have immigrated in recent years and are chronic agitators and advocates of ideas calculated to undermine both our political and our economic structure" (Hull 1948: 1738).

4. Americans were not beyond preferences themselves and were given some for trade with Cuba and the Philippines. This leads Feis (1946: 665) to claim that "our transgression was small" and that the United States could make a claim against Britain "with the enamel of virtue."

5. The issue of trade dependence was clearly understood among the former colonies with respect to imperial preferences. When the European Economic Community (EEC) opened negotiations with its former colonies in Africa, Ghana's President Kwame Nkrumah did not mince his words. He called EEC and imperial preferences as obstacles to economic independence and merely cheap sources of raw materials. He called it "collective neo-colonialism" and "collective imperialism" that merely substituted direct for indirect rule (quoted in Zartman 1971: 21). Zartman notes that Nkrumah advanced the argument that "the Rome Treaty was to neocolonialism what the Berlin Treaty was to colonialism" (ibid.). Germany agreed with this position in opposition to France and Belgium, who advocated for preferences in the creation of the EEC.

6. Unless otherwise indicated, this paragraph summarizes various mentions of the advocacy for infant industry in Irwin et al (2008). The nuclear group included Australia, Belgium, Brazil, Canada, China, Cuba, Czechoslovakia, France, India, Luxembourg, the Netherlands, New Zealand, South Africa, and the United Kingdom. The meaning of *developing country* was different then, and Australia was considered to be developing.

7. Australian economists had long been involved in refining Ricardo's central insights about factor endowments and comparative advantage. In the 1920s, "the Australian case for protection" had relied on the distributional consequences of free trade for export industries that also faced diminishing returns. It was, however, unclear how protection would raise incomes for the diminishing returns factor (Irwin 1996: chapter 11).

8. Clayton wrote to the International Commerce Committee in New York to argue that even though the United States won in the Cuba Case, GATT's decision making showed that the United States did not apply direct power pressures.

9. Hudec (1987: 30–32) also notes that the developed world became pragmatic in granting Article XII and other waivers to developing countries. They received 116 of the 169 waivers from GATT given until November 1983.

10. Curzon (1965: 211n1) cites several studies.

11. Raúl Prebisch's ideas on infant industry borrowed from Keynesian thought and were critiqued by the left in Latin America. Nevertheless, in the McCarthy era, with its distrust of government intervention of any sort, both the CIA and the FBI investigated the ECLA (Helleiner 2014, 268).

12. Committee I was on multilateral tariff negotiations, and Committee II was on agricultural trade.

13. The group included Brazil, Burma, Cambodia, Chile, Cuba, Malaysia, Rhodesia and Nyasaland, Ghana, Greece, Indian, Indonesia, Pakistan, Peru, and Uruguay.

14. Hudec (1987: 30) points out that developing country requests based on Article XII on balance of payments difficulties did meet "pro forma" reviews as opposed to those for developed countries, whose difficulties were beginning to wane by the late 1950s.

15. Later, the Soviet Union began to provide its own system of preferences to the developing world. Although geopolitical interests obviously shaped the mirror image on both sides of the Iron Curtain, the original impetus for this policy came for the developing world's advocacy for market access.

16. UNCTAD now has several annual flagship reports. Since 1981, it has been published as the *Trade and Development Report* and since 1991 as the *World Investment Report*.

17. Australia was the first country to provide the GSP in 1967.

18. NIEO, however, parted company with the promarket advocacy in the GATT, and this had much to do with Raúl Prebisch and his more leftward post-Keynesian orientation.

19. For my notion of public reasoning and deliberation, please see Risse (2000) and Heller and Rao (2015)

20. Historically, "Colonies had been taught by their parent countries that economic benefit was maximized by controlling trade and suppressing competition from alternative suppliers" (Hudec 1986: 12).

21. The Coalition for GSP renewal in the United States—which came into being after the GSP expiration in July 2013—featured a host of trade associations and small and middle-sized manufacturers, who have been vocal about the losses to the U.S. economy because of the GSP. The coalition included thirty trade associations and 679 firms in 295 congressional districts and forty-six states. The measure to renew the GSP, H.R. 1295, passed favorably with a vote of 295 to 138 in the House. The coalition for GSP argued that the taxes they had to pay for imports after the GSP expired cost companies $2 million for each day the GSP was not renewed after July 2013. These taxes were reimbursed after renewal in July 2015.

Chapter 4

1. The usage here is a variation of Sylvia Ostry's (2008) description of the Round's outcome. She writes that the "grand bargain" of the Uruguay Round was that the textiles and agriculture agreements the developed world signed were a return for the developing world's acquiescence on the intellectual property, services, and investment agreements. The reciprocity of the grand bargain, therefore, was across issues, what Ostry calls the

"implicit deal" (287). This chapter questions this reciprocity. As Chapter 2 noted, Ostry did know that the outcome was a bum deal.

2. The Uruguay Round negotiations concluded on December 15, 1993, when the U.S. president's trade promotion authority expired. Therefore, the press releases from 1994 are not analyzed here, although the final agreement of the Uruguay Round, which created the WTO, was signed in April 1994.

3. These press releases were obtained from two successive Freedom of Information Act requests to the U.S. Trade Representative in Washington, DC, in 2013 and 2015.

4. An example provided in Chapter 2 is Amy Skonieczny's (2001) analysis of NAFTA, in which Mexico was portrayed as inferior in U.S. newspaper advertisements.

5. As a negotiation scholar, I have often conducted in-depth interviews of negotiators. In the case of paternalism, which is extremely value loaded, I did not think in-depth interviews could yield meaningful measures. The case of developing country negotiators being bullied and manipulated is already well documented, and developed country negotiators are unlikely to admit to paternalism even if they are aware of it. Nevertheless, my conceptualization of the issue reflects many conversations with trade diplomats in Geneva over successive years.

6. See Matz 1971 for GSP, Sell 1998 for intellectual property, and Drake and Nicolaides 1992 for services.

7. These data are aggregations of the country-level data. NVivo can also report on the number of press releases that mention an OECD or a non-OECD country. Although the two are related, the aggregation of country-level data was more appropriate in this case.

8. Goldstein and her colleagues are responding to Rose (2004), who notes that the WTO does not increase trade; one of his examples is GSP. See Chapter 3.

9. Section 301 of the U.S. Trade Act of 1974 authorizes the U.S. president to investigate practices that abrogate treaty obligations or are harmful toward the United States.

10. See Weber (1990) for a description of these methodological issues in content analysis.

11. The data include a few countries that acceded after the Uruguay Round.

12. The early 1990s were turbulent years, but 1990 allows for relatively stable alliance politics to be captured through the UNGA voting records before the fall of the Soviet Union in 1992.

13. Further information on each of these indices can be found at Hofstede et al. (2010) and the Hofstede Centre: http://geert-hofstede.com/national-culture.html.

14. Trade diversification indices have become increasingly sophisticated since the early days of the Herfindahl-Hirschman Market Concentration Index, which examined only the number of trade partners. See Newfarmer, Shaw, and Walkenhorst (2009) for an overview of these issues. Chapters 6 and 7 of that work explain the logic of using the export market concentration index employed here.

15. Several other negotiation variables that did not yield any meaningful results are not reported here. These included a dummy variable for the Latin America group and a proxy for country expertise measured through number of years of GATT membership.

However, G10 is reported because the statistical insignificance of this coalition in all the models is important in itself.

16. The UN affinity index is not used here due to multicollinearity (the reason for undertaking the factor analysis in the first place).

17. As noted earlier, it makes sense conceptually to include a European colony as a proxy for G77. The other reason is practical. Despite literature searches and several requests to G77 offices, I was not able to obtain a list of G77 members during the Uruguay Round.

18. This is the only place in the book that confirms the "grand bargain" thesis.

19. Hufbauer and Wong (2004), Wong (2004), Petras (2005), and Bown and McCulloch (2005).

20. Farm and textile lobbies in the United States often hold U.S. legislators hostage to frontloading import protectionism and subsidies as the price of approving trade promotion authority for the U.S. president. President Reagan renewed the MFA in 1981 before receiving trade promotion authority (TPA) for the planned new GATT round that was to begin in 1982.

21. "Take some more tea," the March Hare said to Alice, very earnestly.

"I've had nothing yet," Alice replied in an offended tone, "so I can't take more."

"You mean you can't take *less*," said the Hatter: "it's very easy to take *more* than nothing." (Lewis Carroll, *Alice in Wonderland*)

22. The Scott and Wilkinson (2011) reference to Bangladesh in Chapter 1 is, in fact, about Bangladesh's garment industry, which accounted for over 86 percent of the county's exports. An Oxfam report in 2004 warned that many developing countries such as Bangladesh and Sri Lanka, the latter with 54 percent of its merchandise exports in apparel and textiles, were dangerously exposed and ill prepared for the post-MFA era (Barber, Gowthaman, and Rose 2004). However, both Bangladesh and Sri Lanka have fared well in textile and apparel exports.

Chapter 5

1. Sugar rate quotas affixed quantitative restrictions on export of sugar to the United States in the GATT era. In the EC, sugar was first covered through imperial preferences and a variety of quantitative restriction arrangements thereafter.

2. Please see Chapter 4 for further explanation on the quantitative measures, operationalizations, and the models employed here.

3. In reality, the former colonizers were always quick to kick ex-colonies to the curb, especially in agriculture. The Common Agricultural Policy of the European Community is an example. The former colonizers included important members of the European Economic Community, which in the past wanted to preserve imperial preferences, but, as the CAP evolved, they wanted to preserve their own agricultural tariffs and subsidies (van Reisen 2007).

4. Significant exceptions include Iran and Thailand.

5. Other tests, not reported here, also show a negative and statistically significant relationship between being a European colony and concessions received.

6. ASEAN's negative sign is important but not significant. Therefore, to maximize the use of multiple variables, ASEAN was included in only two models.

7. The affinity index also does not stay robust for predicting agriculture concessions with multiple variables and is collinear with the export market concentration index.

8. See Singh and Gupta (2016) for the ways in which India has hedged it proliberalization and antiliberalization interests through its membership of various Doha Round coalitions.

9. In 2013, the CAP budget was less than 40 percent of the EU budget. The 1980 figures are for EU 10, while the 2013 figures are for EU 27. Figures retrieved from European Commission, Agriculture and Rural Development (2015).

10. Froese (2015) codes 259 regional trade agreements to discern which provisions are excluded in RTAs from dispute settlements, implying that these measures are to be found in the WTO agreements. The two topping the list are competition policy (forty-nine exclusions) and SPS (thirty-seven exclusions). The URAA, therefore, provided for fairly comprehensive measures for SPS in agriculture.

11. The original members of the Cairns Group were Argentina, Australia, Brazil, Canada, Chile, Colombia, Fiji, Hungry, Indonesia, Malaysia, New Zealand, the Philippines, Thailand, and Uruguay.

12. Brazil was also a member of the hard-line G10 coalition that opposed the developed world on inclusion of new issues, which delayed the launch of the new Round (see Chapter 4).

13. The Round was held up at the last minute in December 1993 when the French refused to concede to the U.S. push for liberalization of audiovisual (cultural goods) exports (Singh 2011).

14. LMG held on to unity within its ranks despite remarkable pressures from the developed world to break its unity. See Narlikar and Odell 2006.

15. G20 members in 2014 were (Cairns Group in *italics*, others underlined) *Argentina*, *Bolivia*, *Brazil*, *Chile*, China, Cuba, Ecuador, Egypt, *Guatemala*, *India*, *Indonesia*, Mexico, Nigeria, *Pakistan*, *Paraguay*, *Peru*, *the Philippines*, *South Africa*, Tanzania, *Thailand*, *Uruguay*, Venezuela, and Zimbabwe.

16. DR-CAFTA, for example, obtained minor concessions in sugar.

17. Sugar cultivation is generally traced back to New Guinea starting in 8000 BCE and sugar refining to India nearly 2,500 years ago. The word *sugar* comes from Sanskrit. Sugar cultivation was introduced in Spain in the eighth century through the Moors, who were remarkable for growing sugar without slavery, which was prohibited in the Koran. Columbus brought sugar to the New World in 1493 from the Canary Islands, and it began to be cultivated with slave labor, though most of the industrial refining operations were in the North. By the mid-sixteenth century, Santo Domingo plantations generally kept 150 to 200 slaves on an average size of 125 acres. For England, the chief source of sugar became Barbados after its capture in 1627. Sugar was initially a luxury, but after production multiplied

in the colonies, it became a staple food in Europe in the nineteenth century (Mintz 1985: chapter 2).

18. Between 1701 and 1809, there were 252,000 slaves shipped to Barbados and 662,400 to Jamaica (Mintz 1985: 53).

19. CBI was unsuccessful. One of its aims was to counter leftist movements. Instead of preferential trade and foreign aid, instruments that were initially promoted, the United States invaded Grenada in 1983 and Panama in 1989 and sent arms to counterinsurgency movements throughout the Caribbean, including Nicaragua.

20. Marlin-Bennett (2010: 81). Marlin-Bennett also places all agricultural trade preferences in broad worldviews and cultures (10).

21. This section is adapted from Singh 2014b.

22. See WTO (October 12, 2014).

23. This book has not examined the increase or decrease of paternalistic statements in agriculture toward China and India in the Doha Round period. It would be interesting to see if the U.S. stance has become more aggressive and less paternalistic as India and China become major import and export markets. The United States pushed for agricultural concessions in China before its accession to the WTO in 1999, and there is no doubt that, although the United States was paternalistic toward India during the Uruguay Round, this language did not carry over into U.S. agricultural negotiations with other countries such as Japan.

Chapter 6

1. Providing access to exporters in services entails making liberalization commitments for market access and national treatment (same treatment for foreign providers as for domestic ones) and regulatory restructuring. Therefore, the appropriate term for services liberalization is *commitment*, rather than tariff reduction.

2. This section and the next adapt some text from Singh (2008). The interviews referenced in these sections were carried out for the earlier book.

3. There is no comparable data for concessions given and received in intellectual property to test through multiple regressions. However, the depth of commitments to IP from the developing world is well accepted in scholarly and trade accounts.

4. Such "secrecy" is an important feature of IP negotiations, as subsequent analysis will show.

5. Generics come from base processes available in the public domain. Counterfeits are fakes, and infringe intellectual property provisions. However, IP advocates have often not distinguished between the two in making their case. For example, as late as 2009–2010, seventeen shipments of generic AIDS and hypertension drugs from India to Brazil were delayed at transit ports in France, Germany, and Netherlands on the grounds that the ships were carrying drugs that infringed patent protections (Freedman 2010). Not only were the ships carrying generics, but the seizures also infringed on free movement of goods protected in GATT Article V.

6. Interview cited in Singh (2008: 91).

7. A similar hypocrisy, featuring a discrepancy in valuing lives, was on display during the Ebola crisis in West Africa in the early part of 2015. After a couple of American aid workers contracted Ebola, the United States began administering a drug that was under trials at the FDA. However, until the Americans contracted Ebola, the U.S. government was quiet about this drug.

8. The United States had TRIPS+ IP agreements in bilateral treaties with the following countries: Australia, Bahrain, Cambodia, Central American countries, Chile, Colombia, the Dominican Republic, Jamaica, Korea, Laos, Latvia, Lithuania, Morocco, Nicaragua, Oman, Panama, Peru, Singapore, South Korea, Trinidad and Tobago, and Vietnam (Sell 2010: 452).

9. Parties to the agreement include Australia, Canada, the European Union, Japan, Mexico, Morocco, New Zealand, Singapore, South Korea, and the United States.

10. Data from World Bank (May 7, 2015b).

11. G9 was a subpart of the dirty dozen, which also included the United States, Japan, and the EC. Leaving the other three out of agenda setting would marginalize power politics and put the G9 in a neutral light.

12. Oxley (1990) and interview with Felipé Jaramillo, Bogota, June 2007.

13. Interview with Felipé Jaramillo, Bogota, June 2007.

14. In the final GATS agreement, these modes became: Mode 1, cross-border supply; Mode 2, consumption abroad; Mode 3, commercial presence; and Mode 4, presence of natural persons.

15. The proposals from the United States, Switzerland, New Zealand, and Korea proposed the name of the framework: the General Agreement on Trade in Services.

16. Trade officials in Belize portray its commitment differently: as a token commitment, a hard response to the United States to thwart pressures for services liberalization, and even a strategic move to attract neurosurgeons to Belize from Houston and other places to perform their medical operations in a low-cost country (Singh 2005).

17. All of the models in this chapter and elsewhere were also tested for multicollinearity using a variance inflation factor (VIF). Except for a couple of rare circumstances with a VIF of around 2.25, most variables used in this book have a VIF of less than 2.0.

18. When the G10 opposed the services agenda before 1986, it noted that the idea of services trade masked investment issues, which were not part of GATT. However, the idea of services trade is now broadly accepted.

19. See the full list at US Department of State (August 6, 2015).

20. GATS was signed with a built-in agenda, and thus multilateral negotiations could take place outside of a WTO round. Therefore, the telecommunication and financial services negotiations took place in the late 1990s, and GATS 2000 started before the Doha Round.

21. Basic services leave the content of the message, as sent originally by a user, unchanged during transmission. Valued-added services change the content or "add value" to enhance the information. A simple example is voice mail. Once sent, it can be enhanced through distribution channels.

22. In May 1990, telecommunications was one of the nine groups, narrowed down from an initial list of thirteen, within the Group of Negotiations of Services (GNS) chosen for sectoral negotiations. The sectoral working group was "probably the most active and arguably the most crucial of any of the sectoral working groups" (Woodrow 1991: 338). The impetus for a telecommunications agreement came from the United States and the UK, countries with the most significant liberalization underway in their domestic economies.

23. This paragraph cites statistics from WTO February 17, 1997.

24. Interview, April 28, 1999, in Washington, DC. Peter Cowhey was the chief of the International Communication Bureau of the FCC at that time.

25. *Strong domestic liberalization* is taken to mean private competition in voice (thus precluding cases that may have privatization but feature a monopoly operator) and other services and significant presence by foreign operators. *Reasonably strong liberalization* is taken to mean at least liberalization of markets in value-added and specialized services, with some foreign entry for operators and users allowed. In some cases, such as India, liberalization in voice telephony might also be underway. *Weak liberalization* is taken for those countries still waiting to introduce any significant competition in any market segment of telecommunications and waiting to pass major laws changing the role of their monopoly operators.

26. However, Oh and Banjo's (2012) argument is that the need for this paternalism comes from the desire to advance the global "neoliberal" project.

27. The resolution of the issue between the United States and the EU was more complicated, involving the United States signing a Safe Harbor agreement, which obliged the government to regulate firms that were not guarding privacy (see Newman 2008).

Chapter 7

1. This book has avoided survey data findings, although their results are mentioned in places. The claim in this book, on the cultural origins of preferences, in order to have general relevance needed to be situated in historical and more macro data sets than the survey or experimental data sets reveal at present. In doing so, the book has also veered toward the simplicity of ordinary least squares and historically situated case study methods, rather than sophisticated mathematical techniques or the obfuscation of cultural studies jargon.

2. I have worked on an analogous notion of meta-power to explain the meaning formation of issues and identities in political economy. See Singh 2013 and also Burns and Hall 2013. Barnett and Duvall (2005) write of productive power as explaining meanings but productive power is not antecedent in the cultural sense implicit in meta-preferences and meta-power.

3. The *World Development Report 2015* synthesizes many social and behavioral sciences literatures to ascertain the cultural and psychological origins of preferences and the way that they matter in development.

4. Such a bias for writing about happy outcomes goes beyond liberal theory. Many constructivist analyses puzzle in similar ways. Paternalism becomes benevolent in Barnett's (2011) thesis, slavery ends in Crawford (2002), and global oppressions subside in Keck and Sikkink (1998). Nonetheless, such puzzles and outcomes are important for the formulations in this book. I borrow from these analyses to explain the stickiness of an oppressive practice, racism to paternalism, which changes forms through time.

5. As this book heads to press, I'm aware of the xenophobic rhetoric of the left and the right in the United States toward international trade in the U.S. primaries for the presidential election. Republican presidential candidate Donald Trump wants to build walls to keep out everything foreign. Democrat Hilary Clinton backtracks on her earlier favorable impressions of international trade, while Bernie Sanders blames low wages abroad for America losing jobs.

6. This might account for the benign neglect of distributional consequences of regimes for societal actors. What good is the cooperative "order" of an international liberal regime in cotton, sugar, or textiles if it makes a billion people worse off in the developing world, even when the billion accept the broad ramifications of a global liberal order?

7. Therefore, instead of the binary choice of deciding between the merits of causal inference approaching quantitative (King et al. 1994) or qualitative (Brady and Collier 2004), I chose to take best of both worlds as my methodological norm for this book.

8. Hobson (2013) also suggests a similar approach to overcome the reified categories of U.S. international political economy that minimize critical evaluations of social facts and power. Methodologically, he advocates an "inclusive holism" wherein "econometerics should be deployed in addition, rather than as an alternative or substitute to social analysis" (pp. 1078–1079).

9. Shah (2001) cites from several sources, including the two quoted in this footnote, that generally belong to the progressive side of the ideological spectrum. According to economist Robin Hehnel, an opponent of globalization, "Such laws, as well as provisions about labor and environmental standards in WTO treaties given how the WTO operates, can become new vehicles for protectionism and imperial manipulation." "Attempts to enforce labour standards through trade sanctions are likely to cause economic harm to most exporting developing countries" (South Centre, UNCTAD).

10. I am also aware that, in focusing on race, I have overlooked many issues myself—gender and patriarchy being the most important.

11. From grassroots (Scott 1987) to the global level (Odell 2006).

12. Said's (1978) *Orientalism* is a central metaphor to this claim, but English literary scholarship from Mark Twain's *Adventures of Huckleberry Finn* to E. M. Forster's *A Passage to India* have been infused with these racialized assumptions for a much longer period of time.

13. An ideological explanation that brings in notions of do-good manifest destiny, conforming to American puritanical beliefs, also brings us closer to the explanation presented in this book, except that it removes the do-good blinders in favor of no-good paternalism and racism.

14. The case of Bangladesh, with 85 percent of its exports in clothing and apparel, may be more of an outlier.

15. These are merely indicative results. Tables 7.3a and 7.3b also show that, in both cases, the constant term is statistically significant. Poor countries start with negative concessions, whereas the ones with higher income start with a positive constant, meaning that poor countries on average start with a negative "balance" on concessions received whereas those with higher incomes start with a positive balance on average.

16. This volume has not examined these recent changes. The Hofstede cultural index may not be appropriate for cultural distances in the twenty-first century. However, there are many others.

17. Liberal scholarship often points out the influence of systemic factors on national human rights and pluralism (Simmons 2009). This book's claim is different: the extent to which cultural understandings from the grassroots influence the system.

18. Recently, Keohane (2015) has written that symbolic dispositions are important to understand democratic global governance.

References

Aaronson, Susan A. 1996. *Trade and the American Dream: A Social History of Postwar Trade Policy*. Lexington: University Press of Kentucky.

Acemoglu, Daron, and James Robinson. 2012. *Why Nations Fail: The Origins of Power, Prosperity, and Poverty*. New York: Crown Business.

Acemoglu, Daron, and James A. Robinson. 2005. *Economic Origins of Dictatorship and Democracy*. Cambridge, UK: Cambridge University Press.

Aggarwal, Vinod K. 1985. *Liberal Protectionism: The International Politics of Organized Textile Trade*. Berkeley: University of California Press.

———, ed. 1998. *Institutional Design for a Complex World: Bargaining, Linkages, and Nesting*. Ithaca, NY: Cornell University Press.

Ahmed, Syud Amer, Thomas W. Hertel, and Terrie L. Walmsley. 2011. "Outsourcing and the US labour market." *The World Economy* 34(2): 192–222.

Akerlof, George A., and Rachel E. Kranton. 2010. *Identity Economics: How Our Identities Shape Our Work, Wages, and Well-Being*. Princeton, NJ: Princeton University Press.

Albin, Cecilia. 2001. *Justice and Fairness in International Negotiation*. Cambridge, UK: Cambridge University Press.

———. 2015. "The Many Faces of Justice in International Negotiations." *International Negotiation* 20(1): 41–58.

Amin, Samir. 1976. *Unequal Development*. New York: Monthly Review Press.

Amsden, Alice Hoffenberg. 1992. *Asia's Next Giant: South Korea and Late Industrialization*. New York: Oxford University Press.

Anderson, Kym, and Will Martin, eds. 2006. *Agricultural Trade Reform & the Doha Development Agenda*. Washington, DC: The World Bank.

Anderson, Robert D. 2013. "Comment." In Robert C. Feenstra and Alan M. Taylor, eds., *Globalization in an Age of Crisis: Multilateral Economic Cooperation in the Twenty-First Century*, 124–130. Chicago: University of Chicago Press.

Anievas, Alexander, Nivi Manchanda, and Robbie Shilliam. Editors. 2015. *Race and Racism in International Relations: Confronting the Global Colour Line*. London: Routledge.

Armstrong, Chris. 2012. *Global Distributive Justice: An Introduction*. Cambridge, UK: Cambridge University Press.

Arrighi, Giovanni. 1994. *The Long Twentieth Century: Money, Power, and the Origins of Our Times*. London: Verso.

Asuyama, Yoko, Dalin Chhun, Takahiro Fukunishi, Seiha Neou, and Tatsufumi Yamagata. 2013. "Firm Dynamics in the Cambodian Garment Industry: Firm Turnover, Productivity Growth and Wage Profile under Trade Liberalization." *Journal of the Asia Pacific Economy* 18(1): 51–70.

Axelrod, Robert. 1985. *The Evolution of Cooperation*. New York: Basic Books.

Bagwell, Kyle, and Robert W. Staiger. June 1998. *An Economic Theory of GATT*. No. w6049. National Bureau of Economic Research.

———. 2001. "Reciprocity, Non-Discrimination and Preferential Agreements in the Multilateral Trading System." *European Journal of Political Economy* 17(2): 281–325.

———. 2002. *The Economics of the World Trading System*. Cambridge, MA: MIT Press.

———. June 2011. "What Do Trade Negotiators Negotiate About? Empirical Evidence from the World Trade Organization." *The American Economic Review* 101: 1238–1273.

———. 2013. "Can the Doha Round Be a Development Round? Setting a Place at the Table." In Robert C. Feenstra and Alan M. Taylor, eds., *Globalization in an Age of Crisis: Multilateral Economic Cooperation in the Twenty-First Century*, 91–124. Chicago: University of Chicago Press.

Baker, Andy. 2015. "Race, Paternalism, and Foreign Aid: Evidence from US Public Opinion." *American Political Science Review* 109(1): 93–109.

Balassa, Bela. 1965. "Tariff Protection in Industrial Countries: An Evaluation." *The Journal of Political Economy*: 573–594.

Banton, Michael. 2002. *The International Politics of Race*. Cambridge, UK: Polity Press.

Barber, Catherine, Balachandaran Gowthaman, and Jonathan Rose. 2004. "Stitched Up: How Rich Country Protectionism in Textiles and Clothing Trade Prevents Poverty Alleviation." Oxfam Briefing Paper No. 60. Oxford, UK: Oxfam International.

Barkan, Elazar. 1992. *The Retreat of Scientific Racism: Changing Concepts of Race in Britain and the United States between the World Wars*. Cambridge, UK: Cambridge University Press.

Barnett, Michael N. 2011. *Empire of Humanity: A History of Humanitarianism*. Ithaca, NY: Cornell University Press.

———. 2012. "International Paternalism and Humanitarian Governance." *Global Constitutionalism* 1(3): 485–521.

Barnett, Michael, and Raymond Duvall. 2005. "Power in International Politics." *International Organization* 59(1): 39–75.

Bartholomew, David J., Martin Knott, and Irini Moustaki. 2011. *Latent Variable Models and Factor Analysis: A Unified Approach*. Chichester, West Sussex, UK: John Wiley & Sons.

Basevi, Giorgio. 1966. "The United States Tariff Structure: Estimates of Effective Rates of Protection of United States Industries of United States Industries and Industrial Labor." *The Review of Economics and Statistics*: 147–160.

Bauer, Peter T., and J. B. Wood. 1961. "Foreign Aid: The Soft Option." *PSL Quarterly Review* 14(59).

Bayard, Thomas O., and Kimberly Ann Elliott. 1994. *Reciprocity and Retaliation in U.S. Trade Policy*. Washington, DC: Institute for International Economics.

Beitz, Charles R. 1979. *Political Theory and International Relations*. Princeton, NJ: Princeton University Press.

Bell, Duncan. 2013. "Race and International Relations: Introduction." *Cambridge Review of International Affairs* 26(1): 1–4.

Berger, Peter L., and Thomas Luckmann. 1967. *The Social Construction of Reality: Treatise on the Sociology of Knowledge*. Garden City, NY: Anchor Books.

Berridge, G. R., and Alan James. 2003. *A Dictionary of Diplomacy*. Basingstoke, UK: Palgrave Macmillan.

Bhagwati, Jagdish. 2002. *Going Alone: The Case for Relaxed Reciprocity in Freeing Trade*. Cambridge, MA: MIT Press.

Blinder, Alan S. 2006. "Offshoring: The Next Industrial Revolution?" *Foreign Affairs* 85(2): 113.

Bloomberg View. March 13, 2013. "Editorial: That Sickening Sugar Subsidy." Available at www.bloombergview.com/articles/2013-03-13/that-sickening-sugar-subsidy.

Bockman, Johanna. 2015. "Socialist Globalization against Capitalist Neocolonialism: The Economic Ideas behind the New International Economic Order." *Humanity: An International Journal of Human Rights, Humanitarianism, and Development* 6(1): 109–128.

Boulding, Kenneth Ewart. 1961. *The Image: Knowledge in Life and Society*. Ann Arbor: University of Michigan Press.

Bowen, Renee T., George Georgiadis, and Nicolas S. Lambert. February 2016. "Collective Choice in Dynamic Public Good Provision: Real versus Formal Authority." Stanford University School of Business, Unpublished Paper.

Bown, Chad P., and Rachel McCulloch. 2005. "US Trade Policy toward China: Discrimination and Its Implications." Available at SSRN 757124.

Brady, Henry E., and David Collier, eds. 2004. *Rethinking Social Inquiry: Diverse Tools, Shared Standards*. Lanham, MD: Rowman & Littlefield Publishers.

Brander, James A., and Barbara J. Spencer. 1985. "Export Subsidies and International Market Share Rivalry." *Journal of international Economics* 18(1): 83–100.

Brennan, Fernné. 2006. "Time for a Change: Reforming WTO Trading Rules to Take Account of Reparations." In Janet Dine and Fagan Andrew, eds., *Human Rights and Capitalism: A Multidisciplinary Perspective on Globalisation*, 254–283. Cheltenham, UK: Edward Elgar.

Brewer, Anthony. 1990. *Marxist Theories of Imperialism: A Critical Survey*. London: Routledge.

Bridges. July 24, 2014. "WTO's Least Developed Countries Submit Collective Request on Services Waiver." Geneva: International Centre for Trade and Sustainable Development.

Burns, Tom R., and Peter Hall, eds. 2013. *The Meta-Power Paradigm: Impacts and Transformations of Agents, Institutions, and Social Systems*. New York: Peter Lang Publishers.

Busch, Marc L. 1999. *Trade Warriors: States, Firms, and Strategic-Trade Policy in High-Technology Competition*. Cambridge, UK: Cambridge University Press.

———. 2007. "Overlapping Institutions, Forum Shopping, and Dispute Settlement in International Trade." *International Organization* 61(4): 735–761.

Callieres, Francois de. 1716/1963. *On the Manner of Negotiating with Princes; On the Uses of Diplomacy; The Choice of Ministers and Envoys; And the Personal Qualities Necessary for Success in Missions Abroad*. Notre Dame, IN: University of Notre Dame Press.

Cardoso, Fernando Henrique, and Enzo Faletto. 1979. *Dependency and Development in Latin America*. Berkeley: University of California Press.

Carnegie, Allison. 2015. *Power Plays: How International Institutions Reshape Coercive Diplomacy*. Cambridge, UK: Cambridge University Press.

Carothers, Thomas, and Diane De Gramont. 2013. *Development Aid Confronts Politics: The Almost Revolution*. Washington DC: Carnegie Endowment for International Peace.

Carr, E. H. 1964. *The Twenty Years' Crisis, 1919–1939: An Introduction to the Study of International Relations*. New York: Harper & Row.

CEPII. The GeoDist Database. Retrieved on June 6, 2014, from www.cepii.fr/CEPII/en/bdd_modele/bdd.asp.

Césaire, Aimé. 2001. *Discourse on Colonialism*. New York: New York University Press.

Chase-Dunn, Christopher K. 1998 *Global Formation: Structures of the World-Economy*. Lanham, MD: Rowman & Littlefield.

Chase-Dunn, Christopher, and Thomas D. Hall. 1997. *Rise and Demise: Comparing World-Systems*. Boulder, CO: Westview.

Chin, Christine B. 2008. *Cruising in the Global Economy: Profits, Pleasure and Work at Sea*. London: Ashgate Publishing.

Chowdhry, Geeta, and Sheila Nair. 2002. *Power, Postcolonialism and International Relations: Reading Race, Gender and Class*. London: Routledge.

Clapp, Jennifer. 2006. "WTO Agriculture Negotiations: Implications for the Global South." *Third World Quarterly* 27(4): 563–577.

———. 2007. "WTO Agriculture Negotiations and the Global South." In Donna Lee and Rorden Wilkinson, eds., *The WTO after Hong Kong: Progress in, and Prospects for, the Doha Development Agenda*. London: Routledge.

Claude, Inis L. 1956. *Swords into Plowshares: The Problems and Progress of International Organization*. London: University of London.

Conybeare, John A. C. 1985. "Trade Wars: A Comparative Study of Anglo-Hanse, Franco-Italian, and Hawley-Smoot Conflicts." *World Politics* 38: 146–172.

Correlates of War Project. Retrieved August 6, 2015, from www.correlatesofwar.org/data-sets.

Coskeran, Helen, Dan Kim, and Amrita Narlikar. 2012. "Trade in Manufactures and Agricultural Products: The Dangerous Link?" In *The Oxford Handbook on The World Trade Organization*. Oxford, UK: Oxford University Press.

Cowen, Tyler. 1993. "The Scope and Limits of Preference Sovereignty." *Economics and Philosophy* 9(2): 253–269.

Crawford, Neta C. 1994. "A Security Regime among Democracies: Cooperation among Iroquois Nations." *International Organization* 48(3): 345–385.

———. 2002. *Argument and Change in World Politics: Ethics, Decolonization, and Humanitarian Intervention*, vol. 81. Cambridge, UK: Cambridge University Press.

Croome, John. 1999. *Reshaping the World Trading System: A History of the Uruguay Round*. The Hague: Kluwer Law International.

Curzon, Gerard. 1965. *Multilateral Commercial Diplomacy: The General Agreement on Tariffs and Trade and Its Impact on National Commercial Policies and Techniques*. New York: Frederick A. Praeger.

Davis, Christina L. 2003. *Food Fights over Trade: How International Institutions Promote Agricultural Trade Liberalization*. Princeton, NJ: Princeton University Press.

———. 2004. "International Institutions and Issue Linkage: Building Support for Agricultural Trade Liberalization." *American Political Science Review* 98(1): 153–169.

———. 2012. *Why Adjudicate? Enforcing Trade Rules in the WTO*. Princeton, NJ: Princeton University Press.

Davis, Christina L., and Sarah Blodgett Bermeo. 2009. "Who Files? Developing Country Participation in GATT/WTO Adjudication." *The Journal of Politics* 71(3): 1033–1049.

Desmond, Matthew, and Mustafa Emirbayer. 2009. "What Is Racial Domination?" *Du Bois Review: Social Science Research on Race* 6(2): 335–355.

Destler, Irving M. 1992. *American Trade Politics*, 2nd ed. Washington, DC: Institute for International Economics.

dos Santos, Norma Breda, Rogerio Farias, and Raphael Cunha. 2005. "Generalized System of Preferences in General Agreement on Tariffs and Trade/World Trade Organization: History and Current Issues." *Journal of World Trade* 39(4): 637–670.

Doty, Roxanne Lynn. 1993. "The Bounds of 'Race' in International Relations." *Millennium-Journal of International Studies* 22(3): 443–461.

Drahos, Peter. 1995. "Global Property Rights in Information: The Story of TRIPS at the GATT." *Prometheus* 13(1): 6–19.

———. 2001. "BITs and BIPs." *The Journal of World Intellectual Property* 4(6): 791–808.

Drake, William J., and Kalypso Nicolaides. 1992. "Ideas, Interests, and Institutionalization: 'Trade in Services' and the Uruguay Round." *International Organization* 46(1): 37–100.

Drezner, Daniel W. 2007. *All Politics is Global: Explaining International Regulatory Regimes*. Princeton, NJ: Princeton University Press.

———. 2004. "The Outsourcing Bogeyman." *Foreign Affairs* 83(3): 22–34.

Druckman, Daniel, and Cecilia Albin. 2011. "Distributive Justice and the Durability of Peace Agreements." *Review of International Studies* 37(3): 1137–1168.

Eckstein, Harry. 1975. "Case Study and Theory in Political Science." In Fred I. Greenstein and Nelson W. Polsby, eds., *Handbook of Political Science*, vol. 7. Reading, MA: Addison-Wesley.

Economic Times. May 20, 2014. "US Leads the World in Use of Compulsory Licenses: KEI." Retrieved on January 15, 2015, from http://articles.economictimes.indiatimes.com/2014-03-0/news/48402255_1_patent-protection-trips-agreement-countries.

The Economist. September 23, 1999. "White Man's Shame." Retrieved on June 10, 2014, from www.economist.com/node/325062.

Elster, Jon. 1989. *Nuts and Bolts for the Social Sciences*. Cambridge, UK: Cambridge University Press.

Elumenthal, W. Michael. 1970. "A World of Preferences." *Foreign Affairs* 48(3): 549–554.

Emmanuel, Arghiri. 1972. *Unequal Exchange: A Study of the Imperialism of Trade*. New York: Monthly Review Press, 1972.

Erb, Guy. 1974. "The Developing Countries in the Tokyo Round." In James W. Howe, ed., *The U.S. and the Developing World: Agenda for Action 1974*. New York: Praeger.

Escobar, Arturo. 1995. *Encountering Development: The Making and Unmaking of the Third World*. Princeton, NJ: Princeton University Press.

European Commission, Agriculture and Rural Development. "The Common Agriculture Policy After 2013." Retrieved on July 12, 2015, from http://ec.europa.eu/agriculture/cap-post-2013/graphs/index_en.htm.

Evans, John W. 1971. *The Kennedy Round in American Trade Policy: The Twilight of the GATT?* Cambridge, MA: Harvard University Press.

Evans, Peter B. 1979. *Dependent Development: The Alliance of Multinational, State, and Local Capital in Brazil*. Princeton, NJ: Princeton University Press, 1979.

———. 1995. *Embedded Autonomy: States and Industrial Transformation*, vol. 25. Princeton, NJ: Princeton University Press.

Fanon, Frantz. 2008/1952. *Black Skin, White Masks*. New York: Grove Press.

Feis, Herbert. 1946. "The Future of British Imperial Preferences." *Foreign Affairs* 24(4): 661–674.

Ferguson, James. 1990. *The Anti-Politics Machine: "Development," Depoliticization and Bureaucratic Power in Lesotho*. Cambridge, UK: Cambridge University Press.

Finger, J. Michael. 2001. "Implementing the Uruguay Round Agreements: Problems for Developing Countries." *The World Economy* 24(9): 1097–1108.

———. 2002. "Safeguards." In Bernard M. Hoekman, Aaditya Mattoo, and Philip English, eds., *Development, Trade, and the WTO: A Handbook*, 195–205. Washington, DC: World Bank Publications.

———. 2008. "The Uruguay Round North–South Bargain: Will the WTO Get Over It?" In Daniel L. M. Kennedy and James D. Southwick, eds., *The Political Economy of International Trade Law: Essays in Honor of Robert E. Hudec*, 301–305. Cambridge, UK: Cambridge University Press.

———. 2012. "Flexibilities, Rules, and Trade Remedies in the GATT/WTO System." In Amrita Narlikar, Martin Daunton, and Robert M. Stern, eds., *The Oxford Handbook on The World Trade Organization*, 418–440. Oxford, UK: Oxford University Press.

Finger, J. Michael, Merlinda D. Ingco, and Ulrich Reincke. 1996. *The Uruguay Round: Statistics on Tariff Concessions Given and Received*. Washington, DC: World Bank Publications.

Finger, J. Michael, Ulrich Reincke, and Adriana Castro. 1999. *Market Access Bargaining in the Uruguay Round: Rigid or Relaxed Reciprocity?* Washington, DC: World Bank Publications.

Finger, Michael J., and Ludger Schuknecht. 2001. "Market Access Advances and Retreats: The Uruguay Round and Beyond." In Bernard Hoekman and Will Martin, eds., *Developing Countries and the WTO: A Pro-Active Agenda*. Oxford, UK: Basil Blackwell.

Finger, J. Michael, and L. Alan Winters. 2002. "Reciprocity." In Bernard Hoekman, Aaditya Mattoo, and Philip English, eds., *Development, Trade, and The WTO: A Handbook*, 50–60. Washington, DC: The World Bank.

Finn, Daniel K. 2006. *The Moral Ecology of Markets; Assessing Claims about Markets and Justice*. Cambridge, UK: Cambridge University Press.

Finnemore, Martha, and Kathryn Sikkink. 1998. "International Norm Dynamics and Political Change." *International Organization* 52(4): 887–917.

Finnemore, Martha. 1996. "Constructing Norms of Humanitarian Intervention." In Peter J. Katzenstein, ed., *The Culture of National Security: Norms and Identity in World Politics*. Ithaca, NY: Cornell University Press.

Ford, Jane. 2003. *A Social Theory of the WTO: Trading Cultures*. Basingstoke, UK: Palgrave Macmillan.

Forrer, John, Diana Tussie, Marisa Díaz Henderson, Patrick Funiciello, and Kristen Jancuk. June 2005. "The U.S. Sugar Industry and Free Trade Agreements." Unpublished manuscript.

Frank, Andre Gunder. 1966. *The Development of Underdevelopment*. Boston: New England Free Press.

Frank, Thomas. 2005. *What's the Matter with Kansas: How Conservatives Won the Heart of America*. New York: Henry Holt.

Freedman, Jennifer M. May 12, 2010. "India, Brazil Complain at WTO Over EU Drug Seizures." *Bloomberg Business*. Available at: www.bloomberg.com/news/articles/2010-05-12/india-brazil-complain-at-wto-over-generic-drug-seizures-by-european-union.

Freire, Paulo. 1985. *The Politics of Education: Culture, Power, and Liberation*. South Hadley, MA: Bergin & Garvey.

Friend, Theodore. 1963. "The Philippine Sugar Industry and the Politics of Independence, 1929–1935." *The Journal of Asian Studies* 22(2): 179–192.

Froese, Marc B. February 2015. "Mapping the Scope of Dispute Settlement in Regional Trade Agreements: Implications for 21st Century Multilateralism." Paper presented at the International Studies Association Annual Convention, New Orleans.

Froman, Michael. 2014. *Special 301 Report*. Washington, DC: Office of the US Trade Representative.

Fukunishi, Takahiro, and Tatsufumi Yamagata. 2013. "Employment and Wages in Export-Oriented Garment Industry: Recent Trends in Low-Income Countries under Trade Liberalization." Tokyo: Institute of Developing Economies, Japan External Trade Organization (IDE-JETRO).

Galeano, Eduardo. 1997. *Open Veins of Latin America: Five Centuries of the Pillage of a Continent*. New York: New York University Press.

Gallagher, Peter. 2000. *Guide to the WTO and Developing Countries*. Geneva, Switzerland: World Trade Organization and Kluwer Law International.

Gartzke, Erik, and Dominic Rohner. 2011. "The Political Economy of Imperialism, Decolonization and Development." *British Journal of Political Science* 41(3): 525–556.

General Agreement on Tariffs and Trade (GATT). 1947. Article XVIII–XXXVIII. Retrieted on January 5, 2016, from www.wto.org/english/docs_e/legal_e/gatt47_02_e.htm.

General Agreement on Tariffs and Trade (GATT). October 1958. *Trends in International Trade: Report by a Panel of Experts.* Geneva:Author.

———. September 14, 1973. *Ministerial Meeting, Tokyo 12–14 September 1973: Declaration.* Press Release. Geneva. GATT/1134.

George, Alexander L., and Andrew Bennett. 2005. *Case Studies and Theory Development in the Social Sciences.* Cambridge, MA: MIT Press.

George, Alexander L., and Timothy J. McKeown. 1985. "Case Studies and Theories of Organizational Decision Making." In Robert F. Coulam and Richard A Smith, eds., *Advances in Information Processing in Organizations* 2, pp. 21–58. Greenwich, CT: JAI Press.

George, David. 1984. "Meta-Preferences: Contemporary Notions of Free Choice." *International Journal of Social Economics* 11(3–4): 92–107.

Giddens, Anthony. 1984. *The Constitution of Society: Outline of the Theory of Structuration.* Berkeley: University of California Press.

Goff, Patricia M. 2007. *Limits to Liberalization: Local Culture in a Global Marketplace.* Ithaca, NY: Cornell University Press.

Goldstein, Joshua S., and John R. Freeman. 1990. *Three-Way Street: Strategic Reciprocity in World Politics.* Chicago: University of Chicago Press.

Goldstein, Judith. 1993 *Ideas and Foreign Policy: Beliefs, Institutions, and Political Change.* Ithaca, NY: Cornell University Press.

Goldstein, Judith L., Douglas Rivers, and Michael Tomz. 2007. "Institutions in International Relations: Understanding the Effects of the GATT and the WTO on World Trade." *International Organization* 61(1): 37–67.

Gorlin, Jacques. 1985. "A Trade-Based Approach for the International Copyright Protection for Computer Software." Unpublished Paper for IBM.

Goswami, Arti Grover, Poonam Gupta, and Aaditya Mattoo. 2011. "A Cross-Country Analysis of Service Exports: Lessons from India." In Arti Grover Goswami, Aaditya Mattoo, and Sebastián Sáez, eds., *Exporting Services: A Developing Country Perspective,* 81–119. Washington, DC: World Bank Publications.

Gotoh, Reiko, and Paul Dumouchel. eds. 2009. *Against Injustice: The New Economics of Amartya Sen.* Cambridge, UK: Cambridge University Press.

Gourevitch, Peter. 1986. *Politics in Hard Times: Comparative Responses to International Economic Crises.* Ithaca, NY: Cornell University Press.

Gowa, Joanne, and Edward D. Mansfield. 1993. "Power Politics and International Trade." *American Political Science Review* 87(2): 408–420.

———. 2004. "Alliances, Imperfect Markets, and Major-Power Trade." *International Organization* 58(4): 775–805.

Granovetter, Mark. 1985. "Economic Action and Social Structure: The Problem of Embeddedness." *American Journal of Sociology* 91(3): 481–510.

Greif, Avner. 2006. *Institutions and the Path to the Modern Economy: Lessons from Medieval Trade.* Cambridge, UK: Cambridge University Press.

Grossman, Gene M., and Elhanan Helpman. 1994. "Protection for Sale." *American Economic Review* 84(4): 833–850.

———. 2002. *Interest Groups and Trade Policy.* Princeton, NJ: Princeton University Press.

Grubel, Herbert G., and Harry G. Johnson. 1967. "Nominal Tariffs, Indirect Taxes and Effective Rates of Protection: The Common Market Countries 1959." *The Economic Journal*: 761–776.

Guisinger, Alexandra. 2009. "Determining Trade Policy: Do Voters Hold Politicians Accountable?" *International Organization* 63(3): 533–557.

Guyer, Jane I. 2004. *Marginal Gains: Monetary Transactions in Atlantic Africa.* Chicago: University of Chicago Press.

Hafner-Burton, Emilie M. 2005. "Trading Human Rights: How Preferential Trade Agreements Influence Government Repression." *International Organization* 59(3): 593–629.

Haggard, Stephan. 1990. *Pathways from the Periphery: The Politics of Growth in the Newly Industrializing Countries.* Ithaca, NY: Cornell University Press.

Haley, Stephen L., and Mir B. Ali. 2007. *Sugar Backgrounder.* Washington, DC: U.S. Department of Agriculture, Economic Research Service.

Hamilton, Gary, and Cheng-shu Kao. Forthcoming. *Making Money: Taiwanese Industrialists and the Making of the New Global Economy.* Stanford, CA: Stanford University Press.

Hampson, Fen Osler, with Michael Hart. 1995. *Multilateral Negotiations: Lessons from Arms Control, Trade, and the Environment.* Baltimore: Johns Hopkins University Press.

Hardt, Michael, and Antonio Negri. 2000. *Empire.* Cambridge, MA: Harvard University Press.

Harvard Law Review. 1967–1968. "Free Trade and Preferential Tariffs: The Evolution of International Trade Regulation in GATT and UNCTAD." *Harvard Law Review* 81: 1806.

Hausman, Daniel M. 2012. *Preference, Value, Choice, and Welfare.* Cambridge, UK: Cambridge University Press.

Helleiner, Eric. 2014. *Forgotten Foundations of Bretton Woods: International Development and the Making of the Postwar Order.* Ithaca, NY: Cornell University Press.

Heller, Patrick, and Vijayendra Rao, eds. 2015. *Deliberation and Development: Rethinking the Role of Voice and Collective Action in Unequal Societies.* Washington, DC: The World Bank.

Henderson, Errol A. 2013. "Hidden in Plain Sight: Racism in International Relations Theory." *Cambridge Review of International Affairs* 26(1): 71–92.

Herrmann, Richard K., Philip E. Tetlock, and Matthew N. Diascro. 2001. "How Americans Think about Trade: Reconciling Conflicts among Money, Power, and Principles." *International Studies Quarterly* 45(2): 191–218.

Higgott, Richard A., and Andrew Fenton Cooper. 1990. Middle Power Leadership and Coalition Building: Australia, the Cairns Group, and the Uruguay Round of Trade Negotiations. *International Organization* 44(4): 589–632.

Hiscox, Michael J. 2002. *International Trade and Political Conflict: Commerce, Coalitions, and Mobility*. Princeton, NJ: Princeton University Press.

Hobson, John M. 2012. *The Eurocentric Conception of World Politics: Western International Theory, 1760–2010*. Cambridge, UK: Cambridge University Press.

———. 2913, "Part 2—Reconstructing the non-Eurocentric Foundations of IPE: From Eurocentric 'Open Economy Politics' to Inter-civilizational Political Economy." *Review of International Political Economy* 20(5): 1055–1081.

Hoda, Anwarul, and Ashok Gulati. 2007. *WTO Negotiations on Agriculture and Developing Countries*. Baltimore: Johns Hopkins University Press.

Hofstede, Geert. 2015. *Dimension Data Matrix*. Retrieved on March 1, 2015, from www.geerthofstede.nl/dimension-data-matrix.

Hofstede, Geert, Gert Jan Hofstede, and Michael Minkov. 2010. *Cultures and Organizations: Software of the Mind*. Revised and expanded 3rd edition. New York: McGraw-Hill

Holliday, George D. 1997. *Generalized System of Preferences*. Washington, DC: Congressional Research Service, Library of Congress.

Horwitz, Robert Britt. 1991. *The Irony of Regulatory Reform: The Deregulation of American Telecommunications*. New York: Oxford University Press.

Hudec, Robert E. 1987. *Developing Countries in the GATT Legal System*. London: Trade Policy Research Centre.

Hufbauer, Gary Clyde. October 2, 2014. "A Good Deal Settles the Brazil Cotton Dispute." Peterson Institute for International Economics. Available at http://blogs.piie.com/realtime/?p=4525.

Hufbauer, Gary Clyde, and Yee Wong. 2004. *China Bashing 2004*. Washington, DC: Peterson Institute for International Economics.

Hughey, Matthew. 2012. *White Bound: Nationalists, Antiracists, and the Shared Meanings of Race*. Stanford, CA: Stanford University Press, 2012.

Hull, Cordell. 1948. *The Memoirs of Cordell Hull*. Vols. 1 & 2. New York: The Macmillan Company.

Hurd, Ian. 1999. "Legitimacy and Authority in International Politics." *International Organization* 53(2): 379–408.

Hurrell, Andrew. 2007. *On Global Order: Power, Values, and the Constitution of International Society*. Oxford, UK: Oxford University Press.

Huxley, Julian. 1947. *UNESCO: Its Purpose and Philosophy*. Washington, DC: American Council of Public Affairs.

Ingco, Merlinda D., and John D. Nash, eds. 2004. *Agriculture and the WTO: Creating a Trading System for Development*. Washington, DC: The World Bank.

International Negotiation. 1998. Special Issue on Reciprocity.

International Cotton Advisory Committee. 2006. "Production and Trade Policies Affecting the Cotton Industry." Washington, DC: Author.

Irwin, Douglas A. 1996. *Against the Tide: An Intellectual History of Free Trade*. Princeton, NJ: Princeton University Press.

Irwin, Douglas A., Petros C. Mavrodis, and Alan O. Sykes. 2008. *The Genesis of the GATT.* Cambridge, UK: Cambridge University Press. Kindle Edition.

Jackson, John H. 1997. *The World Trading System: Law and Policy of International Economic Relations.* Cambridge, MA: MIT Press.

———. 2000. "Comment." In Alan V. Deardorff and Robert Mitchell Stern, eds., *Social Dimensions of U.S. Trade Policies,* 232–235. Ann Arbor: University of Michigan Press.

Jawara, Fatoumata, and Aileen Kwa. 2003. *Behind the Scenes at the WTO: The Real World of International Trade Negotiations.* London: Zed Books.

Jensen, J. Brad, and Lori G. Kletzer. 2006. "Tradable Services: Understanding the Scope and Impact of Services Offshoring." In S. M. Collins and L. Brainard, eds., *Offshoring White-Collar Work,* Brookings Trade Forum, 75–134. Washington, DC: Brookings Institution Press.

———. 2007. "Measuring Tradable Services and the Task Content of Offshorable Services Jobs." NBER–CRW Labor in the New Economy Conference Paper. Cambridge, MA: National Bureau of Economic Research.

Jones, Vivian C. December 2014. *Generalized System of Preferences: Background and Renewal Debate.* Washington, DC: Congressional Research Service.

Kahler, Miles. 1998. "Evolution, Choice, and International Change." In David A. Lake and Robert Powell, eds., *Strategic Choice and International Relations.* Princeton, NJ: Princeton University Press.

———, ed. 2009. *Networked Politics: Agency, Power, and Governance.* Ithaca, NY: Cornell University Press.

Kapstein, Ethan B. 2008. "Fairness Considerations in World Politics: Lessons from International Trade Negotiations." *Political Science Quarterly* 123(2): 229–245.

Karsenty, Guy, and Sam Laird. 1987. "The GSP, Policy Options and the New Round." *Weltwirtschaftliches Archiv* 123(2): 262–296.

Keck, Margaret E., and Kathryn Sikkink. 1998. *Activists beyond Borders: Advocacy Networks in International Politics.* Ithaca, NY: Cornell University Press.

Kelsey, Jane. 2008. *Serving Whose Interests? The Political Economy of Trade in Services Agreements.* London: Routledge.

———. 19 June 2014. "Analysis Article—Secret Trade in Services Agreement (TISA)—Financial Services Annex." Wikileaks. Available at https://wikileaks.org/tisa-financial/analysis.html.

Kennedy, Paul. 1987. *The Rise and Fall of the Great Powers: Economic and Military Conflict from 1500 to 2000.* New York: Random House.

Keohane, Robert O. 1984. *After Hegemony: Cooperation and Discord in the World Political Economy.* Princeton, NJ: Princeton University Press.

———. 1986. "Reciprocity in International Relations." *International Organization* 40(1): 1–27.

———. 2015. "Nominal Democracy? Prospects for Democratic Global Governance." *International Journal of Constitutional Law* 13(2): 343–353.

Kheir-El-Din, Hanaa. 2002. "Implementing the Agreement on Textiles and Clothing." In Bernard M. Hoekman, Aaditya Mattoo, and Philip English, eds., *Development, Trade, and the WTO: A Handbook*, 186–194. Washington, DC: World Bank Publications.

Kindleberger, Charles P. 1978. *Economic Response: Comparative Studies in Trade, Finance, and Growth*. Cambridge, MA: Harvard University Press.

King, Gary, Robert O. Keohane, and Sidney Verba. 1994. *Designing Social Inquiry: Scientific Inference in Qualitative Research*. Princeton, NJ: Princeton University Press.

Krasner, Stephen D. 1983. *International regimes*. Ithaca, NY: Cornell University Press.

———. 1985. *Structural Conflict: The Third World against Global Liberalism*. Berkeley, CA: University of California Press.

———. 1991. "Global Communications and National Power: Life on the Pareto Frontier." *World Politics* 43(3): 336–366.

Krueger, Anne O. 1988. *The Political Economy of Controls: American Sugar*. No. w2504. Cambridge, MA: National Bureau of Economic Research.

Krugman, Paul R. 1987. "Is Free Trade Passé?" *The Journal of Economic Perspectives* 1(2): 131–144.

———. 1997. "What Should Trade Negotiators Negotiate About?" *Journal of Economic Literature* 35(1): 113–120.

Kuhn, Thomas S. 2012. *The Structure of Scientific Revolutions*. Chicago: University of Chicago Press.

Lake, David A. 2009. *Hierarchy in International Relations*. Ithaca, NY: Cornell University Press,

Lanoszka, Anna. 2009. *The World Trade Organization: Changing Dynamics in the Global Political Economy*. Boulder, CO: Lynne Rienner Publishers.

Larson, Deborah W. 1998. "Exchange and Reciprocity in International Negotiations." *International Negotiation* 3(2): 121–138.

Laurent, Pierre-Henri. 1983. "Partnership or Paternalism: A Critical View of the EC–ACP Conventions." *The Round Table* 72(288): 455–465.

Lévi-Strauss, Claude. 1958. *Race and Culture*. Paris: UNESCO.

Lewis, W. Arthur. 1954. "Unlimited Supplies of Labour." *Manchester School* 22: 139–91.

Lijphart, Arend. September 1971. "Comparative Politics and Comparative Method." *American Political Science Review* 65(3): 682–698.

Ling, Lily. 2004. "Cultural Chauvinism and the Liberal International Order: 'West versus Rest' in Asia's Financial Crisis." In Geeta Chowdhry and Sheila Nair, eds., *Power, Postcolonialism and International Relations: Reading Race, Gender and Class*, 115–141. London: Routledge.

Lopez-Acevedo, Gladys, and Raymond Robinson. May 2012. "The Promise and Peril of Post-MFA Apparel Production." Poverty Reduction and Economic Management Network, Economic Premise No. 84, Washington, DC: The World Bank.

Low, Patrick, Roberta Piermartini, and Jurgen Richtering. October 2005. "Multilateral Solutions to the Erosion of Non-Reciprocal Preferences in NAMA." World Trade Organization, Economic Research and Statistics Division, Working Paper ERSD-2005-05.

Mansfield, Edward D., and Rachel Bronson. 1997. "Alliances, Preferential Trading Arrangements, and International Trade." *American Political Science Review* 91(1): 94–107.

Mansfield, Edward D., Helen V. Milner, and B. Peter Rosendorff. 2001. "Free to Trade: Democracies, Autocracies, and International Trade." *American Political Science Review* 94(2): 305–321.

Mansfield, Edward D., and Diana C. Mutz. 2009. "Support for Free Trade: Self-Interest, Sociotropic Politics, and Out-Group Anxiety." *International Organization* 63(3): 425–457.

Marchetti, Juan, and Martin Roy. 2008. "Services Liberalization in the WTO and in PTAs." In Juan Marchetti and Martin Roy, eds., *Opening Markets for Trade in Services; Countries and Sectors in Bilateral and WTO Negotiations*, 61–112. Cambridge, UK: Cambridge University Press and WTO.

Marchetti, Juan, Martin Roy, and Laura Zoratto. 2012. *Is There Reciprocity in Preferential Trade Agreements on Services?* WTO Staff Working Paper No. ERSD-2012-16. Geneva: World Trade Organization (WTO), Economic Research and Statistics Division.

Marlin-Bennett, Renée. 2010. *Food Fights: International Regimes and the Politics of Agricultural Trade Disputes*. New York: Routledge.

Matz, James R. April 1971. "Generalized Tariff Preferences for the Developing Countries." *Journal of Maritime Law and Commerce* 2(3): 645–659.

Mazower, Mark. 2009. *No Enchanted Palace: The End of Empire and the Ideological Origins of the United Nations*. Princeton, NJ: Princeton University Press.

McCloskey, Deirdre N. 2010. *Bourgeois Dignity: Why Economics Can't Explain the Modern World*. Chicago: University of Chicago Press, 2010.

McGillivray, Fiona. 2004. *Privileging Industry: The Comparative Politics of Trade and Industrial Policy*. Princeton, NJ: Princeton University Press.

McPhate, Mike. November 17, 2005. "Outsourcing Outrage / Indian Call-Center Workers Suffer Abuse." *The San Francisco Chronicle.*

Mearsheimer, John J. 1991. *The Tragedy of Great Power Politics*. New York: W. W. Norton & Company.

Mehta, Uday Singh. 1999. *Liberalism and Empire: A Study in Nineteenth-Century British Liberal Thought*. Chicago: University of Chicago Press.

Meier, Gerald M. 1980. "The Tokyo Round of Multilateral Trade Negotiations and the Developing Countries." *Cornell International Law Journal* 13: 239–256.

Meyers, William P. September 12, 2012. "Cordell Hull's World." Retrieved on April 3, 2013, from www.iiipublishing.com/blog/2012/09/blog_09_12_2012.html.

Michalopoulos, Constantine. 2000. *The Role of Special and Differential Treatment for Developing Countries in the GATT and the WTO*. Policy Research Working Paper 2388. Washington, DC: The World Bank.

Milner, Helen V. 1997. *Interests, Institutions, and Information: Domestic Politics and International Relations*. Princeton, NJ: Princeton University Press.

———. 1999. "The Political Economy of International Trade." *Annual Review of Political Science* 2(1): 91–114.

Milner, Helen V., and Keiko Kubota. 2005. "Why the Move to Free Trade? Democracy and Trade Policy in the Developing Countries." *International Organization* 59(1): 107–143.

Milner, Helen V., and Dustin H. Tingley. 2010. "The Political Economy of US Foreign Aid: American Legislators and the Domestic Politics of Aid." *Economics & Politics* 22(2): 200–232.

Milner, Helen V., and David B. Yoffie. 1989. "Between Free Trade and Protectionism: Strategic Trade Policy and a Theory of Corporate Trade Demands." *International Organization* 43(2): 239–272.

Mintz, Sidney Wilfred. 1985. *Sweetness and Power*. New York: Viking.

Mittelman, James H. 2009. "The Salience of Race." *International Studies Perspectives* 10(1): 99–107.

Moravcsik, Andrew. 1997. "Taking Preferences Seriously: A Liberal Theory of International Politics." *International Organization* 51(4): 513–553.

Morton, Kathryn, and Peter Tulloch. 1977. *Trade and Developing Countries*. London: Overseas Development Institute.

Mosley, Layna, and Lindsay Tello. 2015. "Labor Rights, Material Interests, and Moral Entrepreneurship." *Human Rights Quarterly* 37(1): 53–79.

Muthu, Sankar. 2003. *Enlightenment against Empire*. Princeton, NJ: Princeton University Press.

Narlikar, Amrita. 2003. *International Trade and Developing Countries: Bargaining Coalitions in the GATT and WTO*. London: Routledge.

———. 2005. *The World Trade Organization: A Very Short Introduction*. Oxford, UK: Oxford University Press.

———. 2006. "Fairness in International Trade Negotiations: Developing Countries in the GATT and WTO." *The World Economy* 29(8): 1005–1029.

Narlikar, Amrita, and John Odell. 2006. "The Strict Distributive Strategy for a Bargaining Coalition: The Like Minded Group in the World Trade Organization." In John Odell, ed., *Negotiating Trade: Developing Countries in the WTO and NAFTA*, 115–144. Cambridge, UK: Cambridge University Press.

Narlikar, Amrita, and Diana Tussie. 2004. "The G20 at the Cancun Ministerial: Developing Countries and Their Evolving Coalitions in the WTO." *The World Economy* 27(7): 947–966.

Newfarmer, Richard S., William Shaw, and Peter Walkenhorst, eds. 2009. *Breaking into New Markets: Emerging Lessons for Export Diversification*. Washington, DC: World Bank Publications.

Newman, Abraham. 2008. "Building Transnational Civil Liberties: Transgovernmental Entrepreneurs and the European Data Privacy Directive." *International Organization* 62(1): 103–130.

Newman, Carol, John Page, John Rand, Abebe Shimeles, Mans Söderbom, and Finn Trap. 2016. *Made in Africa: Learning to Compete in Industry*. Washington, DC: Brookings Institution Press.

North, Douglass C. 1990. *Institutions, Institutional Change and Economic Performance.* Cambridge, UK: Cambridge University Press.

North, Douglass C., and Robert Thomas. 1973. *The Rise of the Western World: A New Economic History.* Cambridge, UK: Cambridge University Press.

Nye, Joseph S. 1990. *Bound to Lead: The Changing Nature of American Power.* New York: Basic Books.

Odell, John S. 2000. *Negotiating the World Economy.* Ithaca, NY: Cornell University Press.

———. 2001. "Case Study Methods in International Political Economy." *International Studies Perspectives* 2(2): 161–176.

———, ed. 2006. *Negotiating Trade: Developing Countries in the WTO and NAFTA.* Cambridge, UK: Cambridge University Press.

Odell, John S., and Susan K. Sell. 2006. "Reframing the Issue: The WTO Coalition on Intellectual Property and Public Health, 2001." In John S. Odell, ed., *Negotiating Trade: Developing Countries in the WTO and NAFTA,* 85–114. Cambridge, UK: Cambridge University Press.

Oh, David C., and Omotayo O. Banjo. 2012. "Outsourcing Postracialism: Voicing Neoliberal Multiculturalism in Outsourced." *Communication Theory* 22(4): 449–470.

Olson, Mancur. 1982. *The Rise and Decline of Nations: Economic Growth, Stagflation, and Social Rigidities.* New Haven, CT: Yale University Press.

Organisation for Economic Co-Operation and Development (OECD). 2008. *The Economic Impact of Counterfeiting and Piracy.* Paris: Organisation for Economic Co-Operation and Development.

Ostry, Sylvia. May 23, 2001. "Global Integration: Currents and Countercurrents." Walter Gordon Lecture, Massey College, University of Toronto. Available online at www.sun .ac.za/english/faculty/economy/spl/Documents/2014%20Study%20Tour%20to%20 Brazil/GlobalIntegration.pdf.

———. 2008. "The Uruguay Round North–South Grand Bargain: Implications for Future Negotiations." In Daniel L. M. Kennedy and James D. Southwick, eds., *The Political Economy of International Trade Law: Essays in Honor of Robert E. Hudec.* 285–300. Cambridge, UK: Cambridge University Press.

Oxley, Robert. 1990. *The Challenge of Free Trade.* London: Pearson Higher Education.

Özden, Çaglar, and Eric Reinhardt. 2005. "The Perversity of Preferences: GSP and Developing Country Trade Policies, 1976–2000." *Journal of Development Economics* 78(1): 1–21.

Parekh, Bhikhu C. 1995. "Liberalism and Colonialism: A Critique of Locke and Mill." In Jan Nederveen Pieterse and Bhikhu Parekh, eds., *The Decolonization of Imagination: Culture, Knowledge and Power,* 81–98. London: Zed Books.

Pepinsky, Thomas B. 2015. "Trade Competition and American Decolonization." *World Politics* 67(3): 387–422.

Persaud, Randolph B. 2015. "Colonial Violence: Race and Gender on the Sugar Plantations of British Guiana." In Alexander Anievas, Nivi Manchanda, and Robbie Shilliam, eds. *Race and Racism in International Relations: Confronting the Global Colour Line,* 117–138. London: Routledge.

Persaud, Randolph B., and R. B. J. Walker. 2001. "Apertura: Race in International Relations." *Alternatives*: 373–376.

Petras, James. October 22. 2005. "China Bashing and the Loss of US Competitiveness." *Counterpunch*. Available at www.counterpunch.org/2005/10/22/china-bashing-and-the-loss-of-us-competitiveness/.

Petrazzini, Ben. 1996. *Global Telecom Talks: A Trillion Dollar Deal*. Washington, DC: Institute for International Economics.

Pfeifer, Kimberly, Gawain Kripke, and Emily Alpert. 2004. "Finding the Moral Fiber: Why Reform Is Urgently Needed for a Fair Cotton Trade." *Oxfam Policy and Practice: Agriculture, Food and Land* 4(3): 1–48.

Pomeranz, William. January 25, 2006. "United States: A Legislative Status Report on Outsourcing." *Mondaq*. Retrieved on August 7, 2015, from www.mondaq.com/unitedstates/x/37312/Federal+Law/A+Legislative+Status+Report+on+Outsourcing.

Popper, Karl. 2002. *The Poverty of Historicism*. London: Routledge

Preeg, Ernest H. 1995. *Traders in a Brave New World: The Uruguay Round and the Future of the International System*. Chicago: University of Chicago Press.

Raghavan, Chakravarthi. 2002. *Developing Countries and Services Trade: Chasing a Black Cat in a Dark Room, Blindfolded*. Penang, Malaysia: Third World Network.

———. 2014. *The Third World in the Third Millennium CE: THE WTO—Towards Multilateral Trade or Global Corporatism?* Penang, Malaysia: Third World Network.

———. July 17, 2015. "How the US Is Using a Secret Agreement on Services to Wriggle out of Its WTO Obligation." *The Wire*. Retrieved on August 6, 2015, from http://thewire.in/2015/07/17/how-the-us-is-using-a-secret-agreement-on-services-to-wriggle-out-of-its-wto-obligations-6459/.

Raiffa, Howard. 1982. *The Art & Science of Negotiation*. Cambridge, MA: Harvard University Press.

Rattansi, Ali. 2007. *Racism: A Very Short Introduction*. Oxford, UK: Oxford University Press.

Ravenhill, John. 1985. *Collective Clientelism: The Lomé Conventions and North–South Relations*. New York: Columbia University Press.

Reinert, Kenneth A. 2000. "Give Us Virtue, but Not Yet: Safegaurd Actions under the Agreement on Textiles and Clothing." *The World Economy* 23(1): 25–55.

Reuters. September 30, 2014. "Exclusive: U.S. to Pay $300 Million to End Brazil Cotton Trade Dispute—Officials." Available at www.reuters.com/article/2014/10/01/us-usa-brazil-trade-idUSKCN0HQ2QZ20141001.

Rhodes, Carolyn. 1989. "Reciprocity in Trade: The Utility of a Bargaining Strategy." *International Organization* 43(2): 273–299.

Richardson, Ben. 2009. *Sugar: Refined Power in a Global Regime*. Basingstoke, UK: Palgrave Macmillan.

Ricupero, Rubens. 2001. "Rebuilding Confidence in the Multilateral Trading System: Closing the 'Legitimacy Gap.'" In Gary P. Simpson, ed., *The Role of the World Trade Organization in Global Governance*, 37–58. Tokyo: United Nations University Press.

Risse, Thomas. 2000. "'Let's Argue!': Communicative Action in World Politics." *International Organization* 54(1): 1–39.

Rivoli, Pietra. 2014. *The Travels of a T-Shirt in the Global Economy: An Economist Examines the Markets, Power, and Politics of World Trade*. New York: John Wiley & Sons.

Rogowski, Ronald. 1989. *Commerce and Coalitions: How Trade Affects Domestic Political Alignments*. Princeton, NJ: Princeton University Press.

Rose, Andrew K. 2004. "Do We Really Know That the WTO Increases Trade?" *American Economic Review* 94: 98–114

Rosenau, James R. 1990. *Turbulence in World Politics: A Theory of Change and Continuity*. Princeton, NJ: Princeton University Press.

Rosendorff, B. Peter. 2005. "Stability and Rigidity: Politics and Design of the WTO's Dispute Settlement Procedure." *American Political Science Review* 99(3): 389–400.

Rothstein, Robert L. 1979. *Global Bargaining: UNCTAD and the Quest for a New International Economic Order*. Princeton, NJ: Princeton University Press.

Roy, Martin. 2011. "Services Commitments in Preferential Trade Agreements: An Expanded Dataset." Geneva: Economic Research and Statistics Division, World Trade Organization. Available at www.wto.org/english/res_e/reser_e/ersd201118_e.pdf.

Roy, Martin, Juan Marchetti, and Hoe Lim. 2007. "Services Liberalization in the New Generation of Preferential Trade Agreements (PTAs): How Much Further than the GATS?" *World Trade Review* 6(2): 155–192.

Sabet, Shahrzad. 2012. "Feelings First: Non-Material Factors as Moderators of Economic Self-Interest Effects on Trade Preferences." Annual Meeting of the International Political Economy Society, Charlottsville, VA.

Said, Edward. 1979. *Orientalism*. New York: Vintage.

Schattschneider, Elmer Eric. 1935. *Politics, Pressures and the Tariff: A Study of Free Private Enterprise in Pressure Politics, as Shown in the 1929–1930 Revision of the Tariff*. New York: Prentice-Hall.

Scott, James. 1987. *Weapons of the Weak: Everyday Forms of Peasant Resistance*. New Haven, CT: Yale University Press.

———. 2007. "How the Poor Pay for the US Trade Deficit." In Donna Lee and Rorden Wilkinson, eds., *The WTO after Hong Kong: Progress in, and Prospects for, the Doha Development Agenda*, 97–118. London: Routledge.

———. 2010. "Developing Countries in the ITO and GATT Negotiations." *Journal of International Trade Law and Policy* 9(1): 5–24.

Scott, James, and Rorden Wilkinson. 2011. "The Poverty of the Doha Round and the Least Developed countries." *Third World Quarterly* 32(4): 611–627.

Sebenius, James K. 1983. "Negotiating Arithmetic: Adding and Subtracting Issues and Parties." *International Organization* 37(2): 281–316.

Sell, Susan. 1998. *Power and Ideas: North–South Politics of Intellectual Property and Antitrust*. Albany: State University of New York Press.

———. 2003. *Private Power, Public Law: The Globalization of Intellectual Property Rights*. Cambridge, UK: Cambridge University Press.

———. 2010. "TRIPS Was Never Enough: Vertical Forum Shifting, FTAS, ACTA, and TPP." *Journal of Intellectual Property Law* 18: 447.

———. 2013. "Revenge of the 'Nerds': Collective Action against Intellectual Property Maximalism in the Global Information Age." *International Studies Review* 15(1): 67–85.

Sen, Amartya. 1987. *On Ethics and Economics*. New York: Oxford University Press.

———. 2009. *The Idea of Justice*. Cambridge, MA: Harvard University Press.

Shah, Anup. February 18, 2001. "WTO Protest in Seattle, 1999." *Global Issues*. Available at http://www.globalissues.org/article/46/wto-protests-in-seattle-1999.

Sharma, Devinder. 1994. *GATT to WTO: Seeds of Despair*. New Delhi: Konark Publishers.

Sherman, Laura. 1999. "'Wildly Enthusiastic' about the First Multilateral Agreement on Trade in Telecommunications Services." *Federal Communication Law Journal* 51: 60–110.

Shipman, Pat. 1994. *The Evolution of Racism: Human Differences and the Use and Abuse of Science*. New York: Simon & Shuster.

Simmons, Beth A. 2009. *Mobilizing for Human Rights: International Law in Domestic Politics*. Cambridge, UK: Cambridge University Press.

Singh, J. P. 2000. "Weak Powers and Globalism: The Impact of Plurality on Weak–Strong Negotiations in the International Economy." *International Negotiation* 5(3): 449–484.

———. 2005. "Services Commitments: Case Studies from Belize and Costa Rica." In Peter Gallagher, Patrick Low, and Andrew L. Stoler, eds., *Managing the Challenges of WTO Participation: Forty-Five Case Studies*, 78–94. Cambridge, UK: Cambridge University Press.

———. 2006. "Coalitions, Developing Countries, and International Trade: Research Findings and Prospects." *International Negotiation* 11(3): 499–514.

———. 2008. *Negotiation and the Global Information Economy*. Cambridge, UK: Cambridge University Press.

———. 2010. "Development Objectives and Trade Negotiations: Moralistic Foreign Policy or Negotiated Trade Concessions?" *International Negotiation* 15: 367–389.

———. 2011. *United Nations Educational, Scientific, and Cultural Organization (UNESCO): Creating Norms for a Complex World*. London: Routledge.

———. August 5, 2014a. "India's Multi-Faceted WTO Refusal." Monkey Cage. *The Washington Post*. Available at www.washingtonpost.com/blogs/monkey-cage/wp/2014/08/05/indias-multi-faceted-wto-refusal/.

———. October 2014b. "The Land of Milk and Cotton." Snapshots. *Foreign Affairs*. Available at www.foreignaffairs.com/articles/africa/2014-10-23/land-milk-and-cotton.

———. 2015. "Diffusion of Power and Diplomacy: New Meanings, Problem Solving, and Deadlocks in Multilateral Negotiations." *International Negotiation* 20(1): 73–88.

———. forthcoming. *Development 2.0: How Technologies Can Promote Inclusivity in the Developing World*. New York: Oxford University Press.

Singh, J. P., and Mikkel Flyverbom. July 2016. "Representing Participation in ICT4D Projects." *Telecommunications Policy* 40: 682–703.

Singh, J. P., and Surupa Gupta. 2016. "Agriculture and its Discontents: Coalitional Politics at the WTO with Special Reference to India's Food Security Interests." *International Negotiation* 21(2): 295–326.

Skocpol, Theda, and Vanessa Williamson. 2012. *The Tea Party and the Remaking of Republican Conservatism*. New York: Oxford University Press.

Skonieczny, Amy. 2001. "Constructing NAFTA: Myth, Representation, and the Discursive Construction of US Foreign Policy." *International Studies Quarterly* 45(3): 433–454.

Smith, Adam. 1991/1776. *The Wealth of Nations*. Edited by Andrew S. Skinner. Vol. 3. New York: Prometheus Books.

Spinanger, Dean. 1999. "Textiles beyond the MFA Phase-Out." *The World Economy* 22(4): 455–476.

Srinivasan, Thirukodikaval N. 1998. *Developing Countries and the Multilateral Trading System: From the GATT to the Uruguay Round and the Future*. Boulder, CO: Westview Press.

Steil, Benn. 2013. *The Battle of Bretton Woods: John Maynard Keynes, Harry Dexter White, and the Making of a New World Order*. Princeton, NJ: Princeton University Press.

Steinberg, Richard H. 2002. "In the Shadow of Law or Power? Consensus-Based Bargaining and Outcomes in the GATT/WTO." *International Organization* 56(2): 339–374.

Stolper, Wolfgang F., and Paul A. Samuelson. 1941. "Protection and Real Wages." *The Review of Economic Studies* 9(1): 58–73.

Tambe, Ashwini. 2011. "Climate, Race Science and the Age of Consent in the League of Nations." *Theory, Culture & Society* 28(2): 109–130.

Taylor, Ian, and Karen Smith. 2007. *United Nations Conference on Trade and Development (UNCTAD)*. London: Routledge.

Tobin, Jennifer L., and Marc L. Busch. October 2014. "When Trade as Aid Isn't: GSP, the GATT/WTO and Trade." Unpublished Paper, Georgetown University, Washington, DC.

Toye, Richard. 2010. *Churchill's Empire: The World That Made Him and the World He Made*. New York: Henry Holt.

UNESCO. 1950. *The Race Question*. Paris: UNESCO Publishing. Retrieved on October 8, 2013, from http://unesdoc.unesco.org/images/0012/001282/128291eo.pdf.

U.S. Department of State. Bilateral Investment Treaties. Retrieved on August 6, 2015, from www.state.gov/e/eb/ifd/bit/117402.htm.

U.S. Trade Representative. April 3, 1986a. "Administration Statement on the Protection of U.S. Intellectual Property Rights Protection Abroad." Washington, DC: Executive Office of the President. Office of the US Trade Representative.

———. April 7, 1986b. "Statement by Ambassador Clayton Yeutter Concerning Intellectual Property Rights Protection." Washington, DC: Executive Office of the President. Office of the US Trade Representative.

———. December 15, 1986c. "USTR Announces Country-by-Country Sugar Allocations." Washington, DC: Executive Office of the President, Office of the U.S. Trade Representative.

———. February 26, 1988. "Yeutter Releases Results of Intellectual Property Study." Washington, DC: Executive Office of the President. Office of the US Trade Representative.

———. January 19, 1989. "U.S. Denies Thailand Duty-Free Benefits on Imports Worth $165 Million." Washington, DC: Executive Office of the President. Office of the US Trade Representative.

———. January 23, 1991. "U.S.–Mongolia Free Trade Agreement." Washington, DC: Executive Office of the President. Office of the US Trade Representative.

———. February 26, 1992. "USTR Finds India's Patent Regime Unreasonable and Leaves Door Open to Trade Action." Washington, DC: Executive Office of the President. Office of the United States Trade Representative.

———. June 2015. Statement by Ambassador Michael Froman on Congressional Passage of TPA, AGOA, and Preference Package. Washington, DC: Executive Office of the President. Office of the United States Trade Representative. Retrieved on July 7, 2015, from https://ustr.gov/about-us/policy-offices/press-office/press-releases/2015/june/statement-ambassador-michael-froman.

VanDeVeer, Donald. 2014. *Paternalistic Intervention: The Moral Bounds on Benevolence*. Princeton, NJ: Princeton University Press.

Van Reisen, Mirjam. 2007. "The Enlarged European Union and the Developing World: What Future?" In Andre Mold, ed., *EU Development Policy in a Changing World: Challenges for the 21st Century*, 29–65 Amsterdam: Amsterdam University Press.

Vitalis, Robert. 2000. "The Graceful and Generous Liberal Gesture: Making Racism Invisible in American International Relations." *Millennium: Journal of International Studies* 29(2): 331_356.

———. 2010. The Noble American Science of Imperial Relations and Its Laws of Race Development. *Comparative Studies in Society and History*, 52(04), 909–938.

Voeten, Erik. 2015. "UN Voting." Retrieved on January 5, 2015, from http://faculty.georgetown.edu/ev42/UNVoting.htm.

Waldman, Amy. March 7, 2004. "India Takes Economic Spotlight, and Critics Are Unkind." *The New York Times*.

Wallerstein, Immanuel Maurice. 2004. *World-Systems Analysis: An Introduction*. Chapel Hill, NC: Duke University Press.

Waltz, Kenneth N. 1979. *Theory of International Politics*. New York: McGraw Hill.

Watal, Jayashree. 2001. *Intellectual Property Rights in the WTO and Developing World*. The Hague: Kluwer Law International.

Weber, Robert Philip. 1990. *Basic Content Analysis*. Newbury Park, CA: Sage.

Wellenius, Bjorn, and Peter A. Stern, eds. 1994, *Implementing Reforms in the Telecommunications Sector: Lessons from Experience*. Washington, DC: World Bank Publications.

Wendt, Alexander. 1999. *Social Theory of World Politics*. Cambridge, UK: Cambridge University Press.

Whalley, John. 1999. "Special and Differential Treatment in the Millennium Round." *The World Economy* 22(8): 1065–1093.

White, Flora. 1952. *Review of the World Sugar Situation*. Washington, DC: International Bank for Reconstruction and Development.

White, Mark D. 2011. *Kantian Ethics and Economics: Autonomy, Dignity, and Character*. Stanford, CA: Stanford University Press.

Wight, Jonathan B. 2015. *Ethics in Economics: An Introduction to Moral Frameworks*. Stanford, CA: Stanford University Press.

Wilcox, Clair. 1949. *Charter for World Trade*. New York: Macmillan.

Williams, Frances. December 15, 2005. "Untangling the Emotive Dispute over Trade-distorting Cotton Subsidies." *Financial Times*.

Williamson, Vanessa, Theda Skocpol, and John Coggin. 2011. "The Tea Party and the Remaking of Republican Conservatism." *Perspectives on Politics* 9(1): 25–43.

Winham, Gilbert R. 1986. *International Trade and the Tokyo Round Negotiation*. Princeton, NJ: Princeton University Press.

WITS (World Integrated Trade Solution). 2015. Retrieved on January 30, 2015, from http://wits.worldbank.org/.

Woodrow, Brian R. August 1991. "Tilting toward a Trade Regime: The ITU and the Uruguay Round Services Negotiations." *Telecommunications Policy*. 15(4): 323–342.

Wong, Kent. 2004. "Blaming It All on China." *New Labor Forum* 13(3).

The World Bank. 2008. *World Development Report: Agriculture for Development*. Washington, DC: The World Bank.

———. 2015a. *World Development Report: Mind and Culture*. Washington, DC: The World Bank

———. 2015b. Service, etc., Value-added (% of GDP). Washington DC: The World Bank. Retrieved on May 17, 2015, from http://data.worldbank.org/indicator/NV.SRV.TETC.ZS

World Trade Organization (WTO). July 10, 1991. Services Sectoral Classicfication List. MTN. GNS/W/120. Geneva: World Trade Organization.

———. February 14, 1996. Report on the Meeting of January 26, 1996, S/NGBT/12, para. 6. Negotiating Group on Basic Telecommunications. Geneva: World Trade Organization.

———. April 30, 1996. Report of the Group on Basic Telecommunications. Retrieved in June 2000 from www.wto.org/english/tratop_e/servte_e/tel15_e.htm.

———. February 17, 1997. Data on Telecommunications Market Covered by the WTO Negotiations on Basic Telecommunications. Available at www.wto.org/english/news_e/pres97_e/data3.htm. Retrieved March 15, 2014.

———. November 14, 2001. "Declaration on the TRIPS Agreement and Public Health." Ministerial Conference, Doha, WT/MIN(01)/DEC/W2.

———. September 2014. "Trade Profile: India." Available at http://stat.wto.org/Country Profiles/IN_e.htm.

———. "United States: Subsidies on Upland Cotton." Retrieved October 12, 2014, from www.wto.org/english/tratop_e/dispu_e/cases_e/ds267_e.htm.

———. Retrieved January 25, 2015. "Dataset of Services: Commitments in Regional Trade Agreements (RTAs)." Available at: www.wto.org/english/tratop_e/serv_e/dataset_e/dataset_e.htm.

————. Services Database. Retrieved January 25, 2015, from http://tsdb.wto.org.

Wraight, Christopher D. 2011. *The Ethics of Trade and Aid: Development, Charity, or Waste?* London: Continuum.

Wriggins, Howard. 1976. "Up for Auction." In I. William Zartman, ed., *The 50% Solution: How to Bargain Successfully with Hijackers, Strikers, Bosses, Oil Magnates, Arabs, Russians, and Other Worthy Opponents in this Modern World*. New Haven, CT: Yale University Press.

Yoffie, David B. 1983. *Power and Protectionism: Strategies of the Newly Industrializing Countries*. New York: Columbia University Press.

Zartman, I. William. 1971. *The Politics of Trade Negotiations between Africa and the European Economic Community: The Weak Confront the Strong*. Princeton, NJ: Princeton University Press.

————. 2003. "Negotiating the Rapids: The Dynamics of Regime Formation." In Bertram I. Spector and I. William Zartman, eds., *Getting It Done: Postagreeemnt Negotiation and International Regimes*. Washington, DC: United States Institute of Peace Press.

Index

Aaronson, Susan, 58, 61

Acemoglu, Daron, 33, 148

AFL-CIO, 106, 177

Africa, Caribbean and Pacific countries, 75, 78, 118, 131, 134

Aggarwal, Vinod, 52, 107, 136, 175

Akerlof, George, 16, 32, 44, 174

Amsden, Alice, 79, 193

Andean countries, 86, 88, 90

Andean Trade Preferences Act, 88, 90

Anievas, Alexander, 34–35

Anti-Counterfeiting Trade Agreement, 13, 146–147, 159

Argentina, 9, 89, 98, 100–104, 117, 120, 143, 151, 162, 164, 202

Armstrong, Chris, 22, 29, 73

ASEAN, *see* coalitions

Attlee, Clement, 38, 59

audio-visual services, 157–158, 202. *See also* cultural industries.

Australia: agriculture and Cairns Group, 119–121, 125; GSP, 118, 199; infant industries, 62–63, 198; intellectual property, 147, 151, 159; OECD member, 87; paternalism, 98, 101–102, 114; preferences and dominion status, 57, 59, 61, 76; sugar, 133, 138, 202; telecommunications, 161

Austria, 64, 98, 102, 114, 151

Bagwell, Kyle, 25–28, 30, 43, 76, 82, 193, 195

Bali Accord, 159

Bandung Conference, 68

Bangladesh, 9, 90, 98, 109, 164, 177, 201, 206

barganing power, 48, 50, 52–53, 99, 197. *See also* Best Alternative to a Negotiated Agreement.

Barnett, Michael, 10, 22, 35, 40, 46, 85, 197, 205–206

Bauer, Peter, 67–68

Belgium, 67, 98, 102, 114, 197–198

Belize, 89, 153, 164, 204

Benin, 124, 136

Best Alternative to a Negotiated Agreement (BATNA), 50, 53, 97. *See also* bargaining power.

Bhagwati, Jagdish, 30

Bhutan, 98, 103

Bilateral Investment Treaty (BIT), 87, 90–94, 147, 156, 172

bilateral trade agreements, 23, 86, 93, 132, 147

Blinder, Alan, 167

Bloc diplomacy, 69, 73, 78

Boulding, Kenneth, 180, 196

Brady, Henry, 173, 194, 206

Brazil: agriculture trade, 117–118, 120, 124–125; cotton, 125, 134–137, 175; G10, 100, 166, 202; G20, 133, 202; GATT foundation, 197, 198; GSP, 75, 77; historic trade, 61–63; intellectual property, 142–143, 145, 149, 203; negotiation strength, 49, 138; paternalism, 89, 98, 102–103; PTAs, 3, 13; services trade, 150–151, 153, 159; sugar, 132–133; tariff concessions, 9, 102–103; telecommunications, 161–165

BRICs, 49, 159–160, 170, 173

Brunei, 2, 164, 193

Burkina Faso, 98, 124, 136

Busch, Marc, 43, 50, 72, 76

Bush, George H. W., 145

Bush, George W., 167

business processes outsourcing. *See* outsourcing.

C4. *See* coalitions.

café au lait. *See* coalitions.

Cairns Group. *See* coalitions.

Cambodia, 109, 199, 204

Canada: agriculture, 118, 121, 202; intellectual property, 145, 147, 204; merchandise trade, 101; MFA, 107–108; preferences, 57, 59, 61, 76; services, 151, 166

Caribbean Basin Initiative, 7, 75, 88, 130, 147

Caribbean countries, 3–4, 126–127, 130, 133, 162, 193, 203

Carnegie, Allison, 5, 179, 193–194

case study method. *See* methods.

Césaire, Aimé, 15, 39

Chad, 124, 136

Chase-Dunn, Christopher, 177, 197

Chile: G10, 100; G20, 151; GATT creation, 62, 197; as negotiator, 149, 161, 164, 199, 204; OECD member, 87; paternalism toward, 89, 98, 102–103, 114

China: agriculture trade, 124–125, 203; Bandung conference, 68; cotton, 135; emerging power, 49–50; G20, 124–125, 133, 202; GATS, 153, 157; GATT foundation at, 197; infant indsutry, 61, 198; intellectual property, 142, 148–149; outsourcing, 167; paternalism and bashing, 87, 98, 175, 203; PTAs and, 3, 23; sugar, 133; telecommunciations, 165; textiles, 106–107, 109; USTR, 142–143

Chowdhry, Geeta, 34, 178

Churchill, Winston, 15, 56–60

civil aviation services, 139, 153

Clapp, Jennifer, 122–123, 125

Clayton, William, 60, 198

Clinton, Hillary, 136, 206

Clinton, William, 167, 177

coalitions: agricultural negotiations in, 115, 117, 120, 125, 133–134; ASEAN, 97, 100–101, 104–105, 108, 113–115, 144, 162; C4, 124, 135–137; café au lait, 94, 100, 150, 154–155, 165; Cairns Groups, 97, 100–105, 11, 15, 119–124, 133, 169, 172, 202; class-based, 23; cotton in, 137; Doha Round in, 13; Friends of Services, 94; G4, 125, 138; G10, 3, 97, 101–105, 113, 15, 120–121, 150–154, 165–166, 200, 202, 204; G9, 150, 151, 204; G20, 124–125, 133, 137, 150–151, 172, 202; G77, 69, 72–73, 100, 115, 150, 172, 201; G90, 124–125; G110, 125; impact of 172, 181–182; industry-based 43; Like-Minded Group, 123, 202; merchandise negotiations

in, 99–100, 105; negotiation tactic, 48–54; postcolonial, 68–69; sugar in, 130; Uruguay Round, 23

Collier, David, 173, 194, 206

Colombia, 41, 94, 98, 102–103, 125, 150–151, 164, 202, 204

colonialism: civilizing colonies, xii, 14–15, 40, 171; economics of, 13, 96, 99; imperial preferences, 30, 118; infant industry, 63; injustice, 72; neocolonialism or trade as colonialism, 47, 55–58, 61, 111, 126, 153, 198; paternalism and, 14–15, 21, 35, 41, 85, 104; racism and, 1, 14–15, 31–35, 39, 46; sugar and, 126–128, 17

communication services, 158. *See also* telecommunications.

comparative advantage. *See* trade theory.

content analysis. *See* methods.

core-periphery explanations, 5, 46–47, 178–179. *See also* dependency, world-systems.

Coskeran, Helen, 117–118

Costa Rica, 3, 89, 98, 125, 132, 193

Cote d'Ivoire, 89, 164

cotton: Brazil and, 125, 134–137; C4 (West Africa), 22, 124, 136, 137; case study as, 29; colonial trade, 111; developed world exports, 123; dispute settlement and, 11, 134–137, 83; infant industry, 21; subsidies in the United States, 124, 134–137; trade barriers in, 65–66, 70, 119

Crawford, Neta, 10, 14, 35, 37, 40, 196, 206

Croome, John, 144, 151

Cuba, 62–63, 123, 128, 197–199, 202

cultural industries, 157–158, 202

cultural distance, 2–3, 96–97, 99, 104, 113, 207

cultural identity, xi, 42, 44–45, 47–48, 27, 157, 174, 184, 197

cultural preferences: formation, xii, 2, 4–6, 11–13, 16–17, 22, 32–36, 52, 171–177, 179, 184, 194–195, 205; paternalism as, 11–13, 22, 32–36, 111, 178, 183; racism as, 36–41, 180; SDT in, 30, 33–36; sugar in, 126–130; trade theory in, 41–48, 171–177, 194–195

cultural tolerance, 196

Curzon, Gerard, 63, 65–68, 198

Darwin, Charles, 36–37

Davis, Christina, 51, 53

de Callieres, Francois, 31–32

democracy levels, 43, 100, 105, 113, 115–116, 155

dependency theory and history, 12, 46–48, 70, 79, 115, 177–178. *See also* core-periphery explanations, world-systems.

Destler, Irving M., 106, 108

development assistance. *See* foreign aid, trade-capacity building assistance.

Dispute Settlement Mechanism, 10–11, 125, 135, 138–139, 141, 172, 183, 202

Doha Health Declaration. *See* Doha Round.

Doha Round: agriculture and, 122–126; Cancun ministerial, 27; cotton and, 135–137; deadlocks, 9, 13, 23, 77, 84, 10, 172, 175; development round, 11, 17, 30; Doha Health Declaration, 145–146; intellectual property, 13, 145–146; services trade and, 28, 155–159; sugar and, 131–134

Dominica, 162, 164

Dominican Republic, 98, 123, 132, 163–164, 193, 204

Doty, Roxanne, 34, 40

DR-CAFTA, 45, 132, 193, 202

Drahos, Peter, 141, 147

Drezner, Daniel, 50, 167

Dunkel, Arthur, 121, 151–152

Economic Commission of Latin America, 63, 65

economic efficiency: agriculture in, 120, 129, 132–133; hegemony and, 181; industry in, 76; legitimacy and, 3, 25–26; Pareto, 156, 174; trade distortions and, 4, 23–24, 26, 30–31, 43, 129

Ecuador, 90, 98, 202

Egypt, 68, 89–90, 98, 100, 120, 123, 156, 202

Eisenhower, Dwight, 106

Enterprise of Americas Initiative, 88

Escape Clause. *See* Generalized System of Preferences.

ethical considerations: American trade interests and, 60; colonialism and, 14; economics and, 174; future of, 35–36, 183; legitimacy, 31, 183; normative and strategic, 23–24, 29; reciprocity and, 23, 29, 56, 194. *See also* justice, fairness.

Europe: colonialism and, 13–15, 16, 35, 58, 85, 97, 100, 104–105, 113, 115, 196; imperial preferences, 30, 55, 74; paternalism, 21, 35–36; racism, 15, 36, 39; tariffs, 66

European colony variable, 104–105, 113, 115, 201

European Community. *See* EU.

European Economic Community. *See* EU.

European Union: agriculture and CAP, 26, 55, 117–118; Brazil, China, India and, 3; coding results 86–87; data protection, 168; intellectual property, 142, 147; outsourcing, 168; preferential trade, 74–75, 106–108; services, 150–151, 159; subsidies, 124; sugar, 128–130; telecommunictions, 161; trade concessions, 8–9, 48–50; United States and, 26. *See also* Europe.

Everything-But-Arms, 75

export-market diversification and index: as negotiation strength, 99, 104–105, 115–116, 139, 154–155, 165, 182; as paternalistic strengh, 3, 96–97

fairness: basis of trade and, 8–10, 174; implementation issues and, 122; market exchange and 13, 24; negotiations and, 16, 48; paternalism and, 11, 4; reciprocity and, 26–29, 183. *See also* Justice, ethical considerations.

Fanon, Franz, 48, 171

financial services and banking, 27, 139–141, 152–155, 158–160, 204

Finger, Michael, 10, 25, 27, 28, 48, 83, 95, 108, 10, 116, 119, 139, 195

Finland, 98, 102, 114, 151

Finnemore, Martha, 40, 184

foreign aid: burden on consumers, 68, 135; cotton and, 135; Haberler Report and 64–65; merchandise trade and, 101–102; opposite of trade concessions, 12, 25, 67, 108, 116, 136, 194; paternalism and, 14, 16, 35, 46, 54, 176, 179, 181, 203; side payments, 11, 12, 70, 101, 116, 137, 181; soft option, 67–68

Foreign Direct Investment, 49, 86, 90, 139–140, 173

France, 58, 97–99, 102, 114, 129, 197–198, 203

Freire, Paulo, xi

Friends of Services. *See* coalitions.

G4. *See* coalitions.

G9. *See* coalitions.

G10. *See* coalitions.

G20. *See* coalitions.

G33. *See* coalitions.

G77. *See* coalitions.

G90. *See* coalitions.

G110. *See* coalitions.

Gandhi, Mahatma, 1, 39–40, 57–58.

Generalized System of Preferences: agriculture and, 112–116; benevolence and, 4, 11; G77, 72–73, 100; graduation clause, 74–75; history of, 70–79; intellectual property and, 142–143, 145; legitimacy of, 43; nonreciprocity in, 26, 95; paternalism as, 4–5, 181; services and, 156, 170; UNCTAD and, 70–71; U.S. trade policy and sentiment, 86–91, 199. *See also* Special and Differential Treatment.

Germany, 33, 37, 42, 66, 97–98, 102, 107, 114, 198, 203

Ghana, 67–68, 148, 164, 198–199

Goldstein, Judith, 90–91, 195–196, 200

Gowa, Joanne, 2. 193

graduation clause. *See* Generalization System of Preferences.

grand bargain, 26–27, 83–84, 94, 105, 112, 115, 199, 201

Grenada, 87, 163

Grossman, Gene, 4, 43

Guatemala, 98–99, 115, 125, 134, 202

Haberler Report, 64–65, 68–69, 73, 91

Hausman, Daniel, 174, 195–196

Havana, 56, 61, 62

Helleiner, Eric, 62–64, 199

Helpman, Elhanan, 4, 43

Herfindahl-Hirschman Index, 96, 200. *See also* export market diversification.

Hills, Carla, 89–90, 144

Hiscox, Michael, 42, 173, 174

historical method. *See* methods.

Hitler, 15, 40

Hobbes, Thomas, 36, 196

Hobson, John, 34–36, 175–176, 196.

Hofstede, Geert, 13, 96, 97, 99, 200, 207

Honduras, 89, 98, 109, 123

Hong Kong, 75, 79, 107, 109, 124, 162, 164

Hudec, Robert, 48, 67, 70, 73–74, 78, 198, 99

Hufbauer, Gary, 136, 201

Hull, Cordell, 15, 57–60

humanitarian considerations, 10, 35–36, 40, 46, 54, 128, 176–177, 183–184, 197

Hume, David, 174

IBM, 99, 142

Iceland, 98, 102, 114, 151

Imperial preferences, 15, 30, 52, 55–62, 67, 69, 75, 104, 118, 129–131, 172

indentured labor, 12–127, 202

India: agriculture, 112–113, 117–119, 121–134, 201, 202; Bali Accord, 125, 138; Bandung, 68; coalition leader, 62–63, 100, 125, 133–134, 198, 199, 202; decolonization, 57–58, 197–198; Doha Round 23; exports, 99; GATT, 57, 197; intellectual property, 140–149, 203, 204; outsourcing, 140–141, 159–160, 166–170; paternalism, 89, 98, 115, 139, 203; preferential trade, 4, 59, 74–77, 87, 194, 198; PTAs, 3, 13; racism, 15, 39–40, 47, 57, 61, 166–169, 206; services, 149–153, 157, 159, 166–170, 173; sugar, 137–138, 202; telecommunications, 161–165, 205; textiles, 107–109, 177; trade barriers to, 65–67; trade concessions, 10, 101–103, 105; trade restrictions in, 111; trade share, 59

infant industry, 30, 47, 55–56, 62–70, 128, 172, 198

intellectual property: ACTA, 13, 146–147, 159; Article 31, 141–145; coding 86–89; grand bargain, 83, 94, 112; GSP linkage, 75; negotiations, 90, 100, 105, 108, 139–149, 172–175; terms defined, 203; TRIPS+, 140–142, 147–148, 169, 172, 204

International Monetary Fund, 58

International Trade Organization negotiations, 56–61

interst groups, 16, 22, 41, 43, 76, 88–89, 100. *See also* coalitions.

Irwin, Douglas, 57, 59–62, 198

Israel, 38–39, 120

Jackson, John, 25–26, 30, 32

Jamaica, 98, 100–103, 120, 123, 151, 163–164, 203, 204

Japan: agriculture trade, 114, 118–119, 123; great power, 49; intellectual property, 141–142, 145, 147; MFN, 76; paternalism toward, 89, 203; OECD member, 87; services, 151, 161, 168; steel, 86; textiles trade, 59, 106–108

Jaramillo, Felipé, 150–152, 204

Jawara, Fatoumata, 9, 28, 85, 123

Jones, Vivian, 77, 79

justice: American notions, 45; arguments for, 22–23, 26, 54, 73, 183; cotton and, 126; distributive justice, 45, 79, 194; economic injustice and oppression, 6, 10–11, 22, 29, 43, 48, 174, 180; GATT in, 56; GSP and, 79; neoliberalism and, 15, 2, 183; NIEO and, 72; norms for, 28–29; paternalism and, 14, 21–22; reciprocity and, 8, 22, 24, 29; sugar and, 126. *See also* ethical considerations, fairness.

Kant, Emmanuel, 36, 96
Kapstein, Ethan, 7–10, 13
Karsainty, Guy, 74–75, 77
Kelsey, Jane, 9, 140, 153, 159, 163
Kennedy, John F., 67, 107
Kennedy Round, 27, 70, 78, 18, 120
Kenya, 57, 98, 109, 123, 125, 148
Keohane, Robert, 25, 95, 181, 194, 207
Keynes, John Maynard, 60–61, 198–199
Kheir-El-Din, Hanaa, 107, 109
Kindleberger, Charles, 42, 44
Kipling, Rudyard, 21
Korea (South): agriculture trade, 114; concessions received, 10; GSP, 75; GSP graduation, 74, 79; OECD member, 87; paternalistic strength, 98, 102–103; services trade, 204; telecommunications, 162, 164
Krasner, Stephen, 49, 73, 179, 193, 195, 197
Krueger, Anne, 128–130
Krugman, Paul, 30, 43, 193
Kwa, Aileen, 9, 28, 85, 123

labor issues, 41–43, 76, 78, 41–43, 109, 126–127, 174, 202, 206
Laird, Sam, 74–75, 77
Lake, David, 3, 5, 31, 69, 85, 175–176, 193
las Casas, Bartolomé de, 15
Lévi-Strauss, Claude, 38, 142
liberal world order, 1, 5–6, 175, 179–180, 183, 206
Like-Minded Group. See coalitions.
Ling, Lily, 178
Lomé Convention, 75, 118, 131, 133
Luxembourg, 98–99, 102, 114, 197–198

Malawi, 89, 91
Malaysia, 10, 98, 102–103, 114, 123, 164, 199, 202
Mali, 124, 136
Mansfield, Edward D., 3–4, 44, 174–175, 193, 196
Marchetti, Juan, 28, 48, 153, 156, 165
market access: agriculture and, 116, 118; concessions, 3–4, 23; developing country demands for, 9, 11, 29–30, 70, 72–73, 79, 199; GSP and, 70–73; services and, 150, 157; telecommunications and, 160–161
Marx, Karl, 178
Marxian explanations, 16, 47, 176–178, 197. See also core-periphery and world systems.
Mazower, Mark, 6, 39–40, 196
Meade, James, 60, 64

Mearsheimer, John, 85, 181
medicines. See pharmaceuticals.
merchandise trade: concessions, 11, 94–106; data 1960–2010, 7; textiles and apparel in, 106–109; UNGA voting affinity impact, 180; United States trade sentiment, 92–94
methods: case study method, xi–xii, 1, 3–4, 17, 28–29, 57, 172, 205; content analysis, 77, 83–86, 94, 108, 111, 155, 181, 200; departures from paternalism studies, 35–36; historical, xii, 28–29, 32, 39–40, 48, 50, 99, 11, 126–129, 160, 171–172, 173–176, 183, 194, 205; mixed-methods, xii, 1, 17, 28, 53, 171, 176, 194, 196; quantitative methods, xiii, 28–29, 44–45, 47, 111, 12, 166, 172–173, 176, 179, 181, 194, 197, 206; survey research, 34, 44–45, 99, 149, 195, 205
Mexico: GATT and, 78, 202; MFA, 109, GSP, 118, 142; intellectual property, 142, 147; OECD and 87; paternalism and, 45–46, 89, 98, 102–103, 200; telecommunications, 162–164
Michalopoulos, Constantine, 72, 78
Mills, Wilber, 107–108
Milner, Helen, 43, 193, 194, 196
Mintz, Sydney, 111, 126, 178, 202–203
mixed-methods. See methods.
Moravcsik, Andrew, 174, 195
Morocco, 3, 98, 147, 164, 193, 204
most favored nation: definition, 195; imperial preferences and, 56, 61; preferential trade, 72, 76, 147; reciprocity and, 24–26, 55–56; services and, 153, 157, 158, 160
Multifibre Arrangement. See textiles.
multinational corporation, 142, 145, 163

NAFTA, 45, 46, 88, 132, 138, 200
Nair, Sheila, 34, 178
Narlikar, Amrita, 9, 29, 52, 62, 70, 73, 100, 117, 118, 121, 202
negotiation tactics: defined, 49–50; multiple issues and, 51–53; multiple parties and, 5; negotiation process and, 51–52, 172; trade-offs and linkages, 48, 50–53, 97, 99, 115, 145. See also coalitions.
neoliberalism, 15, 178
neorealism. See realism.
Netherlands, 58, 97, 102, 114, 197, 198, 203
New International Economic Order, 69, 72–73, 199

New Zealand: Cairns Group, 120, 202, 204; intellectual property, 147, 151; paternalism and,
98, 102, 114; preferences, 57, 59; telecommunications and services, 161, 204
Nigeria, 67, 98, 120, 202
Non-Aligned Movement, 68, 72
nonagricultural market access, 9, 157, 159
nontariff barriers: agriculture in, 116, 120–122, 136,
197; OECD in, 7–8
    reciprocity and, 27; toward developing
        world, 12–13, 63, 65, 74; types, 27
North American Free Trade Agreement, 45–46,
132, 138, 200
Norway, 98, 102, 107, 114, 148, 151, 197

Odell, John, 4, 8, 28, 60, 146, 202, 206
Olson, Mancur, 42, 148
OPEC, 49, 72, 75
Ordery market arrangement. See trade measures.
Organisation for Economic Cooperation and
    Development (OECD), 87–88, 90–92, 111–112,
    122–123, 143, 147, 150, 155; agriculture in,
    111–112, 122–123; coding category, 87, 200;
    counterfeiting index, 149; GSP issue, 71; in-
    tellectual property, 143, 147–149; paternalism
    from, 88–92; services, 150, 155–156; tariffs
    and trade barriers in, 7–8, 193
Organization of Petroleum Exporting Countries,
    49, 72, 75
Ostry, Sylvia, 26, 27, 195, 199
Other commercial service exports. See
    outsourcing.
Outsourcing, 17, 29, 47, 139–114, 159–160, 165–170
Oxfam, 135, 201

Pakistan, 61, 98, 100, 107, 109, 123, 164, 197, 199, 202
Paternalism Strength Index: defined, 1; effects
    in agriculture, 113–115; effects in services,
    153–157; effects in telecommunications, 165;
    general effects, 173–175, 179–181; measure-
    ment, 96–98; need for, 13; subliminal effects
    measured, 183
Paternalism: Cordell Hull and, 58; defined, 1; elite
    preferences in, 22–33; GSP, 77; hypotheses
    about, 29, 94–98; racism and, 33–42, 169,
    175–178; subliminal influence, 34–35, 96,
    183, 196; sugar in, 127–129; trade theory
    and, 5, 32–48; U.S. trade policy, 84–94,
    111–115. See also Paternalism Strength Index,
    racism.

Persaud, Randolph, 34, 127
Peru, 98, 100–103, 114, 125, 162–164, 199, 202, 204
pharmaceuticals, 121, 134, 144–146
Philippines, 98, 102–103, 114, 128–129, 133, 161, 164,
    198, 202
PhRMA, 145–146
Portugal, 97–98, 102, 114, 129
Prebisch, Rául, 63, 69–70, 198–199
Preeg, Ernest, 27, 108, 137, 152
preferences. See cultural preferences.
preferential trade agreements: agriculture in, 173;
    coercion and trade distortion, 26, 28, 48, 50,
    110, 146, 172; excluding Brazil, China, India,
    3, 13; human rights and, 76; paternalism
    in, 92; pressures for, 125; services in, 140,
    147, 156–157; sugar, 132; trade creation, 91;
    TRIPS+, 140, 146; United States and, 125

quantitative methods. See methods.
quotas: agriculture and, 112, 118, 120, 127, 129;
    paternalism and, 74, 179; reduction as trade
    concession, 12, 172; sugar in, 3, 88, 129–134,
    201; textiles in, 26, 83, 106–107; trade barriers
    as, 27, 55

racism: American Political Science Associa-
    tion and, 33–34; colonial era, 1–2, 14, 31,
    48; economic relations in, 33–36, 41–42;
    foreign affairs and, 33; international rela-
    tions scholarship and, 15–16, 175–177;
    International Studies Association and, 34;
    Nazi Germany and, 15; outsourcing and,
    14, 170; preferences, 21, 24, 32–33, 195–196;
    subliminal, 96; sugar and, 126; UNESCO and,
    15, 38–39
Raghavan, Chakravarthi, 85, 140, 153, 159, 163
Reagan, Ronald, 3–4, 130, 137, 143, 193, 201
realism, 5, 36, 39, 45, 179
reciprocity: agriculture in, 27–29, 111–114; cultural
    lens and, 43–44; defined 1–2, 24–25; de mini-
    mus, 122, 124; diffuse, 25, 27, 124, 195; fairness
    and ethics, 16–17, 29–32, 171, 183–184;
    GATT and, 24; grand bargain and, 83, 199;
    legitimacy of, 26, 29; measurements, 27–29;
    merchandise concessions and, 94–97, 101,
    104, 195; MFN and 72–73; paternalism and,
    21–22, 45, 179, 181; puzzle as, xi–xii, 1–4, 6–11,
    23–24, 174; services in, 29, 157–158; specific
    reciprocity, 25, 27, 94; telecommunications
    in, 165–166

Regional trade agreements, 138, 146–149, 202. *See also* preferential trade agreements.

Regulatory measures. *See* trade measures.

Reinert, Kenneth, 108–109

Ricardo, David, 42, 44, 198

Richardson, Ben, 126, 128, 133

Robinson, James, 33, 148

Roosevelt, Franklin Delano, 15, 56–59

Roy, Martin, 28, 48, 153, 156, 165

Safegaurds provisions and measures. *See* trade measures.

Sanitary and phytosanitary measures. *See* trade measures.

Saudi Arabia, 98, 142–143

Schattschneider, E. E., 41–42

Scott, James, 9, 26, 63, 201, 206

Section 301. *See* trade measures, United States.

Sell, Susan, 9, 28, 14, 146, 147, 200, 204

sensitive product, see trade measures

Sepúlveda, Juan Ginés de, 15

services: BITS and, 156; coding, 86–87; cultural preferences and, 43; export data 1980–2010, 7; G10, 204; GATS negotiations, 149–159, 165, 175, 204; GATS+, 140, 156, 170, 173; grand bargain and, 26, 83, 94, 105; India and, 166, 165–170; measuring commitments in, 28–29; modes, 156, 159; negotiation issue, 23, 100, 172–173, 205; paternalism, 88, 92; Tokyo Round, 150. *See also* cultural industries, financial services, outsourcing, telecommunications, tourism services, civil aviation services, Trade in Services Agreement.

Sherman, Laura, 160–161

Singapore issues, 123

Singapore, 79, 98, 102, 114, 147–148, 161–164, 204

Skonieczny, Amy, 45–46, 200

slave trade, 33, 126–127, 178, 183–184, 202, 203, 206

Smith, Adam, 32, 167, 174, 194

Social constructivism, 175–176, 183, 195

social contract, 5–6, 85

social exchange, 5–6, 24, 31–32

South Africa: colonialism and apartheid in, 39, 57, 196; exclusion from PTAs, 13; G20 member, 202; GATT creation and, 197–198; GSP, 77; imperial preferences, 59; intellectual property advocacy, 145–146; telecommunications in, 162

Soviet Union, 68–69, 73, 91, 107, 129, 199–200

Spain, 97–98, 102, 114, 129

Special and Differential Treatment: Doha Round, 30, 77, 123–124; evolution of, 70–71, 78, 137; in lieu of trade conessions, 12, 172; services, 156; Tokyo Round and, 56, 83; Uruguay Round and, 117, 119–123. *See also* Generalized System of Preferences.

Special products. *See also* trade measures.

Special safeguard mechanism. *See also* trade measures.

Srinivasan, T. N. 9, 78

Staiger, Robert, 25–28, 30, 43, 76, 82, 193, 195

strategic trade. *See* trade theory.

Subsidies: agriculture in, 30, 116–125, 201; amber box, 118, 122; blue box, 118, 122, 124; cotton in, 27, 125–126, 134–137; green box, 118, 122, 123; reduction as trade concession, 12; sugar in, 129–133, 138; Tokyo Round, 78; trade theory and, 43. *See also* trade measures.

Sugar trade: case study as, xi–xii, 1, 29, 126, 172, 178; Chadbourne Agreement, 128–129; colonial history, 33, 111, 126–127, 138, 171, 202; Common Market Organization, 130, 133; dispute settlement, 11, 132–133; European Community and, 130–133; infant industry as, 21; Jones-Costigan Act, 128; liberal order and, 206; quotas and preferences, 3–4, 12, 88, 112, 120–121, 129–131, 201–202; racism and slavery, 33, 127–128, 202; sugar lobby, 3–4, 127, 130–134; tariffs, 8, 119; trade sentiment in the United States toward, 112

survey research. *See* methods.

Sweden, 65–66, 98, 102, 114, 144, 151

Switzerland, 94, 98, 102, 114, 151, 204

Taiwan, 75, 79, 142–143

tariff differential, 67

tariff rate quotas, 118, 131–132

telecommunications services, 27, 152–166, 204–205; as a case study, xi–xii, 17, 29; negotiations, 152–153, 157–166, 204–205; reference paper, 160–161

textiles and clothing: Agreement on Textiles and Clothing, 110, 135; export rates, 107; grand bargain, 26, 112, 199; industry interests, 174, 201; infant industry, 21; Long-Term Arrangement, 107; Multifibre Arrangement, 94, 106–109; preferential trade, 59, 106–109; Short-Term Arrangement, 107; trade restrictions in, 8, 47, 63, 65, 76, 83–84, 106–109, 175

Thailand, 89, 98, 101–104, 121, 132–134, 138, 142–143, 148–149, 164, 177, 201–202; agriculture trade, 121; GSP, 77; intellectual property issues, 142–143, 148–149; paternalism and, 89, 98, 102–103, 114; sugar, 132–134, 138, 177; telecommunications, 164; trade concessions, 10, 101

Tokyo Round: developing world and, 56, 78–79; GSP and Escape Clause, 70–73, 83, 118; MFA, 107; reciprocity, 27; services trade and, 150

tourism services, 139–140, 152, 157–158, 170

trade capacity-building assistance, 12

trade diversification. *See* export-market diversification.

Trade in Services Agreement (TiSA), 76, 159

Trade measures: orderly market arrangement, 108–109; regulatory provisions, 23, 27, 139, 160–163, 203; safeguards provisions and measures, 83, 108, 110, 133, 160; sanitary and phytosanitary measures, 119; Section 301 (U.S. Trade Act, 1974), 86, 89, 91–93, 106, 142–144, 149, 200; sensitive product (SSP), 119, 134; special product, 119, 124, 133; special safeguard mechanism, 124, 129, 133; voluntary export restraints, 106, 108. *See also* preferential trade, special and differential treatment, subsidies, quotas.

Trade theory: comparative advantage, 7, 17, 22, 32, 41–43, 48, 126, 128, 140, 150, 167, 170–173, 198; cultural preferences and, 41–48, 171–177; Heckscher-Ohlin model, 42, 44; reciprocity and, 26–27, 30, 177–178; Ricardo-Viner model, 42, 44; Stolper-Samuelson theorem, 42; strategic trade theory, 2–6, 29–30, 42–43, 78–79; trade externality, 26, 28, 30

Transatlantic Trade and Investment Partnership, 125–126

Trans-Pacific Partnership, 13, 125, 33, 147, 159

Trinidad and Tobago, 98–99, 163–164, 204

TRIPS and TRIPS+. *See* intellectual property.

Truman, Harry, 60–61, 197

Turkey, 10, 87, 89–90, 98, 102–103, 107, 114, 149, 156, 67

UNGA affinity scores, 99, 105, 180–181

United Kingdom: imperial preferences, 52, 56–60, 198; ITO/GATT negotiations, 62–63, 197; paternalism and, 98, 102, 114; racism and

slavery, 39–40, 127; sugar trade, 111, 126, 129, 131, 202; tariffs and imports, 66, 107

United Nations: Atlantic Charter and, 57; developing world advocacy, 50, 68, 72–73; racism and, 15, 39–40; voting, 99, 183

United Nations Conference on Trade and Development (UNCTAD), 68–73, 79, 121, 124, 172, 179, 199, 206

United Nations Educational, Scientific, and Cultural Organization (UNESCO), 15, 33, 37–39

United States trade laws: farm bills, 136–137; Omnibus Trade and Competitiveness Act of 1988, 142, 144; Reciprocal Trade Agreement Act of 1934, 50, 61; Section 301 of the Trade Act of 1974, 92, 142, 144–146; Trade Act of 1974, 72, 89, 141–142, 144, 200; Trade Act of 1984, 75, 142

United States Trade Representative: cotton issue, 124; intellectual propoerty, 142–144; MFA, 108–109; services, 152–153, 155; sugar, 130; Uruguay Round agriculture trade sentiments, 111–112; Uruguay Round merchandise trade sentiments, 83–94. *See also* United States.

United States: ACTA, 13, 147; agriculture trade, 23, 26, 115–138, 174; ASEAN and, 100, 105; authority/leadership, 5, 49–50, 58, 193; BITs, 90–91, 146–147; colonialism, 15; cotton, 134–138, 174; cultural distrance from, 97–98; domestic interests, 44–45, 128–129, 142, 152–153, 201; Europe and, 117–119; export strength, 99; intellectual property, 140–149, 204; ITO/GATT negotiations, 62–63; merchandise trade, 96; outsourcing, 166; paternalism, 21, 84–91, 96–97, 102–103, 115, 168–169, 197; preferential trade, 4, 55–56, 59, 67, 71, 74–77, 125, 193, 199, 203; PTAs 3, 13, 28; racism, 37, 39–40, 168–169; reciprocity, 27, 44–45; Section 301, 92, 142, 144–146; services trade, 76, 149–159, 173, 204; sugar trade, 126–134; tariff rates, 66; telecommunications, 159–160, 205; textiles, 106–108; trade concessions, 8–10, 48; trade sentiments, 84–94

Uruguay Round: agriculture negotiations, 116–122; developing world negotiation skills, 50, 52–53, 99–101, 119–122, 182; grand bargain, 26–27; intellectual property negotiations, 141–145; merchandise negotiations, 94–110; paternallism and racism, 22, 33, 48,

84–94, 112–116; reciprocity, 27; services trade and, 28, 149–155; tariff concessions, 8–10, 23, 28

Uruguay, 98, 100–103, 114, 120, 199, 202

USSR. *See* Soviet Union.

Utility maximization, 2, 23–24, 28, 31, 43–44, 175, 18, 193, 195–196, 199

Venezuela, 98, 102–103, 162–164, 202

Voeten, Erik, 3, 13, 99

Voluntary export restraints. *See* trade measures.

Wallerstein, Immanuel, 177, 197

Wheat trade, 117, 120, 123, 132,

Wilcox, Clair, 60–61

Wilkinson, Rorden, 9, 201

Wilsonian idealism, 36–39

Winham, Gilbert, 50, 73, 79

Winters, Alan, 25–28, 195

World Bank, 41, 58, 63, 74, 96, 99, 116, 164

World Systems explanations, 197

Wriggins, Howard, 49, 73

WTO meetings and ministerials: Bali 2013, 125, 178; Cancun 2003, 27, 123–125, 135, 137; Hong Kong 2008, 124, 162; July 2008 framework negotiations, 22, 124–125, 157; Marrakesh 1994, 160; Nairobi 2015, 125, 159; Punta del Este 1986, 71, 119, 144, 152;Seattle 1999, 122–123, 177

xenophobia, 34, 41

Yeutter, Clayton, 89–91, 130, 143

Yoffie, David, 49, 52, 193

Yugoslavia, 68, 100

Zartman, William, 49, 53, 67, 198

Zimbabwe, 57, 59, 63, 123, 202

Zoellick, Robert, 27, 124